The Black Family
in Modern Society

Amitai Etzioni
Consulting Editor

The Black Family in Modern Society

JOHN H. SCANZONI
Department of Sociology
Indiana University

Allyn and Bacon, Inc., Boston

Contents

Preface

Enormous amounts of both popular and scholarly literature have been addressed to a most crucial domestic issue currently facing American society—black-white relations. At the substantive level, this book represents an effort to extend our knowledge about the black family in urban America. At the theoretical level, it seeks to escape "color lines" and to contribute to the analysis of the general structure and process of family systems in modern society.

Why a book on family relations among blacks? Jessie Bernard, in her recent efforts in this area, argues that "there are serious gaps in our knowledge of marriage and family among Negroes" and that much research is needed to fill these gaps.[1] She contends that the "classic studies" of black family processes by Frazier, Davis, and others need to be updated. It is clear, she says, that "no one can afford to reject or even to ignore them."[2] Yet after the passing of many years and in view of the ferment in Black America, the inexorable question now is: Which of the numerous conclusions of these "classics" remain valid today, and which do not?

Obviously in this small book, only a selected few of the generalizations from these earlier standards can be considered. There is general agreement that the most comprehensive work on the American black family was done by E. Franklin Frazier.[3] The most

salient conclusion from Frazier's voluminous studies, according to
Glazer, is that "with further economic progress the weaknesses
of the Negro family would be overcome."[4] For Frazier there was
an inextricable link between economic resources and black family
structure. *The major objective of this book is to examine this
premise and many of its corollaries.* The linkage, moreover, will
not be examined in the narrow sense of sheer dollars per se, but in
terms of its widest possible meanings and implications.

One of the many stereotypes whites hold about blacks that
is simply not true pertains to black family patterns. As a result
of recent press popularizations, the image that most whites have is
of a family in which the father is gone; the mother supports her
steadily increasing illegitimate brood through welfare; any available
money is "wasted" on such things as color TV and liquor; and
that these family conditions breed delinquency, drug addiction, and
crime. The fact is, however, the majority (67 percent) of metropolitan black households in 1968 were headed by a *man* with his
wife present.[5] *The focus of this book is on that two-thirds majority
for whom these stereotypes clearly do not apply.*

In recent years, there have been several excellent studies of
that approximately one-third of black families characterized by
absence of the husband.[6] The interested reader should consult those
sources if he wishes to obtain an accurate (rather than stereotypical)
picture of those kinds of families. Throughout this book we shall
have occasion to compare them with the "stable" (husband-wife
present), or ongoing, or existing families that are the focus here.
But partially because the situation is less dramatic, the investigation
of majority patterns among blacks (whether familial or otherwise)
has been almost totally neglected by most social scientists.[7] Therefore, as a corrective—theoretically, substantively, and practically—
our concern here is with patterns of family structure and interaction
among the hitherto largely overlooked majority of the black
population in America.

Our ultimate goal, of course, is systematic social theory that
not only subsumes general family patterns, but also accounts for
significant differences by racial subgroups. To help accomplish this

goal, we shall compare the information on ongoing black families gathered for this study with available data for existing as well as dissolved white families, plus data on dissolved black families. The chief source of information on which this book is based was gathered by black interviewers from a sample of 400 black households, husband-wife present, in the city of Indianapolis during the winter months of 1968. (Additional methodological details appear toward the end of Chapter 1 and following Chapter 8.)

The organization of the book is based on a kind of quasi-three generational model. The first few chapters describe and analyze relationships experienced by our respondents with their own parents and with other adults while they were still adolescents. Next, we examine linkages between these background experiences and the current social and economic position in which these husbands and wives find themselves. Concomitantly, in the context of their present socioeconomic circumstances, we look in considerable detail at processes of husband-wife interaction. Finally, we examine some of the ways in which these parents are socializing their own children to participate in the opportunity system of our society.

The book is designed to appeal to a wide range of audiences. The person outside the college setting might wish to focus simply on the substantive conclusions and on their implications for public policy. Within the college or university, this book may be used in any number of courses; e.g., race and ethnic relations, family, social theory, introductory sociology, social problems, Afro-American, etc., with the instructor himself pursuing his own interests and emphases. Finally, for the graduate student and the professional, this book tries to grapple with pivotal theoretical issues linking stratification, socialization, husband-wife interaction, marital stability, the opportunity system, along with acceptance, persistence, and change of family structures within modern society.

One is always indebted to many persons who have contributed in one way or another to the completion of a project as extensive as this one. For help during the early stages, special thanks are due to Robert Johnson, Gail Garinger-Miller, and Miriam Kaplan. Invaluable assistance in coding and data analysis was received from

William Philliber and Jason Sachs. Jane Wellman patiently typed numerous drafts of all the chapters. Colleagues such as Michael Schwartz and Sheldon Stryker contributed helpful suggestions during manuscript preparation. Special thanks are due Clyde O. McDaniel, Jr., Johnnie Daniel, and J. Ross Eshleman for careful readings of and helpful suggestions for all or parts of the manuscript.

A question that naturally arises is whether *any* white social scientist can adequately investigate any aspect of the black community, including its family patterns. Will he be racially biased? Will he lack the *verstehen* (soul) necessary to grasp what is actually taking place? These types of questions could, of course, be legitimately reversed to ask whether a black social scientist, precisely because he is too "emotionally involved," could make an accurate assessment of certain black community patterns. Or could a Jewish sociologist adequately study the structure of American Judaism because he is "too involved," or else could he investigate American Catholicism because he might be biased or poorly sensitized to its actual workings? If carried to extremes, this issue could result in the elimination of much social investigation, either because one is too much of an "outsider," or else too much of an "insider."

Ideally, of course, the solution to the dilemma is that investigations are to be judged on the basis of their own merits, their grounding in theory and method, and not on the basis of ascribed characteristics (skin color, etc.) of the researcher. Nonetheless, personal preferences of the researcher may creep in at any point, and his own training and outlook inevitably predispose him toward certain perspectives. To try to guard against as much "white bias" as possible, blacks were consulted during the stages of research design and interview schedule construction. Black interviewers collected all the data, and black (as well as white) scholars critiqued the manuscript prior to publication. In short, every effort has been made to "think black," as well as to "think sociologically," for there is no inherent contradiction between the two.

A word regarding terminology. We share the feeling of many blacks that the label "Negro" has unfortunate connotations. Therefore, whenever possible the term "black" will be employed throughout. The chief exceptions will be quotations from other sources where we shall maintain the original wording.

NOTES

1. Jessie Bernard, *Marriage and Family Among Negroes*, Englewood Cliffs, N.J.: Prentice-Hall, 1966, p. ix.
2. Ibid.
3. E. Franklin Frazier, *The Negro Family in the United States*, Chicago: The University of Chicago Press, 1966 edition (original in 1939).
4. Ibid., 1966, p. ix, Nathan Glazer, "Foreword." At least one source however, claims that in Frazier's 1932 work, *The Negro Family in Chicago*, "cultural" rather than economic factors were alleged to be at the heart of Negro family difficulties. See William McCord, John Howard, Bernard Frieberg, Edwin Harwood, *Life-Styles in the Black Ghetto*, W. W. Norton & Co., Inc., New York: 1969, p. 22.
5. U.S. Bureau of the Census, *Current Population Reports*, Series P-23, Special Studies, #27, "Trends in Social and Economic Conditions in Metropolitan Areas," U.S. Government Printing Office, Washington, D.C., 1969, p. 12.
6. For instance, see Elliot Liebow, *Tally's Corner*, Boston: Little, Brown & Co., 1967; Lee Rainwater, "Crucible of Identity. The Negro Lower-Class Family," *Daedalus*, 95 (1966), pp. 172–216; plus several works by Hylan Lewis, cited in his "Culture, Class, and Family Life Among Low-Income Urban Negroes," in Arthur M. Ross & Herbert Hill, *Employment, Race & Poverty*, New York: Harcourt, Brace, & World, Inc., 1967, pp. 149–174; Helen Icken Safa, *An Analysis of Upward Mobility in Low Income Families*, Youth Development Center, Syracuse University, Syracuse, N.Y., 1967; Daniel Patrick Moynihan, "Employment, Income and the Ordeal of the Negro Family," *Daedalus* (Fall 1965), 745–769; David A. Schulz, *Coming Up Black*, Englewood Cliffs, N.J.: Prentice-Hall, 1969.
7. See Andrew Billingsley, *Black Families in White America*, Englewood Cliffs, N.J.: Prentice-Hall, 1968, "The Treatment of Negro Families in American Scholarship," pp. 197 ff.

The Black Family
in Modern Society

1

Introduction
and Perspective

IDEOLOGY, VALUES, AND
THE BLACK FAMILY

At all costs, we wish to avoid the ideological controversy which, unfortunately, has attended discussions of the black family ever since the publication of the "Moynihan report."[1] Rainwater and Yancey suggest that Moynihan was simply verifying Frazier's conclusions regarding the deleterious effects of historic and current economic deprivation on family patterns of a certain proportion of American blacks.[2] Yet some members of the press, the government, and especially the Civil Rights Movement, interpreted Moynihan to mean that the ultimate source of the black plight somehow lies within the structure of the black family itself.[3] They perceived him to imply that if the "inherent feebleness" of the black family could be "corrected" then the "Negro problem" in America would be "solved." It seems clear that "fixing blame" on the black family for the suffering of American blacks was never Moynihan's intent, nor is such reasoning even remotely to be inferred from this book.

On the other hand, Rainwater argues that the model of "white cupidity-Negro suffering" held by some activists is "overly simplistic" and "totally inadequate."[4] Such a model, he says, overlooks the *process between* cupidity and suffering. In this process whites, by their greater power, create situations in which Negroes do the dirty work of caste victimization for them . . . . the caste-facilitated infliction of suffering by Negroes on other Negroes and on themselves appears most poignantly within the confines of the family . . . the victimization process as it operates in families prepares and toughens its members to function in the ghetto world, at the same time that it seriously interferes with their ability to operate in any other world.[5]

Partly because of structural conditions largely beyond their control, black persons face difficulties that are enormous in functioning in the white occupational world. Similarly the difficulties blacks face are enormous in maintaining a dominant-type conjugal family pattern (husband-wife present), yet most blacks do conform to this pattern, even when "objective" or tangible material resources are relatively limited.

In trying to understand and ease the suffering of blacks in America, the role of the black family in this total complex process cannot be overlooked. In this regard, certain important proposals before Congress center on the conjugal family. Some pertain to the guaranteed annual income, or family-maintenance program; others point toward a program of "guaranteed jobs," with the government being the employer of "last resort." The conjugal family is, in our society, the focal point for the accumulation of material resources by individuals, as well as for their allocation and consumption. It is the place where personality is developed, where identity is formed, where status is assigned, and where basic values and norms are learned. By looking at black families that can be defined as conforming to the dominant family form, we can get some idea of those conditions that enable certain blacks to cope with and partially overcome "white cupidity." Knowledge of these conditions (economic, social psychological, structural) can serve practical, as well as theoretical, purposes.

The above by no means implies that the dominant conjugal form is necessarily "better" or "worse" than the "matrifocal" family form found among a large segment of severely disadvantaged blacks. Billingsley contends that "many low income Negro families are often forced to choose [due to current ADC procedures] between a father in the home and money in the home, and many make the pragmatic choice for money." Only in this way, he claims, can the wife and children survive and avoid starvation.[6] To black families in the lower class, in short, marital stability is often a "luxury" which simply cannot be afforded. At the same time Billingsley argues that stability "is always a goal, highly to be desired . . ."[7]

Use of the term "stability" implies, for most social scientists, a situation where husband and wife are both present. Some, however, might wish to extend the term to cover the one-parent family where the remaining spouse keeps the children with him or her, and seeks to provide for and to socialize them. This situation is precisely the "adaptation" to reality that many lower-class blacks have evolved. That adaptation could indeed be labeled a "stable" or "constant" situation, but simply to avoid conceptual confusion the term "stable" is used in this book in its conventional sense to refer to a situation in which husband and wife remain together. This pattern is generally termed the *dominant* family form throughout western society—not because it is considered "better" than any other form—but because at the level of *values*, it is what the majority of adults (black and white) prefer, and at the *behavioral* level this is how they in fact live. Questions about "bourgeois marital hypocrisy," alleged trends toward extra-marital patterns, and commune living are, strictly speaking, beyond the scope of this book, though it shall allude to them from time to time, especially in Chapter 8.

Certain white intellectuals go beyond Billingsley's pragmatic position regarding adaptations and, on ideological grounds, denigrate the validity of the dominant family form as a goal for blacks in general. Glazer notes that at a conference where this particular goal was questioned by a "leading social critic," the response of a black woman in the audience was "that it was up to the Negroes to decide whether the goal was worthwhile or not: 'just give us tickets; we'll decide where to get off.' "[8]

On the basis of census data, it is clear that the majority of American blacks are "deciding" to choose the dominant family form. Moreover, as a result of his intensive research, Rainwater claims that even "lower-class Negroes know what the 'normal American family' is supposed to be like, and they consider a stable family-centered way of life superior to the conjugal and familial situations in which they often find themselves."[9] Elliot Liebow and also David Schulz report precisely the same result.[10] For, like it or not, there is an association between possession of resources (the "tickets") that activists would like to see all blacks have, and the dominant American (or Western, or Industrial, or modern-society type) family pattern. Therefore, for important practical, substantive and theoretical reasons, it is necessary to get some initial grasp of structure and interaction within contemporary black families that "fit" the pattern of the dominant society. That "initial grasp" is the goal of this book.

The phrase "initial grasp" should not be lost on the reader. Rather than being a definitive study, this is an exploratory effort designed to fill the void in our knowledge regarding a critical segment of urban family structure. As such, it attempts not merely to report empirical data, but primarily to generate hypotheses for future testing, and most important of all, to contribute toward a theory of family structure in modern society. (It is a well-worn cliché to assert that sociologists have been remiss in their concern for theory development, but it nonetheless remains a valid criticism.) In another place, certain elements of that theory have been spelled out in great detail, and this book will elaborate on those elements whenever necessary.[11] The reader should keep in mind that in sociology, as in all other disciplines committed to the scientific method, there is an ongoing and expanding stream between data, its analysis and interpretation, generation of new ideas, the collection of fresh data to test these new ideas, etc. It is in this spirit of ongoing investigation, rather than "definitive truth" that the following pages should be read.

The current situation of American blacks, and their family system in particular, cannot be understood fully without historical perspective. Numerous surveys of black history provide background for the brief material that follows.[12] The tribes from which Africans were stolen maintained strong and viable family patterns. As in most pre-modern situations, marriage involved not merely two individuals but also two or more large kinship groups. These groups had a stake in the marriage of their young, usually in the form of exchanged goods or services. Marriage and family patterns were organized through a series of ancient, elaborate customs and rituals, which were reinforced by the kin and indeed by the whole tribe. Males maintained a dominant position within these families, although there were clearly defined, though subordinate, roles for women and children. In brief, the ancestors of present-day American blacks experienced a family system characterized by orderliness and continuity.

CAPTURE AND PASSAGE

The traumatic process of capture, the Atlantic-passage, and chattel-slavery seem to have undermined to some extent many ancient African traditions, including some connected with the family.[13] During capture and passage, the process of dehumanization began, and once in slavery the transition to property was complete. The American slavery system, unlike any other arrangement in the history of civilization, was unique in its absolute insistence on the "subhumanness" of its victims. As a result, slave marriages were rarely recognized either legally or informally, except at the whim and often for the advantage of the slave-owner. Husbands and wives could always be separated and sold at will, as could children. Slaves, especially females, had no sexual rights. And, of course, there were no economic rights to earn wages, to use or invest them, to gain status, to gain freedom. The American Dream was shut tight to black slaves, so that for over 200 years they (especially males) had no opportunity to carry out occupational or family patterns practiced and approved by the dominant society.

DENIGRATION OF THE
BLACK MALE SELF-CONCEPT

Being told he was "inferior and incapable of economic achievement," the black male gradually came to believe it. This denigration of his self-concept accomplished during slavery was reinforced during the periods of Reconstruction and Jim Crow (legal segregation). During those periods, blacks were "free," so society held the same expectations for them that it held for whites. Males, in particular, were expected to fulfill the role of provider for their families. Blacks internalized these expectations and made them their own. White society, however, provided little or no opportunity for millions of rural black people to make their way into the white-dominated educational and occupational systems. It is devastating indeed to be told that one can and should be participating in the Dream when concomitantly, those who expect performance severely limit the chances to do so.

Significantly, during this same era (approximately 1865–1914), black females found much greater access into the opportunity structure than did black males. Whether because of their traditional "activist" role stemming from slavery, or because whites felt less threatened by black females than by black males, black women were able to make certain kinds of socioeconomic gains. Even up to the present, for example, black females complete more years in school than do black males and are more represented than they in high status occupations.[14]

One alleged result of this situation is the black male's perception that his chief family role as provider is threatened by greater discrimination against him than against his wife. This feeling becomes most evident among those males who have minimal job skills, who are the last hired and the first fired. Nevertheless Liebow concludes that even within the black lower-class, the dominant norm is accepted that it is

peculiarly the (good) husband's responsibility, not anyone else's [including the wife]. . . . to pay the rent, buy the groceries, and provide for the other necessary goods and services . . . [this] is the sine qua non of a good husband.[15]

THE PERIOD OF URBANIZATION

Beginning with World War I, blacks have been moving to the cities in great numbers so that they are now proportionately more highly urbanized than whites.[16] Blacks moved primarily to share more fully in the promise of the American Dream. Black men came to the cities so they would be better able to carry out the provider role assigned to them by society. But just as job opportunity had been denied them in slavery and in rural areas, it continues to be denied them in urban America. About this era, Moynihan remarks, "Work is precisely the one thing the Negro family head . . . has not received over the past generation."[17]

More accurately, it is the unskilled, lower-class black male who has been unable to find work, whose unemployment rate is twice that of whites. It is among the *most* economically disadvantaged blacks that family dissolution and illegitimacy are highest. Moynihan and others have amassed reams of data to document such generalizations as, "nearly a quarter of urban Negro marriages are dissolved"; or "almost one-fourth of Negro families are headed by females"; or "nearly one-quarter of Negro births are now illegitimate"; and "the breakdown of the Negro Family had led to a startling increase in welfare dependency."[18]

On the other hand, Frazier's firm conviction was that as the educational and economic position of blacks improved, their conformity to dominant family patterns would increase. Frazier foresaw, for instance, a developing black middle-class comprised of salaried professional and white-collar workers. This development he claimed, would substantially improve the self-image of these people, and one consequence would be a "middle-class stable" pattern of family life.[19] Likewise for the "black proletariat," i.e., laborers, industrial workers (men who have escaped traditional "Negro pursuits" in domestic service jobs), Frazier was equally optimistic: "It appears that, as the Negro worker becomes an industrial worker, he assumes responsibility for the support of his family and acquires a new authority in family relations."[20]

Currently, the greater proportion of blacks has escaped at least the *depths* of lower-class economic deprivation. Do we find there the corresponding family stability that Frazier predicted? In one real sense, the answer is "yes." Both Goode and Udry, each using census data, argue that as the social and economic position of blacks increases, marital dissolution among them decreases.[21]

Nevertheless, there is a fundamental difference between these investigators when comparisons are made *between* blacks and whites at the same status level. Goode claims that "Negro and white rates of divorce are converging. . . . As a higher proportion of Negroes acquire middle-class patterns, it seems likely that they will resort to the courts more, but their rates will be about the same as those of whites."[22] In effect, Goode is suggesting that Frazier's contentions are falling into place—greater economic resources on the part of black families result in adoption of dominant conjugal patterns in terms of stability and dissolution.

On the other hand, Udry maintains his data show that at each occupational and educational level, blacks have higher rates of marital dissolution than do whites.[23] His conclusions do not coincide with the expectation that increased social well-being among blacks will result in the same levels of family stability as among whites with similar status. These divergent conclusions regarding family stability among more advantaged blacks are extremely significant both practically and theoretically. Practically, of course, the matter contains implications for public policy as how best to satisfy the demands and needs of black Americans for the greatest good of the greatest number of citizens. Theoretically, the issue forces us to examine very closely the full gamut of relationships between economic position and family structure.

When Frazier predicted that economic advancement would promote black family stability, he believed, as did most blacks (and many whites) in the 30's and 40's, that color lines were giving way to economic class lines in the classic Marxist sense: "In his struggle for adequate relief and a living wage, the black worker began cooperating more and more with the white worker and consequently regards his problems less as racial problems."[24] He also saw the black middle-class being "permitted to compete on equal terms with whites. . . . As racial barriers break down, the Negro middle class will become assimilated with the salaried workers in the community."[25]

Frazier's expectations cannot be dismissed as merely utopian.

In an exhaustive study of black employment patterns over the decades of this century, Ginzberg and Hiestand conclude that "Negro men made significant progress in closing the occupational gap with [whites] during the 1940's. . . ."[26] Therefore, writing from his perspective during this same period, Frazier had much reason to believe that the economic position of blacks was embarked on a period of long term upswing, as was true of the white population. But beginning in the early 1950's, the "rate of [economic] progress [of blacks] relative to white men slowed down considerably."[27] The differential between blacks and whites is currently most glaringly evident when comparisons are made by education. In 1963, according to Fein, "if the [average] white had but eight years of schooling his income was $5,454, 20 percent more than for the black high-school graduate. . . . The Negro family whose head had some high school earned less than the white with fewer than eight years of schooling; *the Negro who has attended (but not completed) college earns less than the white with only eight years of elementary school*, the Negro college graduate earns but slightly more than does the white high-school graduate"[28] (italics in original).

The emerging black middle-class that Frazier foresaw is not developing at a pace anywhere near rapid enough to approximate proportions of whites who may be called middle class. "The Negro labor force [remains] substantially concentrated in the semiskilled, unskilled, service and farm occupations. . . . over 70 percent of both Negro men and women are in these occupations."[29] Only 40 percent of whites are found at these same job levels.[30] It is significant to note that, writing in the mid-fifties, Frazier no longer describes assimilation with whites, nor enhanced self-image on the part of middle blacks, nor even of "acceptance" by the white community. Instead, he claims that "the white world . . . refuses to permit the black bourgeoisie to share its life. . . . they are rejected by the white world, and this rejection has created considerable self-hatred, since it is attributed to their Negro characteristics."[31]

Neither did the middle-class black (at that time) identify with the plight of lower-class blacks which, according to Frazier, might give him a solid sense of purpose to compensate for rejection by the dominant white majority.[32] Therefore, lacking either acceptance or mission, many blacks, said Frazier, "seek an escape from their frustrations" through "delusions of wealth or power" or else in "magic or chance, and in sex and alcohol."[33] Incidentally, Frazier's conception of the middle class or "bourgeoisie" includes not only the three Census Bureau categories of white-collar workers, but also the top blue-collar category of craftsmen and foremen.[34]

One point that comes through very clearly in Frazier's later book is that education, job position, even income do not totally "solve" the self-image question for many middle-class blacks.[35] To be sure, the prime hindrance to the solution is still "white cupidity" just as much as when whites exploit lower-class blacks. What is denied to higher status blacks is a sense of worth and prestige based on universalistic achievements in the occupational realm. The fact is that many whites still react even to middle-class blacks on the basis of ascribed physical characteristics defined as inherently inferior. Consequently, some have suggested that while the middle-class black is "objectively" well off, he nonetheless *feels* relatively deprived when compared to whites who may be at the same "objective" status level. Pettigrew, for instance, argues that feelings of *relative deprivation* are especially acute among *advantaged blacks* when comparison is made with the white middle-class.[36]

This line of reasoning suggests that the relationship between social and economic resources and black family structure is far more complex than it appears initially. The feelings of alienation and deprivation among middle-class blacks may, for instance, help to account for Udry's conclusion that blacks tend to exceed whites in family dissolution at all status levels. Increasing the level of economic resources per se available to black families, although critical, may be only part of the issue. The question of social-psychological feeling-states may be equally vital. This book will try to explore some of these pertinent social-psychological factors as well as the more obvious "objective" factors.

THE FAMILY IN SOCIAL PERSPECTIVE

Several observers have noted that a glaring weakness of family studies has been the failure to examine the family in its larger social context. Process and interaction within the family are inextricably linked with forces in the larger society. Relationships between husbands and wives, parents and children, siblings, members of the kin, do not exist in isolation. The nature of these relationships is greatly shaped by certain pervasive social forces of which the persons involved may sometimes be unaware. What are the most critical of these forces? Those having to do with economic-status factors: the occupational system, the opportunity structure. In a recent study, the authors express some surprise by their findings in this regard.

What is amazing is that status can make such a difference within the privacy of the family. Evidently, however, it lies close to our humanity, to the essentially social nature of self, and to our conception of life. We know that men find status important enough to die for. On second thought, then, perhaps its importance in the life of the family is not surprising.[37]

At the same time, Billingsley points out that class position by itself is not totally sufficient to explain black family processes.[38] The American black community, he contends, should also be thought of as an "ethnic subsociety." Drawn from Gordon, this term is defined as a large number of persons with a "shared feeling of peoplehood," usually bound by race, religion, national origin, or some combination of same.[39] Persons in the group share a sense of "indissoluble and intimate identity" with that group. They are also bound together "by common definition and treatment on the part of the larger society." Hence, their self-definition flows in large measure from the definition made of them by the larger society.

The history of white ethnic groups in the United States has

been one of what might be called "selective assimilation" into the dominant society. At the educational and occupational levels (secondary-type associations), most persons in those groups have sought for and eventually gained full participation and equality with members of the dominant society. Concomitantly, many of these groups have diligently sought to maintain "ethnic identity" and a sense of "group pride" through such (primary type) means as intramarriage, kin solidarity, holiday observances and other special occasions, knowledge of group history and native language, and so on. Thus ethnic identity and tradition are carried on by these groups chiefly through primary ties, including the family.

Billingsley agrees with Frazier that up until recently many advantaged blacks who had attained economic and social benefits tried to avoid "black identity," primary relations, and ethnic identification with less advantaged blacks. But as noted above, ethnicity is reinforced and shaped greatly through the treatment accorded by the dominant to the subordinate group. For instance, some older members of white ethnic groups are perturbed to see their distinctive heritage and traditions being eroded, in part because the dominant society finds it no longer simple to make meaningful "we-they" distinctions between white-skinned people. Such a distinction is readily made, however, in the case of black-skinned people. All blacks, therefore (according to Billingsley), whether they be congressman or street-sweeper, physician or panhandler, share a sense of "peoplehood" or identification with each other largely on the basis of the common discrimination and disdain they experience at the hands of white society.

One of the evidences of this discrimination (and thus the pressure towards "we-they") was seen above in the different incomes received by comparably educated black and white men. As a consequence of being rebuffed by white society in their attempts at integration and assimilation, blacks at all class levels, now more than ever before, are reacting by seeking to establish themselves as a recognized and viable ethnic group, with their own sense of identity and racial pride. Consequently, the construct of "ethnic group" becomes useful in analyzing the black American family.

There are many elements, for example, that black and white families at the *same class level* share in common.[40] But they also "have very different histories, very different [caste-like] statuses in society, and very different levels of economic security."[41] These differences are due precisely to their ethnic characteristics which, as Frazier eventually came to believe, white society does not choose to overlook.

Therefore, if the main tool for understanding the black family is social class (or level of possession of economic-status resources), an adjunct to class is ethnicity—particularly in terms of the definitions held and discriminations practiced by the dominant white society against blacks. Class has to do primarily with *achieved* characteristics. American society is formally an open-class society. Blacks are encouraged to fulfill the American Dream, i.e., if they study diligently in school, work hard, they are told they will achieve "success," same as the white person. Ethnicity has to do with *ascribed* characteristics. From the standpoint of the "Dream," ascribed factors such as skin color should not impede achievements. For blacks, however, "what should not be" has been. The subversion of open-class factors through ethnic discrimination is bound to have consequences for the black family. This point inevitably becomes a major theme in this book, especially in the later chapters.

Up to this point, the term "class" has been used somewhat loosely, simply to give the reader a sense of the meanings implied. S. M. Miller notes that sociologists often confound the critical distinctions between working class and lower class. To correct this particular fuzziness, he proposes a simplified typology utilizing two factors: economic security and "life-style" based on family stability.[42] The best indicator, he claims, of the economic security of a family is its income. Economists and sociologists differ among themselves as to what income level is actually "adequate" for the urban family, but the 1966 Census Bureau figure of $3,300 for a family of four was the then accepted lower limit in the range of family security.[43] Families below that figure may be labeled economically "insecure"; those above it, relatively "secure."

There are numerous difficulties with Miller's formulations,

and he freely acknowledges them, but they nonetheless constitute a beginning in unraveling some difficult problems. In his discussion of family stability as the second dimension requisite to distinguishing between working and lower classes, Miller is fully aware that the notion of "familial instability-stability" may involve certain cultural biases, especially if imposed on black people. On the other hand, as seen above, all available evidence points to the conclusion that the overwhelming majority of black and white Americans know about and seem to prefer the stable husband-wife arrangement. Consequently, there is no intent here to seek to impose "white middle-class" values on blacks. Instead, family stability is a situation preferred by most Americans, even in those cases (black or white) where for one reason or other it is not (or cannot be) attained.

Miller states: "The two approaches can be welded together by cross-tabulating the two dimensions of the two variables of economic security and familial stability."[44]

To the degree that the term "lower class" can be divested of its value-bias connotations, Miller suggests that it should be absolutely *restricted* to families in block (4) of Fig. 1–1.[45] These are

Familial

		Stability	Instability
		+	−
Security	+	+ + (1) Stable Poor	+ − (2) Strained
Economic			
Insecurity	−	− + (3) Copers	− − (4) Unstable

Fig. 1–1. Types of economic security and familial stability[a]

[a] Source: S. M. Miller, *Sociology and Social Research* 48 (April 1964). Used by permission.

families which are both insecure economically and unstable conjugally. Families in the remaining three blocks are at various points within the working class. The studies by Liebow, Rainwater, Schulz, Moynihan, and others focused primarily on what Miller terms the lower class, those in block (4). Throughout this book, therefore, lower-class black (or white) families refer to the dual criteria hypothesized by Miller and amply verified through recent empirical efforts.

The chief focus of this investigation, however, is on the kinds of families represented by blocks (1) and (3), plus families whose incomes are substantially beyond mere relative security. For example, the median income of families studied for this book is approximately $6,600 (see chapter 5). This figure places most of our respondents substantially beyond the lower class, using solely the economic dimension suggested by Miller. Furthermore, national census data show that Miller is quite correct in asserting that there is an association of economic security with marital stability that tends to place such families outside the scope of the lower class. *For it is the absence of the husband which tends to be generally associated with the severest black poverty.* In 1967, the median income of urban black families headed by a female (block 4) was $3,270, somewhat below the 1966, $3,300 urban "poverty line."[46] With a male present, the 1967 median income of urban black families was more than double (block 1) $6,778.[47] The same phenomenon may be viewed with respect to children. Seventy-six percent of black children living in families with incomes less than $4,000 do not have both parents present.[48] When black family income is from $4,000–$4,999, only 33 percent lack both parents. When it is $6,000–$7,999, the figure again drops sharply to 20 percent. When income is $15,000 and over, the figure is only 5 percent, virtually the same as for whites.[49] Furthermore, it is precisely those black families in poverty (below $3,300) and headed by a female (block 4) that have the highest numbers of children, which, of course, substantially exacerbates the situation of poverty.

The above obviously does not imply that there are no black husband-wife families who are living in poverty—who are stable but insecure—the "copers" within block (3). In 1969, 22 percent of black households headed by a male had incomes below the poverty level.[50] By comparison, however, almost three times as many, or 58 percent of black female-headed households had 1969 incomes that low.[51] Even more significant are the long-range trends in the rates of poverty-reduction between the two categories. The decade of the sixties—especially the latter years—witnessed steady reductions in the numbers and proportions of black people living in poverty *if they dwelled in a male-headed household.*[52] However, for blacks dwelling in female-headed households, the decade saw considerably *less* change in the proportion of blacks able to escape poverty.[53] For example, from 1968 to 1969 there were 8 percent fewer blacks living in poverty in male-headed households, whereas there was "no measurable change" for those in households headed by a female.[54]

It would appear that if both spouses are present, black family income most often takes a "significant jump upward." Basically, therefore, it makes sense both theoretically and empirically to distinguish families in the black working-class (and above) from those in the black lower-class (block 4). (This in no way vitiates the sense of ethnic identity that blacks at all class levels feel, or the ethnically based reactions that whites emit toward blacks irrespective of their achievements.) This book is about the stable black family located in the working and middle classes, i.e., those strata above the lower class (sometimes referred to as the "underclass"). An operational distinction between working and middle classes is made in Chapter 2. Suffice it to say, however, there is greater similarity and homogeneity between these two strata, than there is between them taken together and compared to the lower class. Increasingly, sociologists are coming to agree that the differences between working- and middle-class families are merely differences of *degree:* differences, for example, in degree of economic-status benefits, consumption patterns, and child-socialization.[55] Conversely, the difference between those strata and lower-class families tends to be one of *kind,* i.e., along the lines suggested by Miller.

It is quite clear that there are certain problems involved when utilizing a scheme such as Miller's. By no means do we intend to bind ourselves to it in any ironclad fashion. Nevertheless, its major strength is that it helps to distinguish the lower class from the levels of social strata that are the main concern of this book. Block 2, for example, subsumes those working-class families that are relatively secure economically, yet where there has been marital dissolution. Those situations are beyond the purview here, except insofar as they serve as a basis for comparison. It is also extremely important to take note of Miller's observation that among blacks who live "in and around the poverty line," there is, during their lifetimes, considerable shifting or mobility between categories 2, 3, and 4. In addition, according to Schulz, the notion of "husband absent or present" is not by itself sufficiently broad or subtle enough to capture the several familial roles that the black male might play who lives in or near the "culture of poverty." At different times, he might be a "monogamous father; discreet free man; indiscreet free man/quasi-father; supportive biological father; supportive companion; pimp."[56] The purpose here, however, is to examine the great majority of urban blacks *who have been able to adopt,* in more or less permanent fashion, what S. M. Miller calls the "stable life-style" characteristic of the regularly employed blue-collar (and white-collar) worker.[57] It is this broad spectrum of black society which has not been investigated much in recent years, and which for numerous reasons deserves our careful scrutiny.

A landmark study of some years ago that included black people beyond the lower class was Drake and Cayton's *Black Metropolis.* Their attempts to describe nonlower-class blacks sound remarkably like Miller's.

The middle class is marked off from the lower class by a pattern of behavior expressed in stable family and associational relationships, in great concern with "front" and "respectability," and in a drive for "getting ahead." . . . It represents a relatively stable pattern that has been emerging since the Flight to Freedom . . . [it is] a "model" . . . which will distinguish a segment of the population from the "crude" and "unpolished" masses. These are people interested in maintaining a stable home life, who want to marry and raise a family, who take steady employment when they find it.[58]

Ignoring any value-appellations in their statement, it is those particular strata of black society that are the focal point of this book. Besides scholarly efforts to describe the lower-class family, there is an excellent journalistic account by Gordon Parks reprinted in *Poverty in America*. That article should be compared with the journalistic account by Wakin of a "middle class" black family.[59] Through astute intuition, these journalists have captured some of the salient differences of these two sets of life-styles. Nevertheless, attempts at rigorous assessment of black life-styles above the lower class have been few in recent years.[60] The following pages are one attempt at such an assessment.

ORGANIZATION OF THE BOOK

The plan for pursuing this study of existing black families above the underclass is straightforward. Given the strong emphasis by Frazier and others on the generational cycle of poverty and dissolution, it seems imperative that we examine the black family in its developmental or cyclical perspective, i.e., to look at the ongoing black family system through a type of three-generational model.

1. Past experiences of respondents—as adolescents in their families of orientation (Chs. 2–3–4).

2. Current situations of these husbands and wives—their economic standing and its impact on marital interaction (Chs. 5–6).

3. Shape of the *next* generation of black Americans—respondents' relationships with their own children (Ch. 7).

One advantage of this kind of developmental perspective is that it facilitates tracing some of the intergenerational processes that contribute to economic and conjugal solidarity. Whatever patterns found *currently* among a sample of families are the consequence of *earlier* family structure and the precursor of behavior still to come.

In Chapter 2, we shall examine the backgrounds of those in the sample to obtain some idea of the educational and occupational levels of their parents. Other important elements considered include experience in the urban milieu and whether both parents were present in the home. If Chapter 2 represents the structure of family background, Chapter 3 describes the functions, or what Winch calls the "functionality" of the family for the individual.[61] "Functionality" simply refers to what the family actually *does* for the child in terms of behaviors and values that will help him in later life. In traditional society, the son learns to hunt food or to farm from his father. Since this particular type of "functionality" is absent in modern urban society, what does the family of orientation *do* for the child—in this case the black child whose parental family has often been deprived compared to white families?

Both family structure and its functionality are, as Winch further argues, linked to identification of the child with his parents. To what extent is this true of certain black adolescents? Chapter 4 explores this question, along with the impact of nonfamilial "significant others" in the life of the black child. These are "role models" other than family members with whom the child may have identified, e.g., school teachers, ministers, YMCA workers, peers. In this connection, the child's experiences in school and church, the institutions most significant to the black youth in addition to his home, must be examined. Childhood identification is important per se, and it is also vital in explaining certain later adult behaviors.

Chapter 5 takes up the question of the *social mobility* of these husbands and wives when compared to the social position of their parents. An attempt is made to link patterns of childhood identification with the degree of their occupational achievement. Social mobility for themselves and especially their children is one of the most urgent goals sought by the vast majority of black Americans. Yet recent evidence indicates that black mobility is severely hampered owing to economic discrimination by white society.[62]

Chapter 6 focuses on the *current* marital patterns of these black men and women. Since modern marriage "stands or falls" on the economic and expressive satisfactions perceived by husbands and wives, this is perhaps the most crucial chapter in the book. Therefore, following a model presented elsewhere, Chapter 6 will examine the linkage of these conjugal families with the economic-opportunity structure.[63] We will consider:

1. This linkage in its *objective* senses—occupation and education of the husband, and family income;
2. The *subjective* feelings of these husbands and wives regarding their position in the opportunity structure—feelings of "economic alienation"; and
3. Relationships between these several economic-status elements and husband-wife primary relations—love and physical affection, companionship, empathy or communication and understanding;
4. The effect of these same economic-status elements on husband-wife authority relations;
5. The impact of wife employment on husband-wife relations;
6. Conditions surrounding family fertility and consumption rationality.

Chapters 1 through 5 build up to Chapter 6, but the process does not end there. The black family system, like any kinship structure, is cyclical: Chapter 2 looks at some of the childhood experiences of these parents and Chapter 7 discusses some of the ways these parents socialize their own children in terms of certain kinds of achievement values and mobility aspirations they hold for them.

From this brief description, it can be seen that the notion of "family" (black or white) in a very wide sense is conceived as an ongoing *social system*. What is in view is not merely the relatively narrow focus of interaction between family members, though that is vital and is investigated. That kind of behavior, however, is placed in the broader perspective of the family as social institution, inherently and intimately linked to ongoing social processes both in other institutions (especially the economic) and in the larger society. If the society is pictured as a total system of intricate, inter-locking parts and units, then we may likewise posit that those sub-elements which are labeled "family" are inseparable from the total system. Those elements exist in terms of ongoing (or generational) processes. Our procedure is to "cut in" to these systemic processes at point X (where a husband or wife is interviewed) and try to observe some of the past, present, and future-oriented systemic linkages to the larger society and to intra-family interaction.

To underscore the fact that we are dealing with an ongoing system of interrelated parts, it is critical to see that what is reported in Chapter 3 builds on the information in Chapter 2, Chapter 4 builds on 3, Chapter 5 rests on Chapter 4, Chapter 6 builds on Chapter 5, and Chapter 7 flows from Chapter 6. It is "as if" we are following each respondent through certain adolescent relationships, then into his (her) position in the occupational world, next into particular relationships within his current conjugal unit, and finally into certain aspects of how he seeks to socialize his own children. To help illuminate the bridges between the ongoing processes described in each chapter, we shall make use of certain multiple correlation procedures. Figure 1–2 presents in simplified, graphic form the overall plan of the book. The diagram seeks to show how the various elements of the family as an ongoing (generational) social system (its structure and process) directly influence certain other parts, always in the context of linkages to elements of the larger social system. The reader, therefore, should constantly keep before him the larger overview which the diagram seeks to convey and refer back to it to clarify relationships between materials in successive chapters.

Chapter 8 tries to tie together the several threads that have run throughout the book, touches on questions that could not be answered by this present study, and makes suggestions for further examination of the contemporary urban black family. Also in that chapter are some practical implications of the study, as well as related suggestions for public policy.

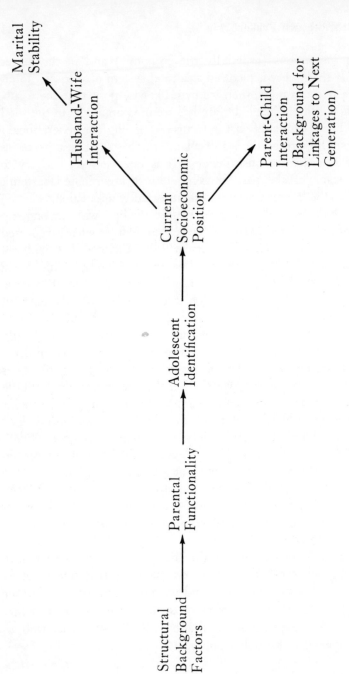

Fig. 1–2. Linkages between selected elements of the black (or white) family as ongoing (generational) social system.

SOURCES OF DATA

This book draws not only on data collected specifically for this study, but also on the many other sources of information pertaining to American blacks, plus the fund of knowledge regarding dominant family patterns in general. The question of what is a "stable" or ongoing social group or system may stir controversy among some sociologists. However, this is not the place to examine the history of the construct, nor the subtleties or intricacies inherent in it. Nor is this necessary, since this book uses the term in a very straightforward sense. A "stable" family (white or black) is described as one in which both husband and wife are currently living together in the same household. To stress process as well as structure, it might also be called an ongoing or existing marriage. In the case of black households in this study, this description is further specified to mean couples married and living together for *at least* five years.

The sampling procedures and data collection for the study were carried out by the *National Opinion Research Center* during the late winter and early spring of 1968, in the city of Indianapolis under a grant from the National Institutes of Mental Health.[64] Following a block-quota sampling technique in all-black neighborhoods, each interviewer (always black) screened potential respondents at the door of the household. If both spouses were not *both* black, or else had not been married *at least* five years, the interviewers did *not* include them in the sample. If they met these criteria, the interview was conducted with only *one* spouse (sex predesignated) from the family, in the respondent's home. This procedure resulted in a total sample size of 400 households.

Use of quota sampling, though far less expensive than a strict probability sample, limits the capability to generalize beyond the sample, either to blacks in Indianapolis or nationally. That is, we cannot be certain of the degree to which the findings that emerge from this sample actually hold within the larger, urban, black community. Nonetheless a start must be made somewhere in a neglected area of investigation. Our findings should therefore be considered initial and basically tentative until there are replications using more rigorous sampling procedures. Until and unless such studies are carried out, however, one may at least *hypothesize* that what we find in our sample might possibly represent the majority of urban (especially in the North and West) black American families *above the underclass*.

An attempt to compare demographic data for the Indianapolis metropolitan area (Marion county) with national data concluded that "the differences in the marital status of the 1960 white and nonwhite population of Marion County paralleled the nationwide trend."[65] That is, in terms of the proportions of whites and blacks who are single, married, divorced, and separated, the greater Indianapolis area does not differ from national proportions of same. However, the report also suggested that blacks in Indianapolis may rank slightly higher than blacks nationally when it comes to levels of income, education, and proportions employed. As we have already seen in this chapter and shall note especially in Chapter 5, when making such comparisons for blacks, one must always take into account rural or urban residence, plus whether or not the husband is present. If one were to exclude rural (Southern) blacks, and those in female-headed households from the national data, it is likely that black husband-wife households in Indianapolis would not deviate much at all from national means and medians when it comes to levels attained by urban American blacks (in the North and West in particular) with respect to occupation, education, and income. Chapter 5 presents comparisons of national data which lend support to that possibility. Strictly speaking, therefore, the generalizations arrived at in this book apply only to this particular sample of urban blacks. Nevertheless, more broadly, they may simultaneously be considered hypotheses which may have potential significance for the understanding of family processes among urban nonlower-class blacks in general.

The rationale for setting the lower limits for sample inclusion at five years is not totally arbitrary. Census data for 1960 indicate that "more than 30 percent of the divorces [in the U.S.] occurred in less than four years and over one-half occurred in less than eight years after marriage.[66] Thus a couple married five years has passed through the initial traumatic phase of marriage, in which a plethora of random and perhaps idiosyncratic elements might combine to bring about dissolution. The marriage as social system has presumably persisted long enough to permit identification of at least some of those sociological elements that systematically account for its "ongoingness." Actually, the median length of marriages in the sample is much greater than five years. Approximately half of those in the sample have been married from five to eighteen years. Thus the claim that we are examining ongoing or "stable" marriages is amply justified.

In sum, the basic objective of the book is to describe and try to analyze the urban black family system above the underclass or lower-class. Following S. M. Miller, families above the underclass are characterized both as conjugally stable and economically secure. That respondents in the sample meet the former criterion of having escaped from the underclass is apparent. That they also meet the latter criterion will be demonstrated in Chapter 5. In conjunction with each other, both dimensions support the contention that we are seeking to explore the broad range of black society extending from the lower working-class through the upper middle-class. To attain the above objective, we shall look at certain aspects of the "life-cycle" of these families, beginning with childhood experiences of husbands and wives, following them into their current economic and marital situations, and then continuing into childhood experiences of their offspring. While no claim is made that focus on the past, present, and future of black families is *the means* to unravel and make sense of the enormous complexities of black-white relations in the United States, it seems clear that the road to theoretical and practical understanding of these kinds of issues cannot by-pass what goes on within the conjugal family.[67]

NOTES

1. The report is a U.S. Department of Labor Document, March 1965, and is reprinted in Lee Rainwater and William L. Yancey, *The Moynihan*

Report and the Politics of Controversy (Cambridge, Mass.: The M.I.T. Press, 1967).

2. Ibid., pp. 17 ff.

3. Ibid., pp. 133 ff.

4. Rainwater, "Crucible of Identity in the Lower-Class Family," *Daedulus* 95.

5. Ibid. (1966): 175–76.

6. Andrew Billingsley, *Black Families in White America* (Englewood Cliffs, N.J.: Prentice-Hall, 1968), pp. 156–57.

7. Ibid.

8. Glazer, Foreword in Frazier, *The Negro Family in the United States*, pp. xiv-xv.

9. Rainwater, "Crucible of Identity," p. 182.

10. Elliot Liebow, *Tally's Corner* (Boston: Little, Brown and Co., 1967); David A. Schulz, *Coming Up Black* (Englewood Cliffs, N.J.: Prentice-Hall, 1969).

11. John Scanzoni, *Opportunity and the Family*, New York: The Free Press, 1970.

12. See Billingsley, 1968; Frazier, 1966; Sidney M. Greenfield, *English Rustics in Black Skin* (New Haven, Conn.: College and University Press, 1966).

13. As Billingsley and Greenfield point up, the Frazier-Herskovits type of debate regarding the extent of "African survivals," is currently unsettled. That the slave trade made some significant inroads on those traditions is beyond question, however.

14. Eli Ginzberg and Dale L. Hiestand, "Employment Patterns of Negro Men and Women," in John P. Davis, ed., *The American Negro Reference Book* (Englewood Cliffs, N.J.: Prentice-Hall, 1966), Ch. 4. Billingsley, pp. 79–87, presents data which indicate that in the urban areas of the North and West, black males are beginning to equal black females both in terms of years of school completed, and also in terms of job status.

15. Elliot Liebow, *Tally's Corner*, p. 129.

16. U.S. Bureau of the Census, *Current Population Reports*, Series P-20, No. 168, "Negro Population: March, 1966" (Washington, D.C.: U.S. Government Printing Office, December 22, 1967), p. 1.

17. Lee Rainwater and William L. Yancey, *The Moynihan Report and the Politics of Controversy*, p. 66.

18. Ibid.

19. Frazier, *The Negro Family in the United States*, p. 333.
20. Ibid., p. 355.
21. William J. Goode, "Family Disorganization," in Robert K. Merton and Robert A. Nisbet, *Contemporary Social Problems* (New York: Harcourt, Brace and World, 1966 edition), p. 514; J. Richard Udry, "Marital Instability by Race, Sex, Education, and Occupation Using 1960 Census Data," *American Journal of Sociology* 72 (September 1966), pp. 203–209.
22. Goode, "Family Disorganization," p. 514.
23. Udry, "Marital Instability."
24. Frazier, op. cit., p. 355.
25. Ibid., p. 333.
26. Ginzberg and Hiestand, "Employment Patterns," p. 225.
27. Ibid.
28. Rashi Fein, "An Economic and Social Profile of the Negro American," *Daedalus* (Fall 1965), p. 833.
29. Ginzberg and Hiestand, "Employment Patterns," p. 209.
30. Ibid.
31. E. Franklin Frazier, *Black Bourgeoisie* (New York: The Free Press, 1957), pp. 24, 26.
32. Ibid., pp. 235–36. It is quite likely that today's black college graduate is more concerned for his lower-class "brother" than was true in the past.
33. Ibid., p. 231.
34. Ibid., p. 47.
35. This same point is made by Billingsley, pp. 169 ff., and by Ralph H. Turner, "Book Review," *American Journal of Sociology* 74 (September 1968), pp. 198–99.
36. Thomas F. Pettigrew, *A Profile of the Negro American* (Princeton, N.J.: D. Van Nostrand, Inc., 1964), pp. 178 ff.; Billingsley, p. 201.
37. William A. Westley and Nathan B. Epstein, *The Silent Majority* (San Francisco: Jossey-Bass Inc., Publishers, 1969), p. 160; see also Billingsley, op. cit.; Scanzoni, *Opportunity and the Family*; Joseph Veroff and Sheila Feld, *Marriage and Work in America* (New York: Van Nostrand Reinhold Co., 1970).
38. Billingsley, *Black Families in White America*, p. 6 ff.
39. Milton Gordon, *Assimilation in American Life* (New York: Oxford University Press, Inc., 1964).
40. Ibid., pp. 172–73.
41. Billingsley, *Black Families in White America*, p. 10.

42. S. M. Miller, "The American Lower Classes: A Typological Approach," reprinted in Arthur B. Shostak and William Gomberg, *Blue-Collar World* (Englewood Cliffs, N.J.: Prentice-Hall, 1964), pp. 9–23.

43. The "poverty line" used in the text is based on 1966 incomes for an urban family with two children. See p. 22 in "Social and Economic Conditions of Negroes in the United States," BLS Report No. 332, *Current Population Reports*, Series P-23, No. 24, October 1967. By 1969 the "poverty threshold" had moved upward to $3,743. See *Current Population Reports*, Series P-60, No. 71, July 16, 1970, p. 2.

44. Miller, "American Lower Classes," p. 14.

45. Miller actually prefers the term, "New Working Class" when talking of the poor, rather than the value-laden term "lower-class." S. M. Miller and Frank Riessman, *Social Class and Social Policy* (New York: Basic Books, 1968), p. 30

46. *Current Population Reports*, Series P-23, No. 24; October, 1967, p. 38.

47. *Current Population Reports*, "Special Studies," Series P-23, No. 27, February 7, 1969, p. 38.

48. Ibid., p. 17.

49. Ibid.

50. *Current Population Reports*, Series P-60, No. 71, July 16, 1970, p. 4. Some "economically poor" families were drawn into our sample. See Table 5–4.

51. Ibid.

52. Ibid., p. 1.

53. Ibid.

54. Ibid..

55. Lee Rainwater and Gerald Handel, "Changing Family Roles in the Working Class," in Shostak and Gomberg, op. cit., pp. 70–80.

56. David A. Schulz, *Coming Up Black* (Englewood Cliffs, N.J.: Prentice-Hall, 1969), p. 145.

57. For a related discussion on the "stable style as a goal" see S. M. Miller and Frank Riessman, "The Working-class Subculture: A New View," especially pp. 29–36.

58. St. Clair Drake and Horace R. Cayton, *Black Metropolis* (New York: Harper & Row, 1962 edition), Vol. 2, pp. 661, 714.

59. Gordon Parks, "The Cycle of Despair," in Louis A. Ferman, Joyce L. Kornbluh, Alan Haber, *Poverty in America* (Ann Arbor: U. of Michigan Press, 1968), pp. 513–18. Edward Wakin, *At the Edge of Harlem* (New York: W. Morrow & Co., 1965).

60. One exception is Warren Tenhouten, "The Black Family: Myth and Reality," *Psychiatry* 2 (May 1970): 145–73.

61. Robert F. Winch, *Identification and Its Familial Determinants* (Indianapolis: Bobbs-Merrill Co., 1962), pp. 40 ff.

62. Peter M. Blau and Otis Dudley Duncan, *The American Occupational Structure* (New York: John Wiley & Sons, Inc., 1967), pp. 207 ff.

63. Scanzoni, *Opportunity and the Family*.

64. Further methodological details are discussed in the Appendix.

65. *The Negro in Indianapolis: A Summary of Local Data*, Community Service Council of Metropolitan Indianapolis, Inc., September 1967, p. 35.

66. "Trends in Divorce and Family Disruption," *Health, Education & Welfare Indicators* (Washington, D.C.: U.S. Public Health Service, September 1963).

67. See William Brink and Louis Harris, *Black and White* (New York: Simon & Schuster—A Clarion Book, 1967), pp. 154–57.

2

Structural
Background Factors

The point has been repeatedly made that minimal economic resources and family instability are part of a vicious, ongoing cycle in which a certain number of blacks are seemingly caught. Born into deprivation, they witness their parents denied economic opportunity and see the bonds of their home gradually dissolve. While their fathers are often forced to leave the home, their mothers either obtain employment or support the family through AFDC.[1] As they grow up, they learn to expect little else for themselves than what they have already seen. Both in terms of the occupational structure and the family system, what they have experienced then becomes normative. "This is the way it is," and seemingly precious little can be done about it.

When they mature physically, sexual activity becomes a mark of identity—of prestige and status. Marriage occurs at a fairly young age and these blacks soon find themselves at the same point in the ongoing cycle that once their parents were in. The husband in particular is denied economic opportunity and since he cannot fulfill his "provider" role adequately, both spouses find that their marriage is becoming "unglued."

But the majority of blacks in American society are not part of this cycle. The families on which this study is based are part of this "black majority." This chapter investigates some of the factors that characterized the social backgrounds of these couples which might have been related to their current capability to maintain ongoing family units.

URBAN EXPERIENCE

Current trends suggest that increasing numbers of blacks are undergoing economic deprivation and marital instability. These trends correspond to the continuing large-scale migration of blacks from the rural South to the ghettos of the urban centers, especially in the North and West. Rainwater remarks,

". . . In the hundred years since emancipation, Negroes in rural areas have been able to maintain full nuclear families almost as well as similarly situated whites. . . . *it is the move to the city that* results in the very high proportion of mother-headed households."[2] (Italics supplied.)

From 1949 to 1962, the percentage of white families headed by a woman changed hardly at all (8.8 to 8.6 percent). But among nonwhites, the proportion increased from 18.8 to 23.2 percent.[3] More recent census data show the proportion of white female-headed families holding at 8.9 percent.[4] And "among white families, death was the most common reason for the husband's absence."[5] On the other hand, the national proportion of nonwhite families headed by a female rose to 26.4 percent in 1968, and to 27.3 percent in 1969.[6] Within the inner city ghetto, the 1968 proportion of female-headed black families is 30 percent, up from 23 percent in 1960.[7] "Among Negro families with a female head, separation and divorce are the most common reasons for the husband's absence."[8] The other commonly used indicator of "stress" within the black (or any) family system is illegitimacy. From an anthropological-sociological standpoint, illegitimacy poses, among other things, a "question" in socialization. If both male and female parents (or their equivalents) are not present, who is responsible for the total training of these "new members" of society?[9] Later we shall look at studies that compare children reared in "whole" versus "other" families. Here we only wish to draw attention to the issue itself, and also to the fact that only 61 percent of black children under 18 in the central city lived with *both* parents in 1968, a drop of from 71 percent in 1960.[10] During this same period, the proportion of white children living with both parents went from 91 to 88 percent.[11]

Likewise, the white illegitimacy ratio (number of illegitimate births to live births) increased from 18.6 to 30.7, while the non-white ratio increased from 202.4 to 235.9.[12] It is not coincidental that since 1948 the number of AFDC cases opened yearly has almost doubled (210,193 to 380,984 in 1963), and that the nonwhite male unemployment rate has likewise doubled (5.1 in 1948 to 10.6 in 1963).[13]

The move to the city and its impact on black family structure is traumatic for many reasons. Perhaps the most significant reason is the undermining of the aspirations that black migrants bring with them to the metropolis. They come with desires to gain more of a share in the American Dream than they have previously known. They expect these aspirations to be realized. For the great majority of first-generation blacks, they are not. Blau and Duncan note that "rural migrants to large cities are better off than they would be had they remained at home," but they also add, "but not so well off as natives or urban migrants there."[14] As Schulz describes it, in the country the life of a sharecropper "pretty well defined" the "occupational fate" and "life-style" of the black couple, and the "wife understood this. In the city, however, they see people doing much better than they. This is likely to create a revolution in expectations (particularly on the wife's part) that can have quite negative consequences for their marriage."[15]

Being born in the South (especially the rural South) is a handicap to occupational achievement for both white and black, but particularly for blacks. Blacks born in the South have significantly inferior educational opportunities than do whites.[16] Those who migrate attempt to make the transition from a way of life vastly different from that found in the city, and discover that they have been ill-prepared for urban living. In addition to processes of discrimination historically and currently practiced by the white majority, the inexorable forces of automation and job obsolescence combine to make the minimally skilled black man less employable than ever before in American history.

When the white worker migrates, it is often because he has had a "job offer" or a "transfer." When the black man migrates, it is most often because he is currently unemployed or else works irregularly, and thus "dreams" of "something better" in the city.[17] In spite of the fact that the city shatters his dreams, available evidence indicates that black *aspirations* continue to remain high. In reality, the actualization of these dreams is minimal. Concurrently, while disillusionment is setting in, the husband's provider-role in the lower-class black family is being undermined. Also settling in, therefore, are the almost inevitable processes of erosion of the bonds of cohesion between husbands and wives.[18]

A fundamental reason the native urbanite does better economically and socially than the rural migrant is because he is better socialized or "acculturated" into the urban milieu. The native urbanite has had access to better schools and possesses greater awareness of viable means to attain valued goals. In more obvious terms he "knows his way around" in the city, even to so commonplace a process as choosing the correct buses to get him to work on time.[19] In a study of black manual workers in Chicago, Stamler found that men born there had absorbed "urban values" to a far greater extent than recent black migrants from the rural south.[20]

Coleman, in his discussion of recent black migrations, suggests that "perhaps the essential characteristic of the individual's relation to society in industrial urban centers is individualism."[21] He further contends that the economic structure under which blacks lived in the rural South "can best be described as modern feudalism." Rural blacks, he claims, have therefore not been socialized in the remotest fashion to adapt to "the most important element. . . . For survival in urban society . . . how to take responsibility for one's self." However traumatic blacks' initial experiences in the city, Stamler's work among others reveals that over time many blacks have shown tenacity and persisted in their efforts at assimilation into the urban milieu. The result is that sheer time in the city enables some blacks to learn how to operate in and to use the urban environment in terms of their own (and their families') interests.

In addition to processes of gradual urban acculturation, the native has another advantage over the recent migrant. According to Blau and Duncan, the native also does better because rural migrants "preempt" the lowest positions in the occupational hierarchy and thus "they provide a structural impetus to upward mobility for the other men in large cities."[22] The influx of rural blacks, in short, seems to push upward the occupational and social status of blacks who have been there for some time. And increased social status increases the likelihood of marital stability.

We might expect, therefore, that husbands and wives in our sample do not come from a rural background. Instead, we would suspect that most of them have not had to face either personally, or else too recently, the trauma of severely shattered expectations as a result of being suddenly transplanted from a rural to an urban atmosphere. They have had enough time to learn what the black man in American society can realistically expect from it and equally fundamental how to "operate" within it. From the following data, it would appear that this assumption is confirmed. Of the 400 respondents in our sample (one spouse per household: 198 males, 202 females) 187 of them or 47 percent reported that during their teenage years, they lived in a "large city of over 100,000 people.[23] The "teen-age years" were specifically spelled out to each respondent as being the 12–18 year interval. (This specification applied to all such questions regarding the teen-age years, and thus enhances the comparability of replies among respondents.)[24] Fifty-eight respondents (15 percent) lived in a "small city," 26 percent (105 cases) lived in a "small town," and only 12 percent (50 cases) grew up on a farm.

Interestingly, of all wives in the sample, 52 percent grew up in a large city, while 48 percent are found in the other three categories. Yet only 42 percent of husbands grew up in a large city, while 58 percent are found in the other categories. Thus while the sample as a whole is predominantly an "urban" sample, the wives represented are perhaps "more urban" than the husbands. Because of the sharp contrasts described by Frazier and others in the role-development of black males and females, our study will contain numerous cross-sex comparisons. Some have alleged that the experiences of black females have been such as to predispose them to "fit" the larger society much more adequately than is so for black males. This allegation is traceable to many factors, e.g., white fears regarding alleged black male sexuality and aggression, being overly dominated by older females in the matriarchate, etc. Whatever its validity, the following pages will examine this assertion and its implications as fully as possible.

Not only have the majority of our respondents not grown up in a rural area, 27 percent of them were born in the Indianapolis metropolitan area and have spent all their lives there. Another 38 percent have migrated to Indianapolis from Kentucky and Tennessee. These border states have racial traditions vastly different from those in the "Deep South." Presumably blacks from these border areas are thus less handicapped in functioning both economically and conjugally in the urban North than would be the case for rural blacks from the Deep South. The difference is probably due to the greater repression and denigration of selfhood that takes place in the Deep South. Concomitantly, border-state educational systems are more adequate for blacks (and whites) than are those in the Deep South.

Finally, when we look at *length* of residence in the Indianapolis area, only 12 percent of the sample have lived there nine years or less. An additional 17 percent have resided there from 10–19 years. The remaining 71 percent have lived there 20 years or more. Thus from *three* standpoints: rural-urban residence during crucial formative teen years; state of birth and subsequent migration; and number of years in the Indianapolis metropolitan area, it may be said that most of our respondents have had substantial experience in urban living. The initial "move to the city," which Rainwater and Coleman have noted is so traumatic for many black families, has not been part of the immediate experience of most our respondents.

The generalization, therefore, that "the occupational achievements of urban men . . . are higher than those of rural men,"[25] may have certain implications for the black family, because of the association between length of exposure to the urban milieu, occupational achievement, and family stability. Unfortunately, we were unable to collect information from one-parent households to provide a *direct* comparison with our husband-wife families. Therefore, our basis for comparison must always be with other studies which do have such information, as well as data collected by the U.S. Census Bureau for both types of households. There are admitted difficulties in this approach, but it is a reasonable one if we keep in mind that our objective is to *explore* relationships, to try to suggest hypotheses, and to build theory rather than to demonstrate definitive conclusions. With regard to the matter of urban tenure, for instance, data available from other sources indicate that there is a tendency for dissolved black families to have been in the urban milieu for a relatively brief period.[26] Our data, on the other hand, at least suggest that length of urban residence may, for the reasons discussed, be *one* of the background factors that contributes to the maintenance of black families.

STATUS ADVANTAGES

Father's Occupation

The preceding paragraphs have implied that urban experience may have positive consequences for later economic and marital situations through the gradual generational improvement of the socioeconomic situation of blacks (males in particular). To examine this possibility more closely, we first want to compare the occupational levels of *fathers* of respondents in the sample with the national occupational levels of black males over the last several decades. Table 2–1 shows these kinds of comparisons based on the main

TABLE 2–1. OCCUPATIONAL LEVELS OF FATHERS OF RESPONDENTS IN COMPARISON WITH BLACK MALES NATIONALLY 1920–1940

Main Census Occupational Category	Fathers of Respondents in 1968 Sample	National Proportions of Black Males		
		1920	1930	1940
Professional, Technical, and Kindred	3.2% (13)	1.2%	1.5%	1.7%
Proprietors, Managers and Officials	3.0 (12)	1.0	1.2	1.4
Clerical and Sales Workers	2.1 (8)	1.5	1.7	2.6
Craftsmen, Skilled Workers, Foremen	11.3 (45)	4.6	4.8	4.4
Operatives (Semi-skilled)	17.5 (70)	7.0	9.0	11.7
Private Household and Service Workers	6.3 (25)	7.1	9.4	13.7
Unskilled Laborers	11.0 (44)	30.9	31.7	23.0
Farmers, Farm Workers	31.6 (127)	46.7	40.7	41.5
Not Ascertained	14.0 (56)			
Total	100% (400)	100%	100%	100%

Source for National Data: U.S. Department of Labor, Bureau of Labor Statistics, "A Century of Change: Negroes in the U.S. Economy, 1860–1960," *Monthly Labor Review* (December 1962), pp. 1363–64. Reprinted in part from Alphonso Pinkney, *Black Americans*, Englewood Cliffs, N.J.: Prentice-Hall, 1969, p. 79.

Census Bureau categories. The median age of respondents in the sample is approximately 45 years. Therefore, a substantial proportion of the sample were adolescents in the thirties. Some were adolescents in the twenties, some in the forties. The table enables us to see the occupational levels of the fathers of our respondents in comparison to the job levels of the black population in general during these decades. The striking feature is that fathers of respondents are weighted more heavily *toward the upper end of the economic and status hierarchy* than was the black population in general during these years.

In the top three white-collar categories, we find that 8.3 percent of respondents' fathers had white-collar positions. In 1920, only 3.7 percent of the general black populace held such positions; in 1930 only 4.4 percent did; and by 1940, the figure had climbed only to 5.7 percent. It is significant to note the greater proportion of respondents' fathers who held *professional* positions as compared to the three census periods, even 1940. But of still greater significance is the proportion of respondents' fathers holding managerial positions, most of them, very likely, in private business. Several observers have noted that while black men are slowly "breaking into" the professions, they are not yet "cracking" the ranks of management.[27] Even the 1960 census showed only 1.7 percent of all employed black males at this level of authority and policy-decision making.[28] Yet fathers of respondents in our sample (3.0 percent) exceed even this recent census figure.

Many sociologists consider foremen and skilled workers as part of the broad middle-class, i.e., the *lower* middle-class. Here too we find that respondents' fathers are greatly overrepresented at this level (11.3 percent) when compared to the general black population. By 1960, only 9.8 percent of all employed black males held these kinds of jobs.[29] Next, the top rung of the working class is occupied by semi-skilled workers and operatives. Here too respondents' fathers (17.5 percent) far exceed the proportions found among blacks as a whole. Only in the lower working-class (service workers, unskilled laborers) and the agricultural workers, do we find that proportions within the larger black population exceed those within our sample.

In short, a substantial number of our respondents came from middle-class and upper working-class homes. They tend to be overrepresented there when compared to the larger black population; they tend to have had higher economic and status benefits than many other black citizens. Furthermore, their spouses also came from homes that tended to be more advantaged than those in the general black populace. For instance, 7.1 percent of their husbands and wives had white-collar fathers; 5.8 percent of spouses had lower middle-class fathers; 14.3 percent had upper working-class fathers; 11.9 percent had lower working-class fathers; and 36.3 percent of spouses had fathers involved in agriculture; the remainder could not be ascertained.

Parental Education

The social-class advantage of these respondents can also be seen when we examine the years of schooling completed by their parents. By the year 1940, it is very likely that all respondents' fathers had completed their formal education, since most Americans have done so by age 25. In 1940, the median years of school completed by nonwhite males ages 25–29 years was 6.5.[30] Very likely if older nonwhite males were included in the computation, the figure would be lower. In any event, the median years of school for *all* fathers (irrespective of age) of respondents in the sample is 8.0, i.e., completion of grade school. The median years of school completed for nonwhite females ages 25–29 in 1940 was 7.5, and for mothers of respondents in the sample it was also 8.0.

Furthermore, we find that there is some connection between urban experience and these apparent status advantages. For instance, males in the sample show a correlation of .37 between fathers' education and years of residence in the Indianapolis area; r = .64 for (non-southern) state of birth, r = .43 for urban adolescent residence. Females show correlations of .19, .41, and .33, respectively. The relationships between occupation of males' fathers and the three factors are .18, .04, and .21, respectively. For occupations of females' fathers, they are .44, .12, and .21, respectively.

Two related points stand out.

1. Respondents in the sample had background status advantages
    (fathers' occupation, education of parents) which exceeded
    those of the larger black population.
2. These advantages are associated with experience in the urban
    milieu.

Urban experience and status advantage combined represent a "syndrome of advantage" in terms of later occupational and conjugal
situations. If there were some way to sort out from the national data
in Table 2–1 rural blacks along with recent urban migrants, it might
be that the remaining proportions would reflect those in our sample.
That is, it may be that to some extent our sample represents a pattern that has been emerging in black, urban society over the last several decades.[31] Gradually, the majority of urban blacks, after a
more or less protracted period of assimilation into the urban milieu,
may have been able *to some degree* to adopt dominant occupational
and conjugal patterns. More concretely, with respect to those in
our sample, having commenced their adult lives with relative
advantages, it is likely that they themselves were subsequently able
to add additional economic and status resources. This possibility
will be examined in later chapters along with its potential implications for current marital cohesion. Although it will be made clear
in Chapter 5, the reader should not get the impression that even
working- and middle-class urban blacks have had anywhere near
the social and economic advantages of urban whites. They have not,
even though they may be "better off" than rural and migrant blacks.

HOUSEHOLD COMPOSITION

Parental Presence

A third type of background feature necessary to examine is the
"composition of the household" in which these husbands and wives
grew up. A central factor in connection with the black family system has been the presence or absence of the father. Frazier has ably
documented the difficulties in our society attached to the adult black

male remaining with his family and functioning in the role of provider. In his summary of the research literature regarding the father-absent family, Winch makes the point that the situation of parental absence or presence—

determines the roles with whose occupants the child has an opportunity to interact, to observe, to admire or to dislike, to be rewarded by, to learn from, to identify. The point is very simple and is reminiscent of Sutherland's principle of differential association: that it is easier to learn from someone who is present than from someone who is not.[32]

The assumption is that the black (or white) child (male, in particular) growing up in a home where the father is absent—either often or permanently—finds it difficult to learn how the dominant society expects adult males to behave or to function both within the conjugal unit and the occupational structure. Lacking these role models, it may therefore be quite difficult for him to fulfill these kinds of behaviors. Elder, however, in his review of the literature of the effects of father-absence on later achievement, makes the telling point that "the effects of father-absence are frequently confounded with economic and cultural factors. . . . when socioeconomic variations are satisfactorily controlled, available data indicate that household structure has little, if any, effect on the academic performance and test scores of children and adolescents."[33] The conclusion seems to be that economic disadvantage seems to have greater negative consequences on school achievement than the fact per se of simply coming from a "broken home."

Father-absence in any household is inevitably linked to limited finances, and without these the child is hampered to some degree in not only the purchase of books and necessary supplies, but also lunch money, clothes, and other "status symbols" necessary for peer acceptance and identification within the context of the middle-class school system. The actual extent to which the child is hampered is strongly related to the amount of income available to the remaining parent. The affluent white child from a broken home, therefore, will be substantially less affected than a poor black child. That blacks in general are so much poorer than whites may be part of the "cause" both of broken homes and of limited school perfor-mance. For example, in 1960 the proportion of nonwhite urban children under 18 who were living without both parents was 35.1 percent; for whites the proportion was 10.1 percent.[34] At ages 7 to 9 years, in 1960, where both parents were present, 96.1 percent of nonwhite males were in school; where only one parent was present the proportion was 95.3 percent—not yet a substantial difference. But by ages 16–17, the proportions were 78.0 and 72.7 percent, respectively, indicating that although many nonwhites have trouble staying in school, those from one-parent homes have an even more difficult time. Nonwhites with neither parent present at ages 16–17 are *most* disadvantaged in terms of being able to remain in school; only 63.2 percent have not dropped out.[35]

Because disadvantage negatively influences school achieve-ment plus remaining in school, it obviously will hinder later occupa-tional attainments. Blau and Duncan conclude that while coming from a "broken home" is a hindrance to occupational achievement, "virtually the entire amount of this handicap . . . can be attributed to the educational disadvantage that such rearing confers."[36] In short, the child from a broken home *where there is financial stress* experiences both educational and later occupational disadvantage.

The other consequence of father-absence that has received con-siderable attention is sex-role development. Factors such as "infan-tile characteristics, greater dependency, and conflict over sex identity expressed in overly aggressive behavior" are said to be found in boys reared without a father present.[37] Pettigrew concludes that black male children reared in "fatherless homes are being socialized into a sex pattern that will later be inimical to the socialization of their own children."[38]

Nevertheless, once again, the critical issue may not be the mere fact of father absent or present, but the economic deprivation that all black males face, significantly those in the lower-class. Schulz notes that even when the lower-class black father is present "he is totally inadequate as a model for achieving mobility in the larger society."[39] This inadequacy results because the father is "likely to be preoccupied with the attempt to cover his own deep sense of failure with a facade of competence and rough hewn masculinity mani-

fested in his physical, if not psychological, domination of his wife."
Boys in these situations, he claims, learn how to be "a man without
assuming full responsibility for a family."[40] In sum, although we
may not overlook the consequences that black father presence or absence has both for achievement and for sex-role learning, it is crucial
to keep in mind that those consequences cannot be separated from
economic-status factors. The fact that white society effectively ex-
cludes many lower-class black fathers from the opportunity structure is at the core both of their rates of absence from the home and
of their alleged inadequacy as a role model if present.

With these perspectives, let us examine our respondents to
discover the extent to which they came from "whole families." In
response to the question, "did you live with both natural parents
during most of your teen-age years," 58.8 percent of those in the
sample (235 of 400) replied affirmatively. If the answer was "no,"
he (she) was then asked if he (she) lived with mother only, or
father only, or else neither parent, but had instead another arrangement. The proportion of those replying "mother only" was 21.8
percent; "father only" was 6.0 percent; and "other" was 13.5 percent. We then probed further and asked those who lived with
"mother only," or "other": "Who acted as your father, that is,
what one man had the most to do with bringing you up?" The
same kind of question was asked of those who replied they had
lived with "father only" or "other": "Who acted as your mother,
that is, what one woman had the most to do with bringing
you up?"

What we were trying to do was to locate any possible parent-
surrogate or substitute—a male in particular but also a female who,
in the perception of the respondent, played the role of father or
mother. Theoretically, such a parent-substitute might be able to
carry out the same kind of socialization as a blood parent, and thus
function in the same way as a role model for the child. Billingsley,
among others, is critical of a simplistic dichotomy of black families
into "female headed," and "husband-wife present" that is not at
least aware of "the variations among Negro families living under
different basic conditions."[41] One of these variations pertains to
precisely this matter of parent-extensions or substitutes. ". . . Ne-

gro families have [always] placed heavy emphasis and reliance on interactions with both relatives and nonrelatives outside the immediate nuclear family . . . to help the family socialize its children."[42] Chapters 3 and 4 will have more to say about the actual place of such role models, but for now it is sufficient simply to underscore both their presence and their potential significance within the black family system.

In addition to the 235 cases who lived with both blood parents, 43 more lived with "natural mother" and a *step-father*, 15 more lived with "natural father" and a *step-mother*. From the legal perspective, these kinds of substitutes are occupying the position of parent. Moreover in Census Bureau terms, they are husband-wife families. If we add these cases (14.6 percent of the total sample) to the 235 cases who lived with both blood parents, we find that 73.4 percent of our respondents lived in husband-wife families during most of their adolescent years. The remaining 26.6 percent experienced a variety of family forms including foster parents, the presence of other male or female relatives (grandfather or grandmother, older brother or sister, uncle or aunt), male or female nonrelatives, only *one* adult (usually mother) present, or else was brought up in some kind of institution.

During the 1930's and 40's when most of our respondents were adolescents, the national proportions of urban black husband-wife families remained fairly constant at around 76 percent.[43] At mid-century (1949) the figure was still 76.8 percent, though by 1962 it had dropped to 72.3 percent.[44] Therefore, any expectation that blacks in our sample would be more likely to come from "whole" families than the black population in general is not borne out.

Nonetheless, only 12.5 percent of the sample (50 cases) could identify no male whatsoever as having played the role of father to them. For about 87 percent of the sample, one of the types of male personages cited above did perform at least some of the behaviors of a father for them. Basically, however, these husbands and wives who are currently maintaining stable families do not differ from the majority of American blacks. Both in the sample and nationally, approximately a quarter of today's adult blacks came from other than "whole" families. Given the great stress in the literature regarding the cyclical nature of black family disorganization, this finding seems significant. That respondents in our sample are able to maintain ongoing family units would not seem therefore to have been particularly influenced by father absence or presence. Instead, what seems to be more central is Schulz's contention that what family experience does to and for the child (i.e., functionality) may be more crucial for him than family "wholeness" per se. In Chapter 3, we shall see in fact that even respondents from "broken homes" had a parent or parent-surrogate who performed valuable functions for them. Those kinds of benefits, as we shall suggest, very likely did have substantial influence on their later economic and conjugal situations.

As we might expect, however, we do find a positive association between family "wholeness" and urban experience, and status factors. For males, the correlation between wholeness and state of birth is .52; residence in the Indianapolis area r = .30; education of father r = .39; education of mother r = .20. For females, the figures are, respectively, .40, .40, .28, .08. In addition, for females, correlations between wholeness and "growing up" in an urban area, and father's occupation, were .16 and .29, respectively. In short, added to the syndrome of urban experience and status advantage is the tendency towards family wholeness. Yet the relationships are far from perfect. There are some in the sample who came from "broken homes" who nonetheless had received certain status and urban exposure advantages. These factors tended perhaps to compensate for lack of a "whole" family as far as later experiences were concerned. That possibility points once again to a basic theme that wholeness is probably less crucial for later attainments than is functionality, i.e., what is done *for* the child, what is provided *to* him.

Number of Siblings

An additional feature of the structure of the household that has definite consequences for the child is the number of siblings with whom he grew up. It is clear for instance that *size* of the household is associated with lower-class black poverty. "In 1960, nonwhite mothers age 35 to 39 with family incomes over $10,000 had 2.9 children; those with less than $2,000 had 5.3."[45] A survey by a government "task force" on men failing to pass the selective service written test showed that 3 out of 4 of the nonwhites failing the test came from families with 4 or more children, 1 out of 2 came from families with 6 or more children.[46] The combined effects of limited economic resources plus limited parental (often only maternal) attention to numerous children could have a deleterious effect on later performances of certain children from large households both in the occupational and conjugal spheres. As Blau and Duncan state:

The proverbial large happy family is not conducive to occupational success. The task of raising many children evidently strains parental resources, with the result that the advantages of a higher education go predominantly to men with few siblings. Men from small families are more likely than men from large ones to continue their education on every level up to college graduation.[47]

What of our respondents in our sample? From what size families did they come? Crude birth rates among nonwhites have been consistently higher than those among whites, at least since 1850. Nevertheless from 1910 to 1947, the trend for *both* groups was toward lowered fertility.[48] The modal (most frequent) number of children in the country as a whole, born to the cohort of 1943–47 was 2. This figure is identical to the number born to the cohort (women of child-bearing ages) of 1920–30. In the cohort 1865–70 the modal number was 4.[49] There was, in other words, prior to and during the lifetimes of the *parents* of our respondents, a movement in the larger society toward smaller family size, with approximately 2 children per family.

The modal background family size for respondents in our sample is 3. Forty-six of our respondents, or 11.6 percent, came from families with three children. Thirty-eight of them (9.5 percent) came from two-child families, and 37 (9.3 percent) were sole children. Therefore, almost a third of the sample (30.4) came from homes with three children or less. A substantial proportion of them cluster at or *near* the modal number of children found in the population as a whole. Another third of the sample (30.5 percent) came from families with 4–6 children, and the remainder came from families with 7 or more children.

Interestingly, the respondents are married to spouses with similar size background families. The modal number of children in the spouse families was also 3 (13.3 percent). Thirty-five percent of the spouses come from families with three children or less; 30 percent from families with 4–6 children, and the remainder from families with 7 or more. Thus a significant proportion of respondents in our sample, plus their spouses, came from families that tended to be slightly larger than those within white society.

Taeuber and Taeuber point out that nationally there is a "net balance [of] an *average* number of children per [black] couple only slightly above the figure for whites."[50] Therefore, the modal number of three for respondents in our sample does not appear to differ from that of the general black population throughout most of this century. This fact means that by and large our respondents did not come from situations where large numbers of siblings placed excessive demands on relatively limited parental resources. They are apparently not representative of the black lower-class where such strains do indeed exist. Therefore, operating in their favor was the fact that available family resources (emotional, material) were less likely to be stretched "too thinly." Instead, each individual was more likely to receive more of whatever resources were available. This factor (or structural feature) therefore, added to those previously discussed, becomes part of their "syndrome of relative advantage," very likely helping to enhance later occupational and conjugal experiences. (For males, the correlation of sibling number with urban adolescent residence was —.19; with fathers' occupation —.20; with family wholeness —.23. For females, respectively, the correlations were —.22; —.28; —.20.)

Before we investigate fully the topic of parental functionality, or resource-provision in Chapter 3, we need to consider one final background factor that might be labeled "structural," but which actually serves as a kind of "conceptual bridge" between structure and functionality insofar as the black family is concerned. The analytic distinction between structure and function must always be arbitrary and sometimes overlapping, e.g., in the above case of both status and sibling number which involve position or structure, but which also involve function in that a *process* of resource-provision is automatically implied. Religion is even more difficult to distinguish in this fashion, for while it may be described as a structural element, it too implies inherent consequences or functions.

PARENTAL RELIGION

Frazier's last study in his well-known series on American blacks focused on the "Negro church." He makes the point that once made a slave, an African native was stripped of all vestiges of his ancient culture, including his religion which formerly had organized his existence and provided a rationale for the meaning of life.[51] The early generations of slaves were not permitted religious assemblage, and after a while their religious traditions largely died out. Even if slave owners had made no efforts to obliviate them, Frazier claims the traditions would have perished anyway due to irrelevancy. That is, the gods they had depended on had failed them, nor had they offered any means for extricating them from their predicament nor, most of all, had they provided the slaves any guidance as to how to live in and with slavery. Lacking any other means of social cohesion, Christianity played the major role "in creating solidarity among a people who lacked social cohesion and a structured social life."[52]

Efforts at proselyting blacks were most successful by the Methodists and Baptists during the decades near the turn of the nineteenth century. Largely because their clergy itself was uneducated, these (then) sects therefore had a strong appeal to "the poor and the ignorant and the outcast."[53] The emotionalism so characteristic of the early camp meetings and revivals provided needed release of pent-up feelings and some sense of emotional solidarity (though temporary) for the otherwise rigidly guarded slaves. Initially some slaveowners worried about the inherent equalitarian implications of Christianity, plus the abolitionist beliefs of many of the circuit riders. Gradually, however, the abolitionist fervor declined and in its place an ideology of acquiescence to slavery was taught to blacks. "Black men were expected to accept their lot in this life and if they were obedient and honest and truthful they would be rewarded in the world after death."[54] As a result the *one* institution that molded plantation slaves to each other and even to their white masters was the Church. After emancipation "an organized religious life became the chief means by which a structured or organized social life came into existence among the Negro masses."[55]

More specifically, "the Churches became and have remained until the past twenty years or so, the most important agency of social control among Negroes."[56] Since, under slavery, monogamous and stable conjugal unions were not allowed to develop, it was the post-slavery church that began to institutionalize and to enforce dominant conjugal patterns among blacks. First at the *ideological* level, free blacks were taught that the Bible commands the father to be "the head of the home." Second at the *economic* level W. E. Dubois was the first to note that economic cooperation among blacks began in connection with church building. "It was in order to establish their own churches that Negroes began to pool their meagre economic resources and buy buildings and the land on which they stood."[57] The church was the first mechanism to begin to instill economic rationality of the American culture variety into black males. They were to be good providers in the economic system because they had an "awesome" responsibility—a duty—both to their family and to their church. Neither obligation could be easily slighted because third, at the *interpersonal* level, strong primary bonds among fellow church members provided meaningful and effective sanctions. Moreover, since almost the entire local black community was involved in a religious group, it was exceedingly difficult for anyone to carry on a subterfuge of any sort and still remain in "good standing" in the church. During the post-slavery period the whole local black community was organized around its churches.

Concomitant with the duty to provide for the church came, fourth, the *privilege* of leadership. The elimination of blacks from the dominant political scene resulted in the church becoming the main area of political activities. "It was the area . . . [where] ambitious individuals could achieve distinction and the symbols of status. . . . where the struggle for power and the thirst for power could be satisfied. This was especially important to the Negro men who had never been able to assert themselves. . . ."[58] The learning of leadership roles plus the confidence gained from enacting them probably carried over, in turn, into more effective male leadership patterns within the black family unit.

Finally the church, according to Frazier, became "a refuge in a hostile white world," i.e., it provided a set of values that enabled blacks to accommodate themselves to the situation of rejection and isolation imposed on them by whites.[59] The core of this value system was quiescence and faithful endurance. Blacks did not seek to overthrow their "white oppressors," but instead to emulate them in the hope that conformity rather than conflict would one day bring valued goals and benefits. The black church was vigorous in establishing all-black schools whose chief purpose was to "uplift" the morals and the work habits of the black masses. As far as conjugal patterns were concerned, black males became more diligent providers, and both sexes began to adopt the sexual norms of the larger society.

In sum, due to all these factors operating together in intricate fashion within black society, church and family structures became closely interlocked and highly interdependent. The religious structure became the vehicle whereby the dominant pattern of the monogamous and stable family, with male as head and provider, became institutionalized among black American culture. The migration to the cities changed the character of the black church and its relations to the family from basic concerns with the after-life to prime focus on the needs of this life. In its current relations to the black family it no longer exercises the strict supervision and effective sanctions it once did. Nevertheless, over the decades of rapid urbanization of blacks, Frazier claims (as do others, e.g., Drake and Cayton) that the church has been the prime institution or means whereby blacks became assimilated into urban life.[60] This fact was due in part at least to the black's systematic exclusion from other segments of urban society. Many first generation migrants chose the *gemeinschaft* (intimate warmth) of the storefront church; while their children and others chose the opposite polar type, i.e., the huge, elaborate and prestigeful (yet *gesellschaft*, or impersonal) black urban church. (The average size of the urban black church is around 800 members.)[61] Significant it is that urban blacks remained in the church, that the church "continues to function as an important element in the organized social life of Negroes," and that it continues to communicate and to reinforce dominant family values and behaviors.[62]

For example, Richardson reports that as late as 1965, there were five major black denominations in the United States, accounting for well over ten million adult members plus almost six million Sunday School members.[63] He also estimates that there are some 800,000 additional blacks who are affiliated with predominantly white denominations. It is difficult to enumerate the number of blacks involved in storefront churches but it is considered to be sizeable, particularly in view of the flood of recent migrants from the rural South. Given that Census Bureau estimates of total black population in 1964–65 were around 19 million, it is clear that an overwhelming preponderance of blacks (above 80 percent) remain to some extent involved in the church.

Frazier and others have noted that in spite of numerical involvement, social control and socialization functions of the church have begun to wane in the last several years, particularly for younger blacks. However, this decline predates the adolescent experiences of respondents in our sample. As youths, they grew up in homes where both parents were highly involved with, and presumably psychologically identified with, religious structures and values. For instance, of males who could locate a father (or father figure) during their adolescent years, 92 percent of them reported their father (or father substitute) attended church.[64] And out of this proportion, 55 percent reported the father attended *at least* once a week. The data for their mothers are, as we might expect, even more striking. The number of males who identify a mother (or mother figure) who also attended church is 186. Of this number, 81.2 percent report she attended *at least* once a week. The proportions of wives in the sample reporting weekly church attendance for their fathers and mothers are similar to those reported by husbands.

Thus, the church played a major role in the lives of our respondents' parents. We may assume, moreover, that it played the kind of role that historically has characterized the linkage between church and black family. Specifically, *it transmitted and reinforced values and behaviors leading to optimum fulfillment of dominant expectations regarding economic and conjugal behavior*. Children from these kinds of homes (our respondents) would quite likely, therefore, tend to share these same kinds of values and behaviors. This is assuredly *not* to say that these kinds of religiously based values operate independently of economic resources. As is true among whites, it appears that less advantaged blacks have less involvement in churches than those who are better off.[65] In other words, lesser resources are associated with lower religious involvement as well as with lower marital stability. The classic interaction of status and religion applies to American blacks as it does elsewhere. Blacks with greater status resources are more likely to be religiously involved, and this involvement is a chief means of transmitting and reinforcing dominant conjugal patterns.

In short, added to urban experience and relative status advantage is the ideological element of sociocultural religion. To be sure it is primarily a correlate of the first two elements, as is family composition. It provided a set of values, beliefs, and norms regarding behavior in two crucial areas of later adult life—occupation and family. (The orientation of the black church toward political activism is not in view here, though as Scheiner puts it, it has been torn continually between protest and accommodation.)[66] Obviously, having these values without economic opportunity will not result in lowered rates of marital dissolution. It is clear, for instance, that many lower-class blacks share dominant ideals regarding marriage and family patterns, yet are hindered from attaining them due to economic deprivations.

Chapter 3 examines the *process* by which certain religious values pertinent to occupation and family are actually transmitted. For now, we may simply assume that parental religious involvement, as a structural feature during the adolescence of most of those in the sample, helped to reinforce the positive consequences of urban experience and status advantage.

SUMMARY

We have looked at four kinds of elements that may have influenced the current economic and family situations of the couples in our sample. Observers have long noted that poverty and instability within the lower-class black family system is cyclical. Generation after generation are caught in a web of economic deprivation and marital dissolution. But most black families both in our sample and nationally have broken the cycle, i.e., they have been able to maintain ongoing marriages for a significant number of years. How might some of the factors discussed in this chapter have aided them in the attainment of that goal?

1. We may suggest that experience in the city is a vital antecedent condition. This might mean that one was born in the urban setting or migrated there in his pre-adolescent period. However, urban experience is by itself insufficient.

2. Even more critical factors are economic and status advantages provided (usually) through a father (or father-substitute) who himself is a steady provider, and/or through parents who, relatively speaking, were "adequately" educated.

3. While of prime significance, status is also associated with religious involvement which tends to reinforce dominant occupational and conjugal values.

4. Social status is also linked to household composition, both in terms of parental presence and number of siblings.

Combined, these four general background factors may be described as a kind of "syndrome of advantage." Chapter 3 will try to describe some of the ways in which parents of respondents, operating in terms of the key elements within this syndrome of advantage, had sought to provide valuable resources for their children. The general kinds of structural patterns described in this chapter are by definition what the black (and white) family *above* the lower class are all about. It is the absence of these very factors (particularly the economic) that often results in lower-class family status. Many blacks migrate to the urban milieu today, for example, and lack both urban experience and occupational skills. Others may have been born in the city, and thus possess some urban experience, yet they may have been born into a lower-class setting. Consequently, they lack status advantage because their fathers may not be present, or else present but subemployed. Numerous siblings may severely strain limited financial resources. Schools are woefully inadequate and the church for them often has retained little moral or ethical significance. Opportunities for meaningful employment are almost nonexistent, thus restricting the possibility of escaping the lower class and establishing a stable family for themselves. A few nonetheless do escape the lower class, but evidently not many.[67] Instead, as cited early in the chapter, the black underclass is actually expanding due to increased rural migration. At the same time, a few blacks slide downward from the working and middle classes into a lower-class setting.[68]

We would not wish to imply that all blacks who possess all the experiences described herein always attain economic security or conjugal stability, or that others who possess only a few of them may not attain the same twin goals. Generally speaking, however, we would expect that possession of these kinds of experiences is likely to predispose persons (black or white) toward attainment of these same valued goals; whereas their absence is likely to be associated with a greater probability of failure to attain them.

NOTES

1. Rainwater, "Crucible of Identity."
2. Ibid., p. 179.
3. Moynihan, in Rainwater and Yancey, *The Moynihan Report*, p. 107.
4. "Recent Trends in Social and Economic Conditions of Negroes in the U.S.," *Current Population Reports*, Series P-23, No. 26, BLS Report No. 347, July, 1968, p. 22.
5. *Current Population Reports*, Series P-23, No. 27, p. 18.
6. 1968 figure from *Current Population Reports*, Series P-23, No. 26, p. 22. 1969 figure from *Current Population Reports*, Series P-23, No. 29, BLS Report No. 375, p. 70.
7. *Current Population Reports*, Series P-23, No. 27, p. 12.
8. Ibid., p. 18.
9. See Goode, "Family Disorganization," p. 484.
10. *Current Population Reports*, Series P-23, No. 27, p. 17.
11. Ibid.
12. Moynihan, in Rainwater and Yancey, *The Moynihan Report*, p. 105.
13. Daniel P. Moynihan, "Employmet, Income and the Ordeal of the Negro Family," *Daedulus* (Fall 1965), 745–69.
14. Blau and Duncan, *The American Occupational Structure*, p. 269.
15. Schultz, *Coming Up Black*, p. 152. Also see Sylvia R. McMillan, "Aspirations of Low-Income Mothers," *Journal of Marriage and the Family* 29 (May 1967): 282–301.
16. Blau and Duncan, *The American Occupational Structure*, pp. 224–25.
17. Walter L. Slocum, *Occupational Careers* (Chicago: Aldine Publishing Co., 1966), p. 163.
18. Descriptions of this erosion are found in Liebow, *Tally's Corner*; Rainwater, "Crucible of Identity"; Safa, *An Analysis of Upward Mobility*, Ch. 6. One study, however, reports that blacks who are native to the urban milieu may be more susceptible to mental illness than newly arrived migrants. See Seymour Parker and Robert J. Kleiner, *Mental Illness in the Urban Community* (New York: The Free Press, 1966).
19. See *Manpower Report of the President* (Washington, D.C., U.S. Department of Labor, April 1968), pp. 90–91; also Safa, *An Analysis of Upward Mobility*, p. 99.

20. Rose Stamler, "Acculturation and Negro Blue-Collar Workers," in Shostak and Gomberg, p. 291.

21. James C. Coleman, "Implications of the Findings on Alienation," *American Journal of Sociology* 70 (July 1964): 76–78.

22. Blau and Duncan, *The American Occupational Structure*, p. 269.

23. Where we ask respondents for information regarding past experiences, we are following the technique described by Hill and Rodgers as "Retrospective history-taking." Although it has certain obvious drawbacks, i.e., how accurate are the respondents' recollections, it has certain advantages in that it serves as an approximation of a longitudinal design without the enormous costs of such a design. Specifically, in this study, we were able to get information on adolescent experiences, plus adult experiences, *for the same respondents*. We then tried to relate the two sets of information to assess the impact of the former on the latter. Although this is less than the ideal of a longitudinal study, it is probably more desirable than *separate* samples of adolescents and adults, in which the connection between adolescent and adult experiences is far less certain and much more tenuous. Hence, until a more ideal design can be executed, this approach probably serves as a useful approximation, if for no other reason than to generate hypotheses to be tested in a longitudinal study. See Reuben Hill and Roy H. Rodgers, "The Developmental Approach," in Harold T. Christensen, ed., *Handbook of Marriage and the Family* (Chicago: Rand McNally & Co., 1964), pp. 204–5.

24. The rationale for focusing on the 12–18 year period is that these are presumably the most significant years for developing conceptions of "appropriate" economic and conjugal role behaviors. What is learned then should have considerable bearing on later behavior in both sets of roles.

25. Blau and Duncan, *The American Occupational Structure*, p. 248.

26. Rainwater, "Crucible of Identity"; see also Safa, *An Analysis of Upward Mobility*, p. 51; Schulz, *Coming Up Black*.

27. Moynihan, "Employment, Income and the Ordeal," p. 754.

28. Ginzberg and Hiestand, "Employment Patterns," p. 210.

29. Ibid.

30. Taeuber and Taeuber, "The Negro Population," p. 145.

31. See Daniel O. Price, *Changing Characteristics of The Negro Population*, Washington, D.C.: U.S. Bureau of the Census, 1969.

32. Winch, *Identification*, pp. 37–38.

33. Glen H. Elder, Jr., "Adolescent Socialization and Development," in E. F. Borgotta and W. W. Lambert, eds., *Handbook of Personality Theory and Research* (Chicago: Rand McNally Co., 1968), pp. 330–31.

34. Moynihan, in Rainwater and Yancey, *The Moynihan Report*, p. 111.

35. *Ibid.*, p. 83.

36. Blau and Duncan, *The American Occupational Structure*, p. 359.

37. Elder, "Adolescent Socialization," p. 330.

38. Quotation is from Bernard, *Marriage and Family*, p. 125, in summing up Pettigrew's discussion in *A Profile of the American Negro*, pp. 17–24.

39. Schulz, *Coming Up Black*, p. 64.

40. Ibid.

41. Billingsley, *Black Families in White America*, p. 16.

42. Ibid., p. 98.

43. Frazier, *The Negro Family in the United States*, 1939 edition, p. 570; 1948 edition, pp. 245–47.

44. Moynihan, in Rainwater and Yancey, *The Moynihan Report*, p. 108.

45. Moynihan, "Employment, Income and the Ordeal," p. 759.

46. Ibid.

47. Blau and Duncan, *The American Occupational Structure*, p. 328.

48. Karl E. Taeuber and Alma F. Taeuber, "The Negro Population in the United States," p. 148.

49. Robert F. Winch, *The Modern Family* (New York: Holt, Rinehart, and Winston, 1963), pp. 185–86.

50. Taeuber and Taeuber, "The Negro Population," p. 150.

51. As noted in Chapter 1, we are aware of the debate over "African survivals." That debate, however, does not invalidate Frazier's major argument regarding the cohesive function of Christianity for blacks both during and subsequent to slavery.

52. E. Franklin Frazier, *The Negro Church in America* (New York: Schocken Books, 1964), p. 6.

53. Ibid., p. 8.

54. Ibid., p. 11.

55. Ibid., p. 30.

56. Ibid., p. 31.

57. Cited in Ibid., p. 34.

58. Ibid., p. 43.

59. Ibid., pp. 44–46.

60. Drake and Cayton, *Black Metropolis*, pp. 412 ff.

61. Frazier, *The Negro Church*, p. 52.

62. Ibid., p. 71.

63. Harry V. Richardson, "The Negro in American Religious Life," in Davis, 1966, p. 402.

64. 154 out of 168 responding.

65. Richardson, "The Negro in American Religious Life," p. 408.

66. Seth M. Scheiner, "The Negro Church and the Northern City," in W. G. Shade and R. C. Herrenkohl, *Seven on Black* (New York: J. B. Lippincott Co., 1969), p. 92.

67. S. M. Miller, Martin Rein, Pamela Roby, and Bertram M. Gross, "Poverty, Inequality and Conflict," in Bertram M. Gross, ed., *Social Intelligence for America's Future* (Boston: Allyn & Bacon, Inc., 1969), pp. 315–16.

68. Ibid. There is likewise upward mobility for blacks—from various levels in the working class to certain middle-class occupations. See our Chapter 5.

3

Parental Functionality

This chapter examines certain aspects of the socialization experiences encountered by respondents in our sample. As much as possible, we shall follow a model devised by Winch in which family structure, functionality, and identification with parents are related to each other and to subsequent attainments. Structure would include the general kinds of elements we considered in Chapter 2. The operation or activity of these structural elements results in outcomes, or consequences, or *functions* for the group per se and for individuals in the group.[1] Functions, Winch notes, are defined as "beneficial to individuals" and thus have "utility" or may be defined as "resources." These resources have "the capacity to satisfy a human want or need."[2]

Within family structure, Winch conceives of the operation of functions or benefits in terms of role relationships. For example, he describes the father in traditional society as "foreman" to his son. In this type of reciprocal role relationship, the son is a worker on the family farm of which the father is chief overseer. Within this setting, the father fulfills a valuable function for his son. By teaching him how to till the soil in preparation for the day when he will assume control of the land, the father has great utility to the son. He provides him with a valuable reward that meets a "core need" or right on the part of the son.

In terms of this model, the parent is seen as functioning to provide certain rewards to the child so that he himself can in turn one day ultimately "function" more effectively within the larger society. Winch defines this as parental "functionality." There are numerous additional subtleties and nuances in Winch's arguments, and we shall draw more fully on these in Chapter 4. But, according to Winch, what the parent does *for* the child precedes and substantially influences identification *by* the child with the parent. Logically, therefore, prior to probing parental identification we must first investigate the functionality of the respondent's parents. *In what ways, if any, did their parents function to provide them with rewards that they could utilize in the larger society?*

Winch makes the point that in modern society in general, the father-son relationship is seldom one of "foreman-apprentice." What then does the father or the mother *do* to prepare the child to function in modern society? Our concern is primarily with parent-child interaction that may be construed as "functional" or useful in enabling respondents to fulfill societal expectations in terms of socioeconomic and conjugal roles. Even when narrowed to within these limits, our particular measures constrict us still further, as we shall see, to only certain aspects of this type of functionality.

LOWER-CLASS SOCIALIZATION PATTERNS

While we lack direct observations of lower-class (see Chapter 1: defined as "economically insecure, conjugally unstable") blacks with which to compare our sample, there is a significant body of literature on black lower-class socialization patterns. We plan, therefore, to use this extensive literature for purposes of comparison with our sample. One of the major findings that seems to emerge consistently from those studies pertains to the gap between socialization practices and desired outcomes or goals. Elder, in a review of some of this literature, remarks:

. . . the data suggest that Negro parents are less effective than white parents in translating their interests and goals into training practices that foster achievement motivation and academic achievement. This ineffectiveness is probably most common among Negro parents who lack a sense of competence and mastery over the environment.[3]

Lewis, from his own work, explains:

. . . low income parents . . . tend to show greater conformity to, and convergence with, middle class family and child rearing standards in what they say they want (or would like to want) for their children and themselves, than in their actual child rearing behavior.[4]

Kamii and Radin conclude that "middle-class and lower lower-class Negro mothers do not differ fundamentally in their child-rearing goals, but they differ considerably in their socialization practices."[5] As Schulz describes it, lower-class black parents are continually trying to control their children (as is normative throughout this and most other societies), but "children constantly question the right of the parents to govern them."[6] Why? Because, in Winch's terms, the parents provide no resources or benefits to their children that would aid them in the larger society—they provide no "reliable information or dependable role models to enable them to better themselves in the world outside the ghetto. . . . The result is a constant threat of insurrection in the home. Parents often [intervene] too late to prevent him from being labeled as a delinquent, a sexual deviant, or a lush."[7]

With resources or functionality comes the capability to control the child or to move him (more or less) toward desired ends. This exchange of resources for conformity is explicit in Winch and is discussed more fully in Chapter 4. The point here is that the lower-class black parent lacks the resources (economic, in particular) to bring about in his children the goals he desires. Inadvertently, as Schultz, Rainwater, and others point up, the lower-class parent does serve as a role model for survival in the ghetto. But development of and facility in the ways of a peculiarly "lower-class lifestyle" are almost always inimical to attainments in the larger society.

There are two related pitfalls that must be avoided in trying to understand lower-class socialization patterns. One is that the situation is the result of some incipient "weakness" in the black family system per se; the other is that there is a "distinctive lower-class culture" that "inevitably" produces those circumstances. The evidence on the contrary (especially that showing acceptance of dominant goals) suggests that "difficulties" encountered by lower-class parents are chiefly the result of being blocked from the resources necessary to bring about desired outcomes in their children's behavior. To the degree that the lower-class black family may be less functional for children in the senses just described, this would be due to its being systematically excluded from the dominant society. If a subsystem is to socialize new members to fit the expectations of the larger system of which it is a part, the linkage of the part to the whole should be as intimate as possible. Yet at every level, particularly the economic, the larger society has effectively excluded blacks from participation in its ongoing processes. It follows, therefore, that certain black adults (especially in the lower class) may be less able to prepare their children to "fit" the expectations of the dominant society.

This possibility touches on an important theoretical, and yet practical, issue that recurs repeatedly throughout this study. In its most general form the question is: "What are the goals of the majority of black people in (white-controlled) America?" More specifically for our purposes, "How are black parents socializing their children?" Young points out that socialization by minority groups (such as blacks) is intimately related to its own long-term goals.[8] *No one could (if he would) dictate to black parents how they should socialize their children.* They themselves must first define certain long-range objectives, and then try to move to attain them. Young lists at least four such objectives:

1. Physical departure from stress caused by the majority group,
2. Maintenance of some degree of external or self-imposed segregation,
3. The removal of majority barriers to assimilation,

4. Lack of any clear plan except to try to meet "troublesome situations as they arise."[9]

The question then becomes: What might predispose blacks to choose one certain objective over another? To answer this, we must reiterate the point made in Chapter 1 that persons who reside in America operate in the context of a modern society, strongly characterized by individualistic occupational achievement. Once minority group families define the rewards of that type of social structure as "good," certain family patterns and processes seem to inevitably follow. All available evidence, for instance, shows that the overwhelming majority of American blacks want to participate as fully as possible in the American Dream, i.e., the notion that status and material benefits are available to all on the basis of *achieved* characteristics. Therefore, most blacks probably seek the third objective above, removal of majority barriers to (selective) assimilation in at least one major sense—assimilation into the "opportunity structure." The opportunity structure refers to a system both of learning and of performance (means and ends).

The individual must have access to appropriate environments for the acquisition of the values and skills associated with the performance of a particular role, and he must be supported in the performance of that role once he has learned it.[10]

There is nothing inconsistent between blacks maintaining a distinctive "ethnic identity" and Afro-heritage and still gaining assimilation into one (major) aspect of our society—the opportunity structure.[11] As we saw earlier, ethnic identity and heritage are mantained chiefly through primary group ties. But assimilation into the opportunity structure means, in public policy terms, first-rate schools for all citizens, equality in job-hiring, equality in pay and advancement. This in practical terms is the American Dream —it is (according to available evidence) what most blacks and whites want for themselves and their children. It is vital to remember that there is nothing intrinsically "white" about the possibilities and opportunities proffered by a modern, industrial society such as the United States or those in Europe or, obviously, Japan.

A black man does not *ipso facto* "betray his people" if he seeks these opportunities. The opportunities are instead, as Emile Durkheim noted, an inherent result of what a modern society is all about—the constant stress on expansion and development.[12] It is to the society's own advantage (as well as to the individual's) "to locate and train the most talented persons in every generation, irrespective of the vicissitudes of birth, to occupy technical work roles."[13] Notwithstanding, American society, to this point in time, has not actively sought out blacks to fill desirable positions. While neither inherently nor inevitably "white," the system of opportunity in America has been controlled by whites, largely for the interests of white-skinned persons. As a result of separation from the opportunity structure, many blacks have become part of a lower-class (or underclass). One consequence has been to lack resources to effectively socialize their children to participate in the system from which they have been excluded.

On the other hand, we would expect that blacks such as those in our sample, who came from families relatively less "cut off" in terms of status advantage, were more likely to have received these kinds of resources. It is likely that they found their parents (or parent figures) to be relatively functional toward them. That is, their parents were probably able to perform valuable "services," and provide them with "rewards" that were "useful" in enabling them to fulfill dominant society expectations *both* in the economic and conjugal realms. Since they are urban residents, the parental services and rewards cannot be construed in any traditional sense, i.e., agricultural skills or other similar behaviors intended to enable the child to live in a simple, ascriptive-type society. Instead they would have had to be "functions" that might enable the child to operate effectively in an impersonal, complex, achievement-oriented setting such as American society.

As indicated earlier, this book is not able to cover the full range of parental socialization that might bring about this goal. But it does focus on the perceptions of these respondents regarding particular values that their parents transmitted *to* them, and also particular behaviors that their parents performed *for* them.

These parental values and behaviors may be described as being "functional" or useful in terms of later economic and conjugal role performance by those in the sample. They are resources transmitted by parents to children that can be effectively utilized by the latter.

EDUCATIONAL VALUES

To apprehend these values and behaviors, we first asked respondents to identify their "natural" father or else their father-substitute. The procedure involved was discussed at length in Chapter 2. The same applied to their "natural" mother or mother-substitute. We then asked questions designed to measure the ways in which they perceived these particular parents (parent-substitutes) had prepared them to function effectively in the larger society. One such question was: "Did your father (father-substitute) ever say that it was especially important for you to get as much education as you could because you are a Negro?" (A separate question probed the same matter in terms of the mother.)

The intent of the question was to determine if their parents had conveyed to them any notion that while education is important for all members of society, it is *doubly* important for blacks. The great disadvantages under which they labor, and the great distance back from which they start, require extraordinary efforts in the educational realm. Throughout the decades of this century, education has been the single most effective means whereby blacks have been able to assuage the effects of white economic discrimination and to attain social mobility.[14] By no means however does education comparable to whites in terms of years completed guarantee comparable rewards for blacks (see Chapter 5). Nevertheless, because other routes to "dominant success goals," such as small business, have been traditionally closed to blacks, education has spelled the difference between some mobility and none at all.

One female respondent, after replying "yes" to the question, made an additional comment: "A Negro had to be twice as good as a white at anything in order to get ahead." The same idea was put in these words by a male respondent. "Yes, I went to an all-white school ('All white' up until the time he integrated it) and you have to be exceptionally good to be thought equal with white people." Or take a male in response to the same query asked about his mother. "Yes, she always said being a Negro would handicap us as far as jobs were concerned." These particular parents stressed that the disadvantaged position of the black person requires *special* concentration on education.

Nevertheless, not all respondents' parents made this "black-white" distinction. As one husband who answered "No," to this question in terms of his father commented: "Not because I was a Negro but because an education was necessary for *anyone* to succeed in our world today." He was saying in effect that, "I must answer 'no' to this question because it clearly implies a greater need for blacks to be educated than for whites. Yet my parents did convey the importance of education, but as equally vital for black and white." In this same vein, other respondents commented, "No. He told me I should try to go to school and learn for my own good." "No, he didn't say it in that way." "No, they never emphasized race—they just wanted me to get an education." "No, not for that reason—not because I was or am a Negro."

Both themes are in fact present among our respondents' families of orientation: on the one hand the belief that education is *especially* crucial to blacks; on the other, the feeling that it is *equally* important to blacks and whites. In terms of actual proportions, the latter theme seems to have been favored by *fathers* of our respondents (see Table 3–1). Sixty-one percent of husbands and also sixty-one percent of wives replied "no" to this question in connection with their fathers; only thirty-nine percent in each case responded "yes."[15] Although their fathers evidently urged our respondents to get as much education as possible, it was not couched in a specific context of racial need. Yet this was less true of respondents' mothers. Forty-eight percent of males in the sample

TABLE 3–1. PERCEIVED PARENTAL STRESS ON EDUCATION

		Male Respondents		Female Respondents	
		Fathers	Mothers	Fathers	Mothers
Did parent	Yes	39.0	48.0	39.0	52.0
urge educa-	No	61.0	52.0	61.0	48.0
tion because	T	100%	100%	100%	100%
of race?	N	(169)	(188)	(179)	(195)
				$x^2 = 5.0$	
			n.s.	$p < .05$; 1 df	

report "yes," their mothers did urge education within a racial context. And 52 percent of females report the same. Consequently, the "push" from mothers toward increased educational efforts due to "relative black deprivation" is greater than that from fathers.

Why this difference should exist is not completely certain. The literature on the black family makes a great deal, of course, about the traditional dominance of the female and especially her greater involvement with the children—particularly female children. If indeed it is true that education is terribly vital to blacks because they are denied access to job opportunities that are open to whites with less training, then of course it is in the best interests of the black child to be aware of this. If these mothers tended to expose their children to this notion more than fathers did, they were perhaps being highly sensitive to the need for sustained educational efforts.[16] It is not that these fathers did not have the best interests of their children in mind; they simply seem to have felt that a marked emphasis on education per se (irrespective of skin color) would serve their children's interests best.

The major point that emerges from Table 3–1, as well as from Tables 3–2 and 3–3, is *that most of these blacks grew up in homes where education was strongly stressed and encouraged in one fashion or the other by both parents.* The significance of this for later economic and conjugal role-performance is enormous. Blau and Duncan argue—

that a positive orientation to education in the family affects educational attainment, and through it occupational chances, by providing inducements to take full advantage of potential resources for obtaining an education. . . . it is the pertinent value orientation that activates potential economic resources and makes them serve as means for achievement and success. . . . A family in which education is valued strengthens the motivation of sons to acquire much education.[17]

EDUCATIONAL HELP

While studies of the black lower-class suggest this kind of value orientation is missing or else muted through lack of appropriate role models, this was not the case among these blacks who presumably represent the majority of American blacks above the underclass. Furthermore, their parents not only talked about the importance of education, but also actually behaved in such a fashion as to implement the value. *Behavior of this kind is clearly other than a lower-class pattern.*[18] Specifically, each respondent was asked: "Do you feel that your father (father-substitute) actually helped you in getting your education, or that he may have hindered you?" The same question was asked separately regarding mothers. Possible responses in each item were "helped," "hindered," "neither" (see Table 3–2). Among males in the sample, 72 percent said that their fathers had been a help to them in getting their education; 77 percent of females responded simi-

TABLE 3–2.   PERCEIVED PARENTAL HELP IN GETTING EDUCATION

| | | Male Respondents | | Female Respondents | |
		Fathers	Mothers	Fathers	Mothers
Did parent	Helped	72.0	79.3	77.0	85.4
help in	Other	28.0	20.7	23.0	14.6
getting	T	100%	100%	100%	100%
education?	N	(168)	(188)	(178)	(192)
			n.s.		n.s.

larly. Once again, however, both males and females were *more* likely to view their mothers as being a "help" than their fathers. Seventy-nine percent of males and 85 percent of females reported that their mothers had helped them in this particular fashion.

Those respondents who said that their fathers or mothers had helped were asked *how* they had done so. These replies fell into two general categories of help: *intangible* and *tangible* (see Table 3–3). More specifically, within the "intangible" category were "interpersonal pressures" involving encouragement, or goading, or continual reinforcement to go to school and to remain there as long as possible. Comments, each from a different respondent, were of the type: "She saw that I went to school." "Lot of times I didn't plan on going and he saw to it I got there." "By persuasion." "He helped me by counseling me and making me go to school." "Encouraged me to go." "Made me go." "She saw that I went." "He kept telling me I needed an education." "Showing me the advantages of an education." "She wanted me to be very smart."

Many adolescents in American society become discouraged with school and perhaps entertain the notion of leaving it at the earliest possible time. This notion was undoubtedly more true during the years when these respondents were young, and it surely varies with socioeconomic position. Black children, more so than white, may have genuine difficulty in perceiving what difference

TABLE 3–3. TYPE OF PARENTAL HELP PROVIDED IN OBTAINING EDUCATION

| | Male Respondents | | Female Respondents | |
	Fathers	*Mothers*	*Fathers*	*Mothers*
Intangible Help	31.7	54.1	47.1	42.0
Tangible Help	68.3	45.9	52.9	58.0
T	100%	100%	100%	100%
N	(123)	(148)	(138)	(162)
	$x^2 = 13.59$			
	$p < .001$; 1 df			n.s.

an education will actually make in terms of achievement and success in society. For instance, in the data compiled by Fein cited in Chapter 1, the black with *some* college earns less than the white with only eight years of school.

Blau and Duncan corroborate this startling evidence. They too claim that:

better educated Negroes fare even worse relative to whites than uneducated Negroes. . . . Since Negroes receive less return in the form of superior occupational prestige and income for their educational investments than whites, they have less incentive to make such investments, that is, to make the sacrifices that staying in school to acquire more education entails. . . . acquiring an education is simply not very profitable for Negroes. . . . *Negroes must be strongly imbued with the basic values of education for them to have improved their educational attainments in recent years despite the comparatively low rewards education brings them.*[19] (Italics supplied.)

Blacks in our sample appear to have been amply "imbued with this basic value." The interpersonal pressures described here —the continual goading and encouragement—would seem to be especially vital in black families. These pressures appear to be a necessity if the black child is to resist the counter-societal pressures to "give up" in school. The fact that rewards from years of education are so dimly perceived stands a good chance of being outweighed through continual parental reinforcement as to the worthwhileness of school. To point out the advantages of education is indeed a crucial parental "function."

Under the "tangible" category, there was one main theme and two subthemes. The main theme was "material aid" (what Blau and Duncan call "economic resources"). In the case of the father, several different respondents answered in these terms: "He provided for us, sent us to high school, and so we didn't have to get out and work." "He went without clothes so I could go to school." "By supporting me he kept me in school or else I might have had to drop out." "He helped me by financing the things I needed for school." The two minor (in terms of proportion of responses), but related, tangible help forms were "help with

homework and lessons," and "keeping clothes clean and neat."
(This last behavior, when it was cited, applied equally to fathers
and mothers.)

In terms of material aid, the comments above suggest that the
father's role was to provide a financial base on which the child
could rely in order to continue his schooling. Within the dominant
society, this familial behavior pattern is taken for granted and its
significance is hardly recognized. But among many black ("disadvantaged") families, where there is often constant struggle for
survival or to "get by," parental behavior of this sort takes on
major proportions. Its consistency during the adolescent period
makes substantial difference whether or not the child can actually
remain in school. Note, incidentally, the kind of role model that
these fathers were able to be, in contrast with what Schulz described earlier in terms of the lower-class father even when he was
present.

Yet material aid by the father was not the whole story in
many of these cases. Forty-five percent (N = 178) of the total
sample report that their mothers worked outside the home during
their adolescent years. Over the decades of the 20's, 30's, and 40's,
when compared to women in general with children 12–18, this is
a high figure.[20] But as Ginzberg and Heistand note, "the proportion of Negro women who work has always tended to be higher
than among white women."[21] At least one reason for this may perhaps be found in the comments of several respondents regarding
their mothers' material help: "She washed and ironed for white
folks and helped out so I could go to school." "She worked to get
money for my clothes." "She helped pay expenses." "She supplied spending money." The need for black women to work when
the father is absent is obvious. But even when he is present and employed, his limited income (relative to whites at the same occupational level) may simply not stretch far enough to keep teenagers
in school. Thus, the mother's added income is often a necessity if
this valued goal is to be attained.

Goode notes that sometimes the less advantaged husband
may resent such an intrusion into his traditional male "bread-

winner" or provider role.[22] He may feel that his wife's working undercuts his already limited prestige and power, since this definition of her employment underscores his inability to meet fully the family needs. Yet there is no indication that, as adolescents, these respondents perceived any such strain between their parents. Chapter 6 suggests that this absence of strain may be owing to the different definitions of wife employment in black compared with white society. In black society, her employment is perhaps more likely to be defined as a "right" rather than an "option" as it often is in white society.[23] So defined by blacks themselves, it consequently introduces less tension into husband-wife relations than is true for whites. In any case, these respondents perceived their mothers' working as a "necessary" means to attain valued ends, and as such is "acceptable." Hence, when respondents report their mothers helped them materially in receiving education, her role was not merely peripheral. It was very likely an essential element in attainment of that goal.

With regard to intangible and tangible forms of educational help, respondents continue to indicate certain differences in the ways their fathers and mothers behaved toward them. Wives report the greater similarity in how their parents helped them in that both fathers and mothers were more apt to have helped them in material or tangible fashion than by interpersonal pressure (see Table 3–3). On the other hand, although two-thirds of husbands also report that their fathers helped them *tangibly*, a majority of them indicate that their mothers were active in the *other* direction, i.e., encouraging them to "keep at it," to stay in school. And these latter differences are markedly significant.

Given the conclusions of many earlier studies regarding the emotional and economic deprivations experienced by black lower-class males, this pattern may have great import. Although as youths these males generally perceived no significant differences between their mothers and fathers as to the *sheer fact* of being helped by them, meaningful differences do emerge as to the specific *nature* of this help. At the economic level, the deprivation of these young males was being alleviated by a father (or other male) active in the occupational system, while the mother played a crucial role in encouraging the youth to remain in school. Together these efforts were complementary—the *economic* means supplied chiefly by the father, and the *social-psychological* motivation supplied chiefly by the mother. It is obviously not the case that the father provided no encouragement, nor that the mother did not often work. But in terms of role emphasis, these males perceived these particular kinds of differences in their parents.

Parsons and others have noted that within the dominant family form this type of instrumental-expressive role differentiation between parents is evident and efficient, and also beneficial for child development. To the extent this is so, the fact that males in our sample have also encountered this kind of parental role differentiation as adolescents, may be a factor in their own later marital experience. At the same time, it is not totally clear why females see *both* parents, particularly their mothers, as more task-oriented than supportive. It may simply be that black female youths experience fewer counterpressures than males to stay in school. Therefore, their parents may have had to exert fewer interpersonal pressures on girls to attain this goal. Consequently, in terms of this level of functionality, females report that they experienced more tangible than intangible aid.

In response to the question regarding whether the parent "helped," "hindered," or did "neither," some 16.5 percent (N = 66) of our respondents indicated the father did "neither," and 14.3 percent (N = 57) said the same about the mother. We did not probe these particular kinds of replies, but it may be assumed that those respondents could not perceive or identify their parents as having been particularly helpful in gaining an education. By the same token, they did not perceive parents as having actually stood in the way of this goal. The parents had been neutral, and neutrality in this realm is actually a *positive* gain when compared to those situations where the parent was reported to have *hindered* the child in getting to school.

Although the numbers are small in the remaining category (fathers who hindered, 6.5 percent, N = 26; mothers, 4.5 percent, $N = 18$), the kind of hindrance reported when we probed was instructive. In almost all cases the complaint was of a combined twofold nature. (1) The parent had *made* the child quit school either to care for younger siblings at home or else to work outside the home to help support the family. (2) There were attitudes of indifference, apathy, and even antipathy on the part of the parent toward school. As one male put it regarding his father: "He hindered us because he wanted us to quit school and go to work; he did not allow us to participate in school activities." And one female said this about her mother being a hindrance: "Because I had to do all the housework, she didn't care if I went to school or not."

As suggested earlier, the effort to keep the child in school required, among black families particularly some years ago, determined and sustained effort. The great majority of these respondents' parents made those efforts at both economic (often with sacrifice) and interpersonal levels. In so doing, they operated as a source of *positive* functionality for their children. At the same time, a small number of these parents behaved in a "dysfunctonal" manner as far as their children's education was concerned. By making them leave school and go to work, or by even putting pressure on the child to do so, they obviously had a negative impact on this kind of goal attainment.

ACHIEVEMENT VALUES

In exploring the positive rewards or benefits provided for these respondents as children by their parents, it is necessary to look at two more kinds of functionality: (1) values and behavior pertinent to achievement and success and (2) behavior specifically relevant to prepare for later conjugal relationships. The actual extensiveness and intensiveness within American society of what has been variously described as the "Protestant work and success ethic," is a matter of debate. Some social observers argue that the ethos of achievement and success is held only weakly, if at all, by those segments of society (many blacks, for instance) that have been excluded from the opportunity structure. Others contend that these values are distributed rather uniformly throughout the class structure, but that expectations concerning their attainment vary directly with degree of opportunity.[24]

In Chapter 2, we found that respondent's fathers tended to hold occupations at levels higher than those found among the general black population. We would expect therefore, that within our sample, the argument over the American success ethos would be resolved in the direction of its being readily accepted. No value judgment on the merits of this ethos is implied, anymore than value judgments are implied regarding the desirability of the dominant conjugal form for blacks. In both instances, the task of the sociologist is to try to "tell it like it is," i.e., What are the values and behaviors that blacks *themselves* hold?

If, as Rainwater and others claim, even lower-class blacks desire the dominant conjugal family form, then it is extremely likely that this desire is associated with an emphasis on dominant values of achievement and success.[25] To determine the extent to which respondents' parents transmitted these kinds of values we first asked: "Did your father ever say it was very important for you to get ahead in life—to make something of yourself?" The same question was asked separately for mothers. From Table 3–4, we see that the great majority of both sexes in the sample report that both parents stressed the American Dream. Their parents sought to convey to them the notion that they *ought* to "get ahead" in life, that they ought to "make something" of themselves. At least two ideas are implicit in this orientation: (1) that such is actually possible and (2) what it means to get ahead.

In the former instance, we may assume that these parents would not likely have conveyed to children that they ought to "get ahead" if they themselves did not believe that it was somewhat possible—at least for their children. In Chapter 7, we shall show how these respondents themselves now *believe* their own children's chances for "success" are much greater than their own were. Presumably, therefore, they are urging their children to

TABLE 3–4.   PERCEIVED PARENTAL STRESS ON GETTING AHEAD

| | | Male Respondents | | Female Respondents | |
		Fathers	Mothers	Fathers	Mothers
Did parent	Yes	77.3	87.8	82.0	88.3
stress get-	No	22.6	12.2	18.0	11.7
ting ahead?	T	100%	100%	100%	100%
	N	(168)	(188)	(179)	(196)

$$x^2 = 6.41$$
$$p < .05; 1 \, df \qquad\qquad\qquad \text{n.s.}$$

"get ahead" in the same way that they were so urged by their parents. The meanings of "getting ahead," "success," "making something of oneself," have been discussed at length elsewhere.[26] There is general consensus that at the very least "getting ahead" is defined in terms of material symbols. The upper middle-class affluent and certain intellectuals may downgrade such material elements, but they are a necessary base on which to build the more subtle evidences of "having arrived."

Conspicuous consumption . . . extends to the lower strata of society and reflects their endeavors to achieve social recognition by displaying the generally valued material symbols of status. The condemnation of such unrefined display by groups whose higher status rests on more secure foundations seems to be an attempt to deny men recognition as equals on the basis of material possessions alone.[27]

For the majority of the population, including most blacks, getting ahead refers to the obtaining of money and its use in purchasing those visible symbols that "prove" one's worthiness in an acquisitive society.

In spite of the general tendency in Table 3–4 of the respondents to see both parents conveying these kinds of values, only husbands report a meaningful difference between parents. Husbands saw their mothers clearly more active toward them in this regard than their fathers were. This pattern complements the one observed in connection with parental emphasis on education. There we saw that mothers stresed the "double value" of education for blacks more than fathers did. Aside from the possibility of greater involvement of black mothers than fathers with their children, the explanation for this may lie also with the frustration of the certain proportion of black adult males. Although the majority may hold to the American Dream, a minority (of respondents' fathers) may have been so discriminated against and so deprived that they no longer had much faith in it. As a result they did not (unconsciously perhaps) bother seeking to communicate it to their sons.

However, the overriding consideration to keep in mind as we examine Tables 3–4, 3–5, and 3–6, is that the great majority of

TABLE 3–5. PERCEIVED PARENTAL HELP IN GETTING AHEAD

| | | Male Respondents | | Female Respondents | |
		Fathers	Mothers	Fathers	Mothers
Did parent	Helped	68.8	78.4	67.0	79.7
help in	Other	31.1	21.6	33.0	20.2
getting	T	100%	100%	100%	100%
ahead?	N	(167)	(185)	(173)	(188)
				$x^2 = 6.82$	
			n.s.	$p < .01$; 1 df	

TABLE 3–6. TYPE OF PARENTAL HELP IN GETTING AHEAD

| | Male Respondents | | Female Respondents | |
	Fathers	Mothers	Fathers	Mothers
Material Help	25.6	24.0	34.8	21.2
Counsel and				
Example	74.4	76.0	65.2	78.8
T	100%	100%	100%	100%
N	(113)	(142)	(112)	(146)
			$x^2 = 6.44$	
		n.s.	$p < .05$; 1 df	

respondents' mothers *and* fathers were highly beneficial in providing the kinds of resources and rewards that would enable their children to achieve and succeed and thereby raise the likelihood of their marital stability. These families fit quite well the following description of the kind of family background that is optimal for later occupational attainments.

In addition to economic support the family of orientation provides the child with diverse forms of social support which range from such subtle factors as furnishing thought patterns and role models and having many books available at home to such explicit ones as encouraging children to study and helping them if they have trouble. . . . The achievement orientation that disposes the man to strive to better himself is acquired by the child largely in his parental family. Conditions [there] tend to determine both whether the child develops the socialized anxiety that drives him to succeed and whether he receives the socio-emotional support to cope with this anxiety without becoming debilitated by it.[28]

ACHIEVEMENT AID

These respondents defined their parents, not only as verbally urging success, but also as *behaving* in such a way toward their children so as to increase the probability of its attainment. From Table 3–5, we may conclude that the majority of respondents did indeed perceive their parents to behave toward them in this positive fashion—their parents did *help* them to try to get ahead. As with education, however, mothers once again seem to play more of a role in this process for both sexes than do fathers. When we probed to find exactly *how* the respondents' parents helped them get ahead, the responses fell into two different, but, as we shall see, not totally unrelated categories.

The majority of respondents indicated their parents helped them get ahead by means of "counsel and example" (see Table 3–6). The nature of this counsel and example can be described as a kind of "anticipatory socialization," i.e., respondents' parents behaved and communicated ideas that were designed, probably consciously, to try to move the respondents *from* a position of relative disadvantage in the total society *to* a position of greater advantage at sometime in the future.[29] These behaviors differ from those under educational interpersonal pressures and goading since they are much broader and generalized. In the former, the objective was simple and straightforward—"stay in school." In the latter, it is more complex and amorphous, yet equally if not more urgent because it is after all (in the minds of most Americans) the chief goal that education is directed toward. From the following comments, it may be seen that respondents' parents accepted the dominant value system of the society regarding achievement and success, and that they wanted their children to internalize it and to be able to fulfill it. In effect, they were trying to influence them to adopt a middle-class (broadly defined) life-style.

One male respondent put it bluntly in terms of his mother: "She had a value system that was a middle-class standard, not like poor people." Other comments (under "counsel and example") included: "He has given me the incentive to get ahead." "She taught me to work and the importance of being a man and standing on my own two feet." "She taught me how to treat and get along with people." "She always taught me to save money—what little I could get hold of—and take advantage of every opportunity that would help me to get ahead." "Taught me to be saving, thrifty, and that helped me to get along in life." "He made me more independent." "Said if you don't *hold* a job you can't get ahead—look out for yourself *and your family*." "I used to jump from job to job, he told me I couldn't get ahead like that—to stay on the job until I could get to know whether I liked it or not." "She encouraged me [a male] to enter office work." "By proving that black was not destined to destruction." "By teaching me manners." "By always telling me how he couldn't, and how he was hindered, and what would probably be available to me." "Taught us how to face life and be prepared for disappointment." "Taught me what I had to face." "Taught me everything I know." And so on, including many comments which were less specific but which subsumed the foregoing ideas by this kind of phraseology: "advice, counsel, example." "The way she carried herself as an example before us and the community."

It seems that respondents' parents were conscious of the relative deprivation of blacks in society, yet, felt nonetheless that their children could somehow share in the "Dream." To do so however, the children would have to conform to dominant norms in terms of work, consumption patterns, and general life-style. Their parents communicated these kinds of norms and sought themselves to conform (i.e., as role models) insofar as possible. The other category of "help" perceived by respondents has been labeled (Table 3–6) "material." All those replying here indicated in one fashion or another that money expended by their parents to send them to school had been the prime factor in their "getting ahead." In about half these cases, however, the school in view was not on the elementary or secondary level as had been true when we looked at tangible educational help. Here it refers to schooling beyond high school, i.e., business or trade school, or college. For example: "She sent me to John Herron Art Institute." "He got me into a trade school." "She had connections with white folks who helped me get into college."

With regard to "getting ahead," parents of these respondents appear to have exhibited a good deal of "functionality" on their behalf. Although this functionality was predominantly in terms of "mobility-type" counsel, it was also in terms of material aid designed to attain education essential to improved social and economic advantage. We learn from Table 3–6 that while males show virtually no differences in behavior of fathers and mothers, females do. Fathers of females gave substantially *more material* help to them than their mothers did, and more than either parent did for males. Females also received less counsel from fathers than from mothers.

This finding may be due to two related factors: (1) As girls, they may have needed more material help than boys, because it was more difficult to obtain part-time work that would pay enough to help defray school expenses. (2) Black females are less prevented than black males from identifying with the middle-class school system and general middle-class values. They may simply have needed less counsel than males regarding the desirability and necessity of adopting particular means to effectively manipulate the world "out there." Instead, their fathers concentrated on providing for them.

As was true for education, when the parent is perceived as *neither* a help nor hindrance, this neutral stance would seem to facilitate the success goal more than when (he-she) is defined as a *hindrance*. Respondents who indicated "parental hindrance" made two kinds of observations: (1) Their parents seemed to be indifferent to the notion of getting ahead. They never counseled nor gave "advice" to their children on how this goal might best be attained. (2) Their parents failed to provide adequate material aid to keep them (as children) in school.

DIRECT PREPARATION FOR THE CONJUGAL SITUATION

Before discussing the relationship of the background factors discussed in Chapter 2 to parental functionality, we need to consider one more way in which these parents were or were not seen as "helping" their children. In wording similar to earlier items we asked: "Do you feel that your father (identical but separate question for mother) helped you to prepare for marriage and a family or do you feel he (she) may have hindered you?" The forms of functionality discussed previously involved parental preparation specifically for the economic-opportunity system. Here we are interested in preparation primarily for the conjugal situation itself.

From Table 3–7, we see that mothers provided more help than fathers did, in the view of both male and female respondents. More males report help from fathers than do females yet reveal differences between parents that are not meaningful. On the other hand, females report differences that are strongly significant. While about half the females report help of this kind from fathers, three-quarters of them see their mothers helping

TABLE 3–7. PERCEIVED PARENTAL HELP IN PREPARING FOR CONJUGAL SITUATION

| | | Male Respondents | | Female Respondents | |
		Fathers	Mothers	Fathers	Mothers
Did parent	Helped	57.2	64.0	51.5	75.6
help prepare	Other	42.8	36.0	48.5	24.4
for conjugal	T	100%	100%	100%	100%
situation?	N	(166)	(186)	(165)	(185)
				$x^2 = 22.01$	
			n.s.	p < .001; 1 df	

in this fashion. There was, in short, a pronounced affinity between these daughters and their mothers in terms of socialization for marriage that did not exist in the father-daughter, father-son, mother-son relationships. Whether this condition would be equally true among whites is not certain. Its occurrence among blacks is not surprising because of traditionally intense mother-daughter ties. These ties have emerged as a result of societal pressures that have often prevented the black male from assuming a significant place within the conjugal unit.

Some observers have compared these mother-daughter ties to a kind of female "alliance" against male family members. This comparison (while probably applicable to the lower class) is unwarranted in the case of these respondents who for the most part represent the working class and above. When we examine the comments of *how* parents helped, it would seem that what both fathers and mothers were chiefly concerned about was to prepare their children for *any eventuality* that marriage might bring. Their parents were evidently aware of the particular vicissitudes that may arise in family interaction as a result of being black and relatively disadvantaged. Consequently, they seemed to try to communicate to their children the general values, plus specific role obligations, which would in fact enable them to cope with the inevitably greater stresses that face black families. Since stresses due to discrimination and frustration based on skin color are obviously absent among white families in American society,[30] these kinds of values and norms are perhaps taken for granted as part of the "normal outcomes" of daily, orderly routines and consequently are communicated less self-consciously. But where order is considered more problematic, transmission of these orientations grows correspondingly more salient.

For instance, in Table 3–8 parental help was categorized into responses that stressed *general* values and overall example, as opposed to those that consisted of the teaching of *specific* norms or role expectations. In the latter grouping, some of the statements were: "He would sit and talk about the obligations of taking care of a family." "She told me once my wife got pregnant I had to think about my family before anyone else." "Talked to me about the responsibilities of marriage and family." "He always said to take care and to do right by your wife and children." "He taught me the responsibilities of a family." "When you marry, he said, treat your wife as a wife and accept your responsibilities." These "responsibilities" and "obligations" were spelled out in some detail by these and other male respondents. The "duties" incidentally often included household-task performance, as well as occupational performance.

A substantial number of husbands replied, for instance, that they learned "all the ways of caring for a family—cook, wash, iron, sew, care for babies, wash diapers, and keep house." Signifi-

TABLE 3–8. Type of Parental Help for the Conjugal Situation

Kind of Socialization	Male Respondents		Female Respondents	
	Fathers	Mothers	Fathers	Mothers
General Values	49.5	46.0	65.0	46.2
Specific role obligations	50.5	54.0	35.0	53.8
T	100%	100%	100%	100%
N	(93)	(112)	(83)	(106)
			$x^2 = 7.00$	
		n.s.	$p < .01$; 1 df	

cantly, some other researchers have found that black men are more helpful around the house than white men are in terms of these kinds of traditionally "female tasks." Billingsley remarks,

"These [Negro] men are considered by the particular researchers to be henpecked or under the domination of their strongly matriarchal wives. . . . [but] One is hard put to substantiate such reasoning. . . . This behavior may be more appropriately interpreted as another example of the strong tendency toward mutual aid and a reflection of the pragmatic qualities in Negro family life."[31]

With regard to occupational performance, several males replied in this fashion: "My mother taught me to work hard and make an honest living for my family." "My father told me to hold the jobs I could manage so I could be able to manage a family."

In brief, the role obligations impressed on these men were twofold: (1) domestic (including both instrumental and expressive duties, i.e., "treat your wife right") and (2) occupational, i.e., "be a good provider." Role obligations impressed on females were chiefly domestic, although of both the instrumental and expressive varieties. It is important to note that apparently parents did not socialize their girls to expect to be economic providers. This kind of expectation was evidently not normative for these parents in spite of the fact that since Emancipation many black females have been *forced* to play this role.

The major point here is the self-conscious stress on role obligations rather than on role rewards. This emphasis is seemingly more true for males than females. In Table 3–8, we see that males reveal no significant differences in the parental pressures they experienced toward role obligations. Instead, *both* parents apply substantial pressures in this direction although those from their mothers exceed those from their fathers. Females perceived significantly *far less* emphasis from fathers on specific role obligations than on general values. Mothers tended to emphasize specific role obligations to girls as well as boys.

This pattern suggests that these parents (especially mothers) were very likely aware of the structurally imposed difficulties that black males often face in fulfilling their provider roles. Wives of black males may in turn tend to feel under-rewarded, to define their economic and status rights as not being met, and hence feel less motivated to fulfill their own conjugal role (expressive) obligations. The result of this complex process is that many black marriages dissolve through gradual erosion of reciprocal role relations.[32] What these parents may have done was to anticipate and to seek to compensate for this by placing great stress on role *duties* to the extent that the underlying notion may be (for both sexes) that even if rewards are minimal, "you should be motivated to carry out your duties anyway." This includes not only minimal rewards through the opportunity system, but also minimal rewards from one's spouse.

By placing great emphasis on the *duty* element of one's role, these parents may have hoped to assuage the disappointments that inevitably come when the "rights segment" is only partially fulfilled. Several respondents in fact remarked that their parents helped them for marriage by "talking and explaining the disappointments of life"; and "she told me what hardships you had to meet." This emphasis on patience, dependability, and perseverance under stress might stem from the days of slavery and legal segregation. Or it may simply be traceable to the traditional belief of the dominant society in the permanence of marriage. The point is, however, that this type of emphasis may be construed as one additional element of functionality contributing toward later marital situations. Feeling they *ought* to perform their role obligations consistently (even when rewards at times are minimal) is quite likely, in turn, to motivate the spouse to do the same.[33] To the extent this is the case, *perceived* satisfactions and rewards are very likely increased, and the probability of maintenance of the marriage is thereby enhanced.

The *general* marital values communicated by these parents, while more global, probably help to accomplish the same end. The following comments are indicative of these kinds of general orientations: "By offering concrete and universal rules of law that govern and bind the family and that are the foundations of civilization." "She would tell me about the rearing of a family—in general what makes a good marriage." Many respondents also used phrases such as "advice and counsel," "example," "taught me to be a good husband (wife)," "how she raised us," "by having that golden rule: do unto others as you would have them do unto you; any girl you go with is somebody else's sister and daughter." Both at a general level as well as at the more specific level, respondents' parents seemed to place emphasis on what one should expect to *do* and how one should *conform* in marriage, rather than on what one should expect to *receive* or how one should *dominate*. And given the negative pressures imposed on black families by white society, it is likely that this type of emphasis has proved a factor in maintaining an ongoing family structure.

Among white families less threatened by society, an overt and strong emphasis of this type is probably not required. Although research is needed to verify it, among black families where dissolution has occurred, this kind of overt parental emphasis might be lacking. Even within our own sample, the proportions in Table 3–7 reporting "other" (parent did nothing or else hindered) are consistently greater than those in the "other" categories in Tables 3–5 and 3–2. Our respondents saw their parents more active in the educational and mobility dimensions than in the marital realm. Moreover, of those indicating "other" in Table 3–7, better than 90 percent had said their parents *neither* helped nor hindered. In this instance, apparently what respondents learned of a positive nature regarding conjugal role relations was not perceived as coming from parents. Finally, in those few cases who replied a parent had hindered, the complaint was a perceived failure on his (her) part to communicate information defined as pertinent: "Didn't help me by telling about men—how to get along with them and what's expected of a woman." "She was shy and she didn't know how to explain things like the facts of life." "She didn't talk about marriage at all." Further research is needed to determine if among dissolved black marriages lack of "overstress" on role duties is *part* of the syndrome accounting for dissolution, or if dissolution occurs anyway, in spite of "overstress" and due to economic impingements.

THE LINKAGE OF FAMILY STRUCTURE AND FUNCTIONALITY

The reader will recall that according to Winch, structure influences functionality. Structural factors such as urban experience, social class, household composition, and religion may have an impact on the level of benefits that the family of procreation is able to provide for its children. To examine this possibility, we shall relate certain of these structural factors (those which past literature indicates are theoretically *most* central) to the kinds of benefits discussed in this chapter. One such prime element is social class as measured by the occupation of fathers of respondents. Most earlier research concurs that class is probably the most fundamental structural feature in terms of resource-provision to children. Black or white, we may certainly expect that the more advantaged the parents (the more resources they themselves possess), the greater the levels of resources they will (be able to) provide for their children.

A second factor that has received considerable attention and that possesses great theoretical and practical importance is family wholeness, i.e., presence of both parents. Some studies suggest that family wholeness per se affects functionality, whereas others indicate that controlling for social class makes differences due to parental absence disappear. These latter studies suggest the generalization that what the remaining parent, or parents, or surrogates are able to *do* for the child may be more central than the mere fact of "wholeness." Billingsley, for instance, argues that father and mother need not necessarily *both* be present to prepare children to compete effectively in society. Many black adults, he asserts, can point to great efforts on the part of only *one* parent or *other* adult which had an enormous impact on their subsequent achievement and mobility.[34]

To try to test the relationships between structure and functionality, we have devised three separate indexes of family functionality based on some of the items discussed in this chapter. In
Table 3–9, the sample is divided by occupation of respondents'
fathers. The "middle class" is composed of Census Bureau categories of professional-technical, managers, clerical-sales, and craftsmen-foremen. The "working class" is composed of the remaining
categories of the labor force.[35] Each of the mean scores under the
functionality of "father," "mother," "total both parents," reflect
their particular contribution to the child, or their functionality for
him in terms of (1) stress on education, Table 3–1; (2) help in
getting education, Table 3–2; (3) stress on getting ahead, Table
3–4; (4) help in getting ahead, Table 3–5; (5) help for later
marriage and family, Table 3–7.[36] The parent(s) who did all of
the foregoing may be said to be highly functional or beneficial for
his (their) children, i.e., the children were provided with a great
deal of resources. Those who did some of the foregoing may be
said to be only moderately beneficial. Those who did few or none
may be said to have engaged in only slight functionality.

By combining the foregoing five items into one index, we have
an index of functionality for fathers, and a separate index for
mothers. By combining these two indexes we then have a third
index, or a measure of the *total parental functionality* or benefits
to which the child was exposed as an adolescent. The higher the

TABLE 3–9. SOCIAL CLASS AND PARENTAL FUNCTIONALITY
(mean scores)

	Middle Class	Working Class	
Father Functionality	15.02	11.87	$F = 15.3$; df $= 1$ & 398
N	(78)	(322)	$p < .001$
Mother Functionality	16.17	15.05	$F = 3.04$; df $= 1$ & 398; n.s.
N	(78)	(322)	
Total Functionality	31.2	26.9	$F = 12.0$; df $= 1$ & 398
N (Both parents)	(78)	(322)	$p < .001$

mean scores in the table, the greater the functionality of the parent for the child. In Table 3–9, we find that the mean functionality (or resource) score for respondents having middle-class fathers is significantly higher than for those having working-class fathers.[37] Fathers here refer not just to "natural" father but to stepfather, foster-father, or other male adults who may have played the role of father to the child. The same notion of a parent-substitute is true for mothers, but there we see that the difference in mean functionality scores between social classes is very slight and not meaningful. When we examine the composite index of the functionality of *both* parents together we find a significantly higher score among middle-class respondents, due very likely to the already observed differences between fathers. Therefore, our expectation that social class would influence the level of resources or benefits provided is only partially confirmed. The middle-class black father is more likely to provide the kinds of resources (stress on education, getting ahead, etc.) than is the working-class black father.

However, social class played little or no part in the functioning of their mothers. Working-class black mothers were just about as contributory as middle-class black mothers and both were equally or more "beneficial" than fathers in either class. But respondents growing up in a middle-class home had the additional advantage of having been more likely to have had a father (or father-figure) who was also quite active with regard to this kind of socialization. Nevertheless, in spite of this difference, respondents from working-class homes have been able to attain certain economic and conjugal goals. Apparently, working-class fathers did provide at least an "adequate" amount of functionality which, added to the extensive efforts of the working-class mother, was sufficient to put them relatively on a par with those from middle-class backgrounds. Hence, as Billingsley remarks, those who sometimes denigrate the role of the black mother as being detrimental to their youth may need to modify their thinking. For at least among these strata (presumably) *above the underclass,* she seems to make a substantial and highly beneficial impact.

Our findings throughout this chapter regarding the positive influence of the black wife-mother are paralleled in a recent study by McCord et al.[38] Their major focus was on black society in general, but they point out that the black woman is a major force in the individual occupational achievement of her children. The black woman is also a major force in the *corporate* goals of the black community, e.g., in protests and civil rights struggles. She has assumed this position partly in response to the greater strictures placed on black males than on black females by white society. Nonetheless, it is likely that as more black men gain greater economic rewards and social status, the relative contribution of each sex to their children, to the black community in general, and to the larger society, should arrive at parity.

Table 3–10 considers relationships between family wholeness and levels of resource-provision. "Whole" families in the table include only those with both *natural* parents. "Other" accounts for all the remaining situations described in Chapter 2 including those who had a *step*-parent. Having a step-parent plus a natural parent means, of course, that one is counted by the Census Bureau as living in a husband-wife family. But we inserted step-parents with the "other" grouping for two reasons. One was practical. We wanted to obtain as much of a balance as possible in the number of cases in the "whole" and "other" categories. Placing step-parents in the "other" group was thus helpful not only in Table

TABLE 3–10. FAMILY COMPOSITION AND PARENTAL FUNCTIONALITY (mean scores)

	Whole Family	Other Situation	
Father Functionality	14.5	9.5	F = 68.3; df = 1 & 398
N	(235)	(165)	p < .001
Mother Functionality	15.9	14.2	F = 11.4; df = 1 & 398
N	(235)	(165)	p < .001
Total Functionality	30.5	23.7	F = 51.2; df = 1 & 398
N	(235)	(165)	p < .001

3–10, but especially in Table 3–11, where class and family composition are combined, and where cases dwindle rapidly in each cell when the number of cells is doubled.

Second, and more important, is the theoretical justification. We did not know how long the child had actually lived with the step-parent, as compared to the natural parent. With more time comes more opportunity to be helpful. Moreover, the popular lore describing both white and black step-parents often paints them in a negative light as not being as vitally involved in the lives of their step-children as are natural parents. The question in short is, are step-parents more like "natural" or "other" parents in terms of what they do for children? Certain respondents hinted (recorded verbatim during the interview) that step-parents more frequently than natural parents were perceived as "hindrances." Therefore,

TABLE 3–11. SOCIAL CLASS, FAMILY COMPOSITION AND PARENTAL FUNCTIONALITY (mean scores)

| | Middle Class | | Working Class | |
	Whole	Other	Whole	Other
Father Functionality	15.6	13.4	14.2	8.9
N	(56)	(22)	(179)	(143)
	$F = 3.6$		$F = 58.4$	
	n.s.		$p < .001$	
	df = 1 & 76		df = 1 & 320	
Mother Functionality	16.8	14.4	15.7	14.2
N	(56)	(22)	(179)	(143)
	$F = 4.9$		$p < .05$	
	$p < .05$		$F = 6.5$	
	df = 1 & 76		df = 1 & 320	
Total Functionality	32.5	27.9	29.9	23.1
N	(56)	(22)	(179)	(143)
	$F = 5.5$		$F = 40.1$	
	$p < .05$		$p < .001$	
	df = 1 & 76		df = 1 & 320	

we placed step-parents in the "other" category on the premise that in most instances they would be more like them than like "natural" parents. In any case, the bias that might occur from this procedure would obviously be in the direction of *equalizing* the degree of functionality between categories.

But instead, Table 3–10 shows strong differences over all three indexes (father, mother, total). Children from "whole" families appear to have received more "benefits" than those who grew up in "other" situations. Hence, growing up in a "whole" family as opposed to some other type of household composition does seem to make a difference in what the family is able to do for the child. While the differences are least in terms of mother's help, they are nonetheless there. In a "whole" family, both parents are present and relatively active. Moreover, they may be able to *reinforce one another* (in a way that is perhaps more difficult when only one "actual" spouse is present) in terms of the values and behaviors that they feel they ought to transmit to their children.

However, lest we be too hasty in assessing the influence of wholeness alone on functionality, we need to combine with it the effects of social class to see if the consequences of family composition are thereby weakened. Looking first in Table 3–11 at father-functionality, we find that in the middle class, mean scores between "whole" and "other" types of family backgrounds are not significantly different. In other words, whether one comes from a "whole" or "other" home is not as crucial in the middle class with respect to *father* impetus toward economic and conjugal attainment. Within the middle class, those males who act as father figures are only slightly less functional than natural fathers. Hence, as this social-class level household composition does fade in importance: regardless of the composition, some male was there to provide ample and generous "help" to the child.

But in the working class, household composition made an extremely large difference. Respondents from whole working-class backgrounds report a mean functionality score of 14.2 for their fathers, as over against a mean score of 8.9 for those from "other" kinds of homes. In the working class, either the father was not there, or if a father-substitute was used by the child, he participated only minimally in these particular phases of the child's socialization, as compared to fathers in whole families. In short, when thinking of resource-provision solely from black fathers, household composition makes little difference in the middle class but makes a great difference in the working class. This conclusion may be partial support for the observation made in Chapter 2 that it is the child from the less advantaged, "broken" home who "suffers" more than the one-parent child from "better" circumstances. Not having the father present is likely to be less detrimental, in terms of later attainments, when the home is relatively well-off than when it is not.

In *both* the middle and working classes (Table 3–11), mothers from whole families were seen as significantly more functional or helpful than mothers from "other" situations. But the mean scores in each social class are not very far apart. Especially among working-class mothers, there is nowhere near the great difference (in terms of whole versus other) that exists between working-class fathers. Working-class mothers, in short, even when they operate as substitutes or surrogates, were likely to be more helpful to children than were working-class fathers in the same situation. Finally, in both the middle and working classes, respondents from whole families report greater *total* parental functionality than those from "other" backgrounds. However, differences in the working class are greater and the significance level much higher than is true for the middle class.

It is apparent that status advantage and family composition are closely intermingled in terms of their impact on resource-provision for children above the underclass. It is perhaps simpler to grasp the situation in the lower class where, due to blocked opportunity, the presence or absence of the father is seemingly less crucial. Even when present, he is not likely to be able to function as an "adequate" role model in terms of attainments in the larger society. In that situation, blocked access to the opportunity structure—rather than family wholeness—is clearly more critical with regard to family functionality.

When we talk about blacks with relatively greater status advantage, the situation becomes more complex. For example, looking at "total-functionality" in Table 3–11, we may construct a continuum of "total parental-functionality" or child-advantage. Following this scheme, children from middle-class, whole families are most advantaged ($\bar{x} = 32.5$) which is to be expected. But next are children from working-class, whole families ($\bar{x} = 29.9$). Hence, children from the latter type of working-class setting are seemingly "better off" than children from middle-class, "other" families ($\bar{x} = 27.9$). By this comparison the effect of wholeness appears to outweigh the influence of father's occupation. Finally, the least advantaged are those from working-class, "other" situations ($x = 23.1$).

Perhaps the point of overriding significance (theoretical and practical) is that just as resource *disadvantage* severely hampers the functionality of parents in the lower class, so relative resource *advantage* enhances the functionality of parents *beyond* the lower class. Differences by father's occupation and family wholeness do exist but only in *degree* of resource provision. There is a far more fundamental difference in *kind* between the "ineffective role model" described in the literature on the black lower-class and the "effectiveness" of the black parents described in this chapter. The comparison is analogous to and a function of the contrast in *kinds* of life-situations and life-chances that distinguish the underclass from the strata above them. As a consequence, the generalization can be offered that family wholeness is less critical to the child (black or white) in the long run, than the social stratum into which the child is born. If he is born into the underclass, wholeness may be largely irrelevant. If he is born into the working or middle classes, wholeness is desirable, but whole or not, there are sufficient resources emanating from other aspects of his total life-situation (including remaining parent and surrogates) which enable him as an adult to participate reasonably effectively in the intertwined opportunity and family structures. Obviously, being born into the middle class upgrades his chances, but the difference is one of degree not of kind.

Using a multiple correlation procedure, there is within our sample some additional evidence for the greater significance of status advantage than of family wholeness. Of particular significance in Table 3–12 are the path coefficients (p) or *Beta weights*. Although causal inferences in sociology are always and inevitably crude and hazardous, the path coefficient would seem to be one of the most adequate tools currently available to try to attain the

TABLE 3–12. THE INFLUENCE OF PARENTAL EDUCATION, FATHER'S OCCUPATION AND FAMILY WHOLENESS ON PARENTAL FUNCTIONALITY

	Males			*Females*		
	p		*r*	*p*		*r*
			Functionality of Fathers			
X	.209		.09	.121		.04
Y	.107		.52	.014		.38
Z	.018		.00	.00		.07
R^2 =		.25			.12	
N =		(130)			(133)	
			Functionality of Mothers			
W	.196		.02	.054		.00
Y	.099		.37	.103		.33
Z	.101		.00	.00		.00
R^2 =		.23			.11	
N =		(140)			(145)	
			Total Parental Functionality			
W	.075		.40	.047		.28
X	.165		.01	.068		.01
Y	.128		.52	.005		.40
Z	.103		.00	.025		.07
R^2 =		.24			.09	
N =		(124)			(128)	

W = Mother's Education
X = Father's Education
Y = Family Wholeness
Z = Father's Occupation

ideal of causal relationship.[39] For example, when the effects of father's education, family wholeness, and father's occupation are run jointly against father-functionality, we find that the p for father's education, like occupation a status factor, is greater (for both males and females) than the p for wholeness.[40] Since this holds both for males and females, father's education would seem to exert the single greatest *path of influence* on resources provided to the child. Even though the simple r's between wholeness and functionality are strong, when the effects of wholeness are controlled, education accounts more directly for functionality of the father. Therefore, in trying to account for paternal resources provided to the black child above the underclass, degree of access to the opportunity-structure rather than composition of the household would appear to be more significant.

The same conclusion emerges when we examine functionality of the mother for males—her own educational level is *a more direct predictor* of resources provided to the son than is family wholeness. This is not true, however, for females where wholeness does seem to have more direct impact on resource-provision than does mother's education. A similar disparity occurs when we look at *total* parental functionality. There appears in fact to be no single meaningful path of influence for females, whereas, for males, father's education remains the most single direct influence on resource-provision. Why the results fall as they do for females is uncertain and requires additional research. Of far greater theoretical import is the influence of father's education on total-functionality received by the *son* when mother's education, along with wholeness, and father's occupation are controlled.

The literature on the lower-class black family is replete with the alleged "inability" of the father to move his sons toward goals valued both by them and the larger society. The cumulative evidence of this chapter culminating with these data suggest this is not so above the underclass. Instead, the father's educational level is apparently more important than the mother's in determining the total level of valued resources the son receives. There is no indication here of alleged "female dominance" or "black matriarchy." In short, in the more advantaged black family, the father (or a surrogate) seems to function toward sons in much the same way as do fathers in the larger society. In spite of deprivation vis-à-vis similarly situated whites, black fathers not only perceive certain economic and conjugal goals as desirable, but also exert considerable positive effort calculated to move their sons along the route of *relative* attainment of these intertwined objectives.

SUMMARY

Important findings from this chapter include:

1. The majority of male and female respondents perceived that both their fathers and mothers provided the kinds of resources, rewards, and benefits that would enable them to begin to conform to dominant economic and conjugal patterns.

2. These resources took the form of pertinent values and norms, plus appropriate behaviors including economic help. Resources were focused on attainment of educational, occupational, and marital goals.

3. Their parents provided both expressive or person-oriented support, as well as instrumental or goal-oriented direction. There was some indication that mothers were more active in the former sphere, fathers in the latter.

4. There is great similarity or convergence in the behaviors of their parents toward them and what we know about the behaviors of white parents toward their adolescent children. Respondents' parents, in brief, give evidence of being just as aware of the "achievement demands" of modern society, and just as active as whites in trying to prepare their children to meet these demands.

5. Respondents who came from middle-class backgrounds seem to have been exposed to greater levels of resources than those coming from working-class backgrounds; and those from "whole" families seem to have been relatively more advantaged than those from "other" types of families.

6. Nevertheless, class background seems to be more significant than family composition in explaining differences in levels of resources received. More specifically, the education of fathers and mothers seems to exert the most powerful and most direct influence on resources provided to children.

In effect, what we are describing here and throughout the book may be said to be family patterns of blacks above the lower class, extending from the working class upward, or what may be defined as the "broad middle-class." These patterns are substantially different from the oft-described black lower-class. It is generally agreed that particular family structures and process are the result of social-class position. Persons (white or black) who move out of the lower class into the working or middle classes tend to adopt the family forms of that class. Economic discrimination, however, keeps a disproportionate number of blacks in the lower class. In Chapters 5 and 6, we shall find that economic discrimination influences the family patterns even of working- and middle-class blacks. The underlying point to remember is that whatever differences emerge between black and white family structures are largely the result of discrimination and differential access to opportunity. They are not due to any racial or biological proclivities. To the degree (and if) discrimination diminishes, we may expect in the future even greater convergence in black and white family patterns. This is, of course, merely a proposition that can be tested by further research and could, therefore, be modified. One hypothesis that might be examined is the possibility of the development of a family form by *advantaged blacks*, not in reaction to economic deprivation and as a means to survival as is the case with lower-class blacks, but as the desired outgrowth of a distinctively black ethnic subculture. We found no evidence whatever of even the slightest hint of such a family form, nor are we aware of any other empirical work that might document its existence. Until such evidence emerges, it seems safe to consider the foregoing proposition as reasonably valid, though in the remainder of the book we shall continue to scrutinize it.

NOTES

1. Winch, *Identification and Its Familial Determinants*, p. 40.
2. Ibid., p. 41. Winch does not go into dysfunctions or negative consequences in detail, but obviously parents may sometimes influence their children negatively.
3. Elder, "Adolescent Socialization," p. 326.
4. Hylan Lewis, "Child Rearing Among Low-Income Families," in Louis A. Ferman et al., *Poverty in America*, p. 435.
5. Constance K. Kamii and Norma L. Radin, "Class Differences in the Socialization Practices of Negro Mothers," *Journal of Marriage and the Family* 29 (May 1967): 302–10.
6. Schulz, *Coming Up Black*, p. 187.
7. Ibid.
8. Donald R. Young, "The Socialization of American Minority Peoples," in David A. Goslin, *Handbook of Socialization Theory and Research* (Chicago: Rand McNally & Co., 1969), p. 1121.
9. Ibid., p. 1121 ff.
10. Richard A. Cloward and Lloyd E. Ohlin, *Delinquency and Opportunity* (New York: The Free Press, 1960), p. 148.
11. See Young, "The Socialization of American Minority Peoples," p. 1124.
12. Cited and discussed in Cloward and Ohlin, *Delinquency and Opportunity*, pp. 79 ff.
13. Ibid.
14. See Billingsley, *Black Families in White America*, pp. 79 ff.
15. The total N in the tables includes those who identify a parent or parent figure and who also respond to the question.
16. See McCord et al., *Life Styles in the Black Ghetto*, pp. 175–178, and p. 168, for a discussion of the impact of the black female on the mobility of her children.
17. Blau and Duncan, *The American Occupational Structure*, pp. 319, 329.
18. See Safa, *An Analysis of Upward Mobility*, p. 55 ff.
19. Blau and Duncan, *The American Occupational Structure*, p. 239. Precisely the same point is made by Albert J. Lott and Bernice E. Lott, *Negro and White Youth* (New York: Holt, Rinehart, and Winston, Inc., 1963), pp. 133–34.
20. Price, *Changing Characteristics*, Chapters 3, 4, and 5.
21. Ginzberg and Hiestand, "Employment Patterns," p. 237.

22. William J. Goode, *After Divorce* (New York: The Free Press, 1956), pp. 62 ff.

23. See McCord et al., *Life Styles*, p. 177; also Anne Steinmann, David J. Fox, Ruth L. Farkas, "Attitudes Toward Marriage, Family Relationships, and Childbearing in Samples of Negro and White Female and Male College Undergraduates in the United States," Paper read at *Seventh International Congress on Mental Health*, London, England, August 1968.

24. See Scanzoni, *Opportunity and the Family*, where numerous sources for this second viewpoint are cited.

25. Rainwater, 1966, p. 182; See also Liebow, and Safa, for a clear statement of this position.

26. See Ephraim H. Mizruchi, *Success and Opportunity* (New York: The Free Press, 1964).

27. Blau and Duncan, *The American Occupational Structure*, p. 438.

28. Ibid., p. 296.

29. See Seymour Martin Lipset and Reinhard Bendix, *Social Mobility in Industrial Society* (Berkeley, California: University of California Press, 1960), pp. 256–57.

30. See Billingsley, *Black Families in White America*, pp. 28–29, for a discussion of some of the unique stresses faced by the black family in our society.

31. Ibid., p. 25.

32. Rainwater, 1966, pp. 193 ff., presents an interesting case study in the process of gradual erosion of reciprocal role relations. See Scanzoni, *Opportunity and the Family*, for a general discussion of economic-expressive role relations between husbands and wives, irrespective of skin color.

33. See Alvin W. Gouldner, "The Norm of Reciprocity: A Preliminary Statement," *American Sociological Review*, 1960.

34. Billingsley, *Black Families in White America*, p. 98.

35. Fathers of respondents not able to provide enough information to code them specifically into one of the Census Bureau categories are nonetheless placed with the working-class for Tables 3–9 and 3–11. This is because on examination of the interview schedules of these respondents, there was clearly enough information to make this type of gross categorization. There was not however, enough information to go beyond this gross dichotomy, and whenever we are forced to become more specific, these cases are dropped from consideration. (See Table 2–1.)

36. The index of "father-functionality" is based on the weights assigned to the responses to the question for fathers cited in the text for Tables 3–1,

3–2, 3–4, 3–5, and 3–7. "Yes" in 3–1 and 3–4 was asigned a weight of four; "No" was assigned zero. In 3–2, 3–5, 3–7, "helped" was assigned "four"; "neither helped nor hindered" was assigned two, and "hindered" was assigned zero. The rationale for assigning a weight of two to "neither" is based on a discussion in the text surrounding Tables 3–2 and 3–3. Compared to being a hindrance, *not* standing in the child's way is a positive gain for the child, and the weighting reflects this notion of *relative* benefit. This "benefit" is relatively less useful to the child than actually being helped, but more "functional" to him than actually being hindered. The index of "mother-functionality" is constructed in identical fashion except that only responses to questions regarding mothers are used. The "total functionality" index is the result of adding the scores of father and mother (as each is present) for each respondent.

37. The technique for comparing mean scores is a simple one-way analysis procedure. This technique is used extensively in this study because so many comparisons of mean scores (see tables from Chapter 4 on) involve more than a mere dichotomy. See Hubert M. Blalock, *Social Statistics* (New York: McGraw-Hill Book Co., 1960), p. 252.

38. McCord et al., *Life Styles*, pp. 168, 175–78.

39. Blalock, *Social Statistics*, pp. 343–46; Blau and Duncan, *The American Occupational Structure*, pp. 171–77. For a discussion of the use of path coefficients with ordinal data, see Richard P. Boyle, "Path Analysis and Ordinal Data," *American Journal of Sociology* 75 (January 1970, part 1): 461–80.

40. While the correlation between father's education and occupation is only .19, this may be owing in part to job discrimination, even against educated blacks, as documented in earlier chapters. That is, compared to whites with similar education, blacks are not permitted to attain similar job levels. (See also our Chapter 5.)

4

Identification
with Parents

Winch has suggested that the structure of a family system is
linked to its functionality, i.e., certain structural situations more
than others will give rise to more functionality. This relationship
was considered in Chapter 3. The next step in Winch's model is
to link functionality and identification. He postulates:

The more functional the parent, the greater will be the identification of
the offspring with that parent.
To the extent that one parent is more functional than the other, the
offspring will tend to identify with the more functional parent.[1]

Winch bases these hypotheses on a form of social exchange
theory. Functionality, as we saw in Chapter 3, is construed as a
set of rewards or resources provided by the parent to the child. As
the level of these resources increases, presumably there will be
reciprocity on the part of the child in the form of increased identification with the parent.[2] The point is that functionality as reward
to child in turn stimulates identification as reward to parent, within
a set of complex, ongoing, reciprocal processes.

Identification is defined by Winch as "the more or less lasting influence of one M (the identificand, in this case the parent)
on the behavior (including attitudes) of I (the identifier, in this

case, the child)." He goes on to make at least two important refinements in the notion of identification that tend to link it to what is broadly known as "reference group theory": (1) identification may be opposite as well as similar, and (2) identification may be positional as well as personal. Positional identification refers to specific and segmental role relationships, while personal identification refers to the personality or nearly total range of M's behavior.[3]

Newcomb, Merton, Hyman, among others, point out that the norms of a reference group (or reference person) may be rejected as well as accepted.[4] Rejection implies "not merely nonacceptance of norms but the formation of counternorms."[5] This notion is akin to Winch's "opposite identification." Merton also makes a vital distinction between "role model" and "reference individual."[6] Merton's idea of role model is virtually identical to Winch's "positional identification," i.e., "denoting a more limited identification with an individual in only one or a selected few of his roles."[7] In contrast to this *partial* identification, *full* or personal identification occurs when "I" seeks "to approximate the behavior and values of that individual (M) in his several roles," i.e., M becomes a reference individual. Merton goes on to remark that taking a person as a role model could eventually lead to adopting M as a reference individual—"I" could make the transition from partial to full identification.[8]

The pertinence of these several theoretical notions to our particular problem is evident. Within the *dominant* family form there is evidence of considerable identification (both positive and negative) of children with parents. In addition, it is clear that white adolescents identify with a wide range of nonconjugal role models and reference individuals. The complex interactions of familial and non-familial identifications appear to have substantial impact on the behavior and development of the child, particularly in terms of later attainments within the economic-opportunity structure.[9] The question here is to what extent do these same kinds of processes operate within the black family system above the underclass.

PARENTAL ROLE MODELS

We must first determine whether or not these respondents used their parents as role models. To ascertain that we asked each respondent: "While you were a teen-ager [defined to R, as in Chapter 2, ages 12–18] did you feel you wanted to be like your father [father-substitute] when you grew up, or different from him?" The same item was asked separately regarding mothers.[10] Being "like" the parent indicates *positive* identification; being "different" indicates *negative* identification. A certain proportion of respondents replied "neither like nor different," suggesting neither type of identification with the parent at least on the level of role model.[11]

Looking at Table 4–1, we find that both sexes identified to a considerable extent with each parent or parent figure. However, there was more *positive* identification with mothers than with fathers, and conversely, more *negative* identification with fathers than with mothers, by both male and female respondents. Males were more apt than females to identify positively with fathers, al-

TABLE 4–1.   USE OF PARENTS AS ROLE MODELS

		Be Like Parent	Be Different	Neither	T	N
Identification with Father	Males	36.0%	35.9	28.1	100% (167) n.s.	
	Females	29.2%	37.6	33.2	100% (178)	
Identification with Mother	Males	48.3%	22.0	29.7	100% (168) $x^2 = 16.7$ $p<.01$; 2 df	
	Females	56.1%	31.5	12.4	100% (187)	

though the differences are neither great nor significant. On the other hand, female respondents were more apt than males to identify more positively *and* more negatively with mothers, and these differences are significant.

On the basis of these findings, we may suggest that most of our respondents did indeed use their parents as *role models*. By earlier definition, this refers to some rather specific behavior or value of the parent with which the child identified in *either* a positive or negative fashion. To get at these more or less specific characteristics, respondents who replied they wanted to be *like* a parent were asked *why*, as were those who said they wanted to be *different*.

In Table 4–2, we examine those who replied they wanted to be *like* their parents; and in Table 4–3 we examine those who replied they wanted to be *different*. The responses of those explaining why they identified positively with parents were coded into two categories: goal-oriented behavior (instrumental), and person-oriented behavior (expressive). Examples of the former kind of comments are as follows: "I wanted to be reliable and dependable and have people trust in me as they did her." "He was ambitious and so am I." "In many ways he was a go-getter, wasn't lazy at all." "She was well known and I wanted just that." "She always

TABLE 4–2. REASONS FOR POSITIVE PARENTAL IDENTIFICATION

		Positive Goal-Oriented Behavior	Positive Person-Oriented Behavior	T	N	
Father Figure	Males	34.4%	65.6	100%	(64)	
	Females	30.2%	69.8	100%	(53)	n.s.
Mother Figure	Males	10.8%	89.2	100%	(83)	$x^2 = 6.5$
	Females	26.9%	73.1	100%	(108)	$p < .05$ 1 df

wanted the best—as far as her neatness, appearance, the house, and *everywhere*."

These comments fit the widely accepted definition of instrumental behavior as that which is goal- or task-oriented. In these instances the behavior was evidently directed toward the goal of some type of individual attainment. Expressive behavior, on the other hand, is generally defined as person-oriented or primary-type interaction. There is no goal in view extrinsic to the socioemotional support of those involved in the relationship. Respondents' comments of this kind are as follows: "She was good and kind and I wanted to be like her." "She was gentle and kind with everybody." "She was a good Christian woman, a loving mother." "Because he was unselfish." "Because he was a fine, kind person." "She was a religious woman and she taught me to love everyone." "I wanted to be kind like my father—walk in his footsteps." "He was a good and kind, religious father." "He was a strong man with sincere opinions."

In Table 4–3, comments of those replying they wished to be different from parents fell into two categories which are the exact converse of those just discussed. *Negative* instrumental or goal-oriented behavior refers to parental behavior defined by the respondent as inadequate in terms of individual attainments. It has to do with parental goals in life that, as a child, the respondent

TABLE 4–3.   REASONS FOR NEGATIVE PARENTAL IDENTIFICATION

		Negative Goal-Oriented Behavior	Negative Person-Oriented Behavior	T	N	
Father Figure	Males	62.7%	37.3	100% (59)		
						n.s.
	Females	50.7%	49.3	100% (63)		
Mother Figure	Males	47.2%	52.8	100% (36)		
						n.s.
	Females	50.0%	50.0	100% (62)		

felt were too limited. Such respondents believed, in other words, that their parents were not ambitious enough, did not want or expect enough from life, were too content or satisfied with their lot, and were not willing, anxious or aggressive enough to try and change it. The child was not satisfied with his parents' outlook and behavior and wanted "to do better."

Sample comments include: "She was satisfied with nothing—just her surroundings." "I wanted to have more, see more than she did." "Because of his laborer's occupation, and lack of education." "I did want to do more and accomplish more than he and live better than he did." "She was a beautician and I wanted to be a nurse." "Wanted to be better than she was." "Because he didn't have the things I always wanted—like a nice home and clothes." "Wanted better life than he had." For these particular respondents, their parents were clearly *negative* role models with regard to achievement and success in society. In Merton's terms, rejection here goes beyond nonacceptance of parental norms to encompass the formation of *counter-norms*.[12]

Likewise, certain parents were *negative* role models at the expressive, or person-oriented level. We saw that perceptions of kindness, gentleness, warmth, unselfishness, etc., were linked to a positive expressive identification. Opposite comments such as the following suggest a negative or counter-identification: "He was too mean and I never wanted to be like him." "He had funny ways, one day he was nice, the next day he wasn't." "She wouldn't let me alone—always nagging me." "She was too bossy." "Never paid much attention to us kids." "Always beat me for no good reason." At the interpersonal, psychic, socioemotional level, these parents behaved in a fashion defined as "bad" or unkind or overbearing by these respondents. Hence, the feeling developed within them that they did *not* want to emulate these kinds of characteristics. Instead, they wished to behave in a contrary fashion at the interpersonal level.

Combining the information from Tables 4–1, 4–2 and 4–3, let us first trace identification with the father. About the same proportions of males used him as a positive role model as used him in a

negative sense, while females were more apt to use him as a negative rather than as a positive role model. Only a minority of both
sexes did not identify with a father figure at all. Since reasons for
nonidentification were not probed, there is little we can say here
about that situation except to note that a few volunteered the comment, "I just wanted to be me, that's all."

Of those respondents who did identify *positively* with *fathers*,
most (about two-thirds) of each sex wished to emulate their expressive, person-oriented behavior. Approximately one-third of
each sex used the father as a role model in terms of individual
achievements or attainments. Among *males* using the father as
a negative role model, two-thirds rejected his ambitions for
achievement and mobility as being too low. Among *females* who
viewed the father negatively, about half rejected his instrumental
behavior, half his expressive behavior.

These patterns of positive and negative father identification
differ somewhat from those that pertain to *mother* identification.
First, there is more positive identification with mothers than with
fathers, especially by girls. Second, this positive identification is
overwhelmingly at the expressive level. Males use the mother
strongly as an expressive role model, and hardly at all as an instrumental role model. By way of contrast, females used the
mother in a positive instrumental, as well as in a positive expressive fashion. Finally, when it comes to *rejecting* the mother, males
are divided rather equally between their use of the mother as a
negative instrumental and also negative expressive role model, in
contrast with their use of the father primarily as a negative instrumental role model. *Females* were about evenly divided in their
rejection of instrumental and expressive roles of both parent
figures.

Since social class and family "wholeness" influenced the degree of benefits the child received, do these two elements influence
his identification with his parents? Although we might expect, for
instance, that coming from a middle-class background might lead
to significantly greater use of parents as positive role models,
this does not seem to be the case. Of middle-class respondents,

35 percent wanted to be *like* their fathers, 32 percent different, 33 percent neither. In the working class, the proportions were 32, 38, and 30 percent, respectively.[13]

When it came to mother-identification, there were hardly any differences at all. (Middle class: "like" mother, 53 percent; "different," 26 percent; "neither," 22 percent. Working class: "like," 52 percent; "different," 28 percent; "neither," 20 percent.)[14] Evidently, the differences by social class in resources enjoyed by the child were not great enough in degree or in kind to alter the pattern of identification with parents. Within both strata, basically similar processes of parental identification were operative.

Likewise, family wholeness produced no meaningful differences in father-identification. The proportion of those from whole families wanting to be "like" their fathers was 33 percent; "different," 37 percent; "neither," 31 percent. From "other" families, the proportions were 31, 38, 31 percent, respectively.[15] Interestingly, family composition did produce significant differences in type of mother-identification. Those from whole families were more likely to identify *positively* with her; those from "other" families were more apt to identify *negatively*. (Whole 56, 22, 22 percent, respectively; other 47, 35, 18 percent, respectively.)[16]

Aside from this latter finding, it would seem that what are "objectively less desirable" situations (working-class, "other" family background) have consequences similar to "more desirable" situations. In short, among these black respondents, representing strata above the lower class, what determines identification with parents is not so much class or family composition, but rather the behavior per se of parents. And though this behavior is somewhat different in *degree* between these groupings, it is not distinct enough in *kind* to produce greatly different outcomes. This same conclusion that was also indicated in Chapter 3 will emerge again shortly when we examine the linkage of functionality and identification.

Several generalizations emerge from the discussion so far. First, to the extent that our sample may be representative of stable black families in America above the lower class, *there is substantial*

identification between parents and children. Although this identification is somewhat more frequent with regard to mothers than to
fathers, black fathers in these strata are by no means bland or
"inadequate" figures. It is an error to attribute to them the kinds
of characteristics that might apply to lower-class fathers. As adolescents, many male respondents, for instance, identified with some
father figure who provided a role model in terms of achievement,
success, and social mobility, and in terms of socioemotional support
as well.

Certainly, a proportion of males used the father as a *negative*
role model, i.e., they rejected what they considered to be his
"inadequate" goals. But in terms of impetus toward occupational
attainments, this formation of "counter-norms" can be just as
effective as a *positive* identification. There are some studies that
show that within the dominant society positive identification is
conducive to attainments, while others suggest that negative identification is beneficial.[17] Both sets of conclusions are correct if differing background situations (see Chapter 5) are considered. The
point is that both processes are apparently at work within the black,
as well as within the white, family system.

In addition to identifying (in one fashion or the other) with
the instrumental impetus from their fathers, males also identify
with the expressive support and warmth provided by their
mothers. There was evidence of this in Chapter 3, in terms of
parental functionality, and it is quite clear that these families were
similar to the pattern found within the dominant family form. The
general assumption, based on a wide range of studies, is that the
optimum situation for the young male in terms of attainments is
precisely that of the instrumental father and the expressive mother.
As Blau and Duncan explain—

Conditions in the family of orientation tend to determine both whether
the child develops the socialized anxiety that drives him to succeed [task-
oriented identification] and whether he receives the socio-emotional support [person-oriented identification] to cope with this anxiety without
becoming debilitated by it.[18]

Females identified with their parents in generally similar fashion, although there were some variations. Overall, the patterns of identificaton that emerged for them can also be construed to "fit" dominant conjugal patterns. Therefore, with respect to child-identification of parents as role models in terms of the two major components (instrumental-expressive) of parental roles, respondents' behaviors did not appear to differ substantially from patterns found within dominant family structure. *There was identification, both positive and negative, toward both parents, and on both types of role levels.* (Obviously, fathers were not *totally* instrumental toward their children, nor were mothers totally expressive.) Very likely, therefore, this too is one more significant factor in the chain of elements positively influencing later economic and marital goal-attainment.

RESOURCES AND IDENTIFICATION

Winch, it will be recalled, predicts that as functionality (benefits) increases so will identification. As resources are increased to the child, he in turn will respond by using the parent as a role model. So far, having established the presence both of functionality (Chapter 3) and of identification within the backgrounds of these black respondents, the next step is to see if these two elements vary together as predicted. From Table 4–4, we discover that indeed they do.

Male respondents who report they want to be *like* their fathers show a signficantly higher father-functionality score than those who say they want to be *different* from their fathers. Those who said they wanted to be *different* report greater father-functionality than those who said they wanted *neither* to be like their father nor to be different from them. The same pattern holds true for females in terms of their fathers. It is also true for both sexes with respect to their *mothers*, except that the mean differences in functionality, though significant, are not quite as great as are those for fathers.

TABLE 4–4.   PARENTAL FUNCTIONALITY AND TYPE OF ROLE-MODEL
IDENTIFICATION

	Father-Functionality (Mean scores)		Mother-Functionality (Mean scores)	
Male Identification	Like Father	16.1 (60)	Like Mother	16.7 (81)
	Different	13.8 (60)	Different	16.1 (37)
	Neither	7.3 (68)	Neither	11.6 (61)
	(F = 44.6; p < .001; df = 2 & 185)		(F = 2.08; p < .001; df = 2 & 176)	
Female Identification	Like Father	16.0 (52)	Like Mother	17.1 (105)
	Different	13.7 (67)	Different	15.1 (59)
	Neither	9.2 (75)	Neither	11.3 (29)
	(F = 22.0; p < .001; df = 2 & 191)		(F = 19.4; p < .001; df = 2 & 190)	

Generally, therefore, we may say that as adolescents, *the more their parents did for them, the more they wanted to be like them.* Their parents were providing them with rewards and resources in the form of values and behavior that would aid them in their education, in getting ahead in life, and in their later family situations. In exchange for these rewards, many respondents used their parents as positive role models. Both in terms of instrumental and expressive behaviors, they wanted to emulate them, to be like them, to behave as they did.

When their parents provided *fewer* rewards—when they were less functional to their children—the respondents tended to want to be *different* from their parents. Failure to provide a high enough level of rewards weakened bonds between parents and children. This condition is the essence of exchange theory, i.e., increased reciprocal rewards strengthen the bonds of a relationship, decreased rewards weaken it. Furthermore, we saw that when children wanted to be different, it was also because their parents were behaving in an "undesirable" manner as far as the children

were concerned. They failed to have "high enough" success aspirations, or else they were personally overbearing toward their children. Therefore, concomitant with not giving enough *positive*
rewards, certain parents were also emitting *negative* attitudes and
behaviors. Acting together, these different sides of the same coin
result in a *negative* identification with parents.

But as noted earlier, this situation should not be taken as
necessarily inimical to later economic and conjugal attainments.
Seeing their parents behave in a way that they define as "bad,"
could lead them to want very much to adopt *opposite* behavior
patterns and therefore *enhance* later attainments. For this reason,
it is quite proper to speak of their parents too as role models—
negative to be sure—but role models nonetheless since they provide definite impetus to certain *contrary* behaviors. It is possible,
in short, that some black children who use their parents as *negative*
role models could be just as effective in the larger society as black
children who use parents as *positive* role models.[19] In the latter
case, their parents have adopted dominant values and norms and
transmit them directly to their children. In the former instance,
the failure of parents to adopt dominant orientations is somehow
sensed, and this in itself prompted them as children to seek something "different and better."

Just how, as adolescents, these respondents might have received this "sense of things," will be discussed when we look at
potential role models outside the family. But first note that consistently in Table 4–4, when functionality is *least*, we find *neither*
positive nor negative identification. Providing minimal rewards,
plus not behaving in either a positive *or* a negative fashion toward
children, results in *minimal* identification by the child.[20] In effect,
not "being involved" with the child (either positively or negatively) leads in turn to the child's not "being involved" with the
parent—either negatively or positively. The question then emerges
which is similar to that just raised for those with *negative* parental
identification. How did black adolescents, with little or no parental
identification, come to internalize expectations held by the dominant society regarding economic and conjugal roles?

The answer to this question may lie in part with sources outside the family, i.e., extra-familial role models. But before pursuing that, we should note that the basic conclusions just reached regarding functionality and role-model identification apply *equally* to those with working-class and middle-class backgrounds, and also to those who come from "whole" as well as from "other" families. For example, while there are differences of degree in the functionality provided by middle- and working-class families, nevertheless, in both *settings,* positive identification is related to maximum rewards and benefits, lesser rewards account for negative identification, and least rewards are linked to a neutral stance toward parents as role models.[21] Among these black respondents who represent those strata above the impoverished lower-class, that fine line distinguishing middle from working class did not affect basic processes of parent-child identification. Throughout this broad spectrum of black society, the conclusion is the same: the greater the parental functionality, the greater the likelihood of identification by the child.

Moreover, the same basic types of processes were at work, regardless of whether blacks in the sample came from "whole" or from "other" families.[22] Hence, if neither class nor family composition alters the fundamental identification process in kind within the "dominant" black society, and in view of all the negative pressures imposed on its family system, then we may be safe in assuming the same kinds of processes operate throughout similar strata in the more advantaged white society. This assumption implies additional indication of basic similarity between black and white family systems above the lowest stratum. Black or white, whole or other family form, middle or working class—the greater the parental resources, the greater the positive child identification. Lesser amounts of resources result in negative identification, and where resources are least, there is little or no identification at all.

Thinking back to Figure 1–2, the reader will recall that we had expected that background factors would influence functionality which would, in turn, influence identification. Table 3–12 confirmed a "path of influence" between parent's education and his functionality. Table 4–5 reveals the direct impact of resource-

TABLE 4–5. INFLUENCE OF PARENTAL FUNCTIONALITY ON CHOICE OF PARENT AS ROLE MODEL, CONTROLLING FOR OTHER INFLUENCES.

	Identification With Father				Identification With Mother			
	Males		Females		Males		Females	
	p	r	p	r	p	r	p	r
Father-Functionality	.350	.07	.215	.03	—	—	—	—
Mother-Functionality	—	—	—	—	.261	.03	.253	.06
Occupation of Father	.086	.20	.103	.01	.035	.13	.018	.09
Family Wholeness	.032	.23	.130	.11	.039	.20	.194	.04
Education of Father	.020	.35	.090	.20	—	—	—	—
Education of Mother	—	—	—	—	.080	.27	.087	.27
$R^2 =$	.36		.28		.28		.35	
$N =$	(125)		(127)		(130)		(142)	

provision by parents on identification with them. In each of the four equations in the table, the strongest p (path coefficient) is consistently the one from the functionality of the parent. In short, controlling for critical status factors plus family wholeness, there seems to be a *direct linkage* (not merely an association) between what the father or mother *does for* the male or female child, and in exchange, identification by the child with the parent.

As we go on, we shall add further paths of influence that build on parental identification in much the same way as identification builds on functionality. This method is in keeping with the objective of which Figure 1–2 is illustrative, i.e., to try to examine the black family *qua system* (above the underclass) in a kind of developmental sequence. We assume that one set, or chain, or path of sociological factors that influenced the respondents' current ongoing marriages are those described to this point. But before we discuss current husband-wife interaction, several additional elements must be considered, and the remainder of this chapter plus the next are devoted to them.

EXTRA-FAMILIAL RESOURCES

Billingsley argues that black Americans who have been able to gain benefits from and make attainments within our society owe this to several kinds of elements. First, he says, is the individual's own personality and fund of inherited talents and abilities. Second, is what he calls a

strong family life. . . . Strong families are often highly influenced by the religious convictions and behavior, the education or educational aspirations of one or more members. They often have an economic footing more secure than the average Negro family in their community. They often have strong social and emotional ties. These factors—religion, education, money or property, jobs, family ties, and other community-centered activities—are the chief ingredients of strong family life. . . . it need not be a great deal of money or education to . . . provide a head start for its young members. . . . Negro families have shown an amazing ability to survive in the face of impossible conditions. They have also shown remarkable ability to take the barest shreds of opportunity and turn them into the social capital of [marital] *stability* and *achievement*. (italics supplied)[23]

His description of the type of family background that leads to stability and achievement certainly corresponds to the conclusions reached so far regarding blacks in our sample. But for part of this chapter, we want to look at additional factors that, he claims, also influence marital stability and occupational achievement, i.e., persons and structures providing resources from *outside* the family. These, he says, might include such persons as neighbors, Sunday school teachers, school teachers, or other community figures. In these several capacities, they have been able to function as role models to black youth at both the task-oriented and supportive levels we have already observed in the case of parents.[24]

Persons

To learn more about this type of situation, we asked respondents: "While you were a teen-ager, was there ever anyone like a minister, school teacher, a Sunday school teacher, a social worker who really took an interest in you and helped you?" Fifty-five percent of our male respondents replied there was such a person, as did fifty-four percent of female respondents. Moreover, neither social class nor family composition made any difference whatsoever. Irrespective of whether one came from middle or working class, or from a "whole" or "other" family situation, the proportion of those responding "yes" to this remained at 54 or 55 percent.

Next, we asked those who replied affirmatively to name as many such persons as there were who "took this interest in them." Table 4–6 shows the frequency with which respondents chose that kind of community figure (some named more than one). The one picked most frequently was school teacher, followed by minister, then Sunday school teacher. Although they were asked about

TABLE 4–6. KINDS AND FREQUENCY OF ADULTS WHO TOOK INTEREST IN RESPONDENTS (AS ADOLESCENTS)

Type of Adult Role Figure	Frequency of Choice By Males*	Frequency of Choice by Females*
Minister	20% (40)	18% (37)
School Teacher	27% (54)	33% (66)
Sunday School Teacher	14% (27)	11% (22)
Social Worker Plus Others	7% (13)	4% (9)
	Total N = 198	Total N = 202

* Some respondents made more than one choice.

possible "others," only a small percentage said there were any. Some of these "others" included an agricultural supervisor, a girl friend's mother, a church deacon, "a lady who stayed with family," a police officer, a gambler, "a white friend of daddy."

In short, more than half our respondents can look back on their adolescent years and pick out someone outside the family who took a "personal interest" in them, and who "lent them a helping hand," i.e., provided valuable resources in their efforts to penetrate white society. What is more, these persons overwhelmingly represented the two institutions in society that evidently "cared most" about black youth, the religious and educational institutions. There were few representatives of economic or political structures in the community who took such an interest, nor does the literature on American treatment of blacks give any hint that one should expect to find that they had. In addition to the family, church and school provided the greatest impetus to our respondents to attain in both the economic and conjugal spheres.

That these parental "extensions" did in fact provide such impetus emerges if we examine the comments received when those who said somone had been interested in them, were queried further as to *how* the person(s) named had actually *helped* them. Thirty-four percent of these males and the same proportion of females indicated they had received instrumental or task-oriented help from the person(s) who helped them.

For instance, some of these kinds of comments were: "The teacher would make me stay after school and get my lessons." "The minister's wife tried to help me in keeping myself clean, personal hygiene." "The police officer had a chance to lock me up but he didn't. He took me to his home and talked to me, showed me I was wrong." "My art teacher always encouraged me and took me places to show off my ability and helped my mother get a loan so I could go to art school. He helped me get an award when I graduated." "He told me that if there was anything I needed to let him know and that if I ever wanted to go back to school he would help me because he wanted to see me make something of myself."

In Chapter 3, we looked at parental functionality of this same sort. Now we see that certain figures other than parents also provided resources, benefits, rewards of an instrumental nature. These benefits would clearly aid young blacks in attempts at achievement and mobility, and thus in their later family experiences as well. The same conclusion applies even more to expressive, or person-oriented resources. Some 66 percent of these males and also of these females reported they received this kind of help. Examples of these kinds of comments were: "He just took time out to talk to young people and encourage them." "Just talked to me—talk with your minister will help." "He used to take time to talk to me a lot. He encouraged me to read and believe in the Bible." "During summers the teacher would just talk to me and encourage me."

Notice the consistent emphasis here on socioemotional and psychological support. These parental extensions simply took the time to *be* with our respondents, to *talk* to them, to provide some sort of solace, support, comfort, and meaning to their existence as black adolescents. In a discussion of black youth of earlier decades (when our respondents were young), Pierce points out that the major lesson they had to learn was a "defense system which was an all-inclusive umbrella against any onslaught which might serve to humiliate, shame, degrade, or provoke anxiety or wrath."[25] This was necessary, he claims, for them even to survive, to say nothing of mobility.

It may very well be that the teachers, ministers and others named by our respondents played an important part in this type of supportive learning process. Parents also obviously helped. But these extra-familial figures provided *additional* resources. They reinforced the self-esteem of many of these youth. In spite of being relatively important personages in their communities, these adults were willing to expend time and energy on behalf of these adolescents. And though young, and though they might have been terribly confused as to what it means to be a black adolescent in a white world, these adults supplied to these youth vital encouragement, counsel, and direction. This was no small benefit, and added to whatever task-oriented prodding they may have received from such figures, plus the resources provided by parents, the outcome is a substantial amount of "functionality" received by these youth from "significant adults" both parental and nonparental.

Religion

The question of identification of nonfamilial figures will be discussed later in this chapter. But first we want to look more closely at the adolescent involvement of respondents in church and school. We need to see if additional light can be cast on just how these institutions *as such* (insofar as a distinction can be made between structures and the performance of role-occupants within the structures) have aided them in later economic and conjugal role performance. Both Frazier and Billingsley stress the historic and current importance of the church to young blacks (see Chapter 2). And this stress seems warranted since 80 percent of males in our sample attended church at least once a week as adolescents, and 88 percent of females did the same. Only 6 cases out of the total sample never attended at all. Of all those who ever attended, about 70 percent went to a Baptist group; 15 percent were Methodists; 2.5 percent were Catholics; and the remainder belonged to small Holiness and Pentecostal groups. The great preponderance of Methodist and Baptist backgrounds can be traced back to the work of the early circuit riders described by Frazier.

We then asked those who had attended church: "Do you feel that the Church or religion helped you in any way to prepare for your marriage?" Sixty-eight percent of males and also of females replied that it did; 22 percent of each sex said that it had not; and 11 percent did not know. Hence, in the perception of more than two-thirds of these blacks, the church itself had been a significant force in preparing them for their later conjugal experiences. To get more specific as to the nature of religious influence, we asked: "Why do you feel that way?" Our interest was in discovering *why* some said it helped, and *why* others said it did not.

Responses of those indicating it did help fell into three

categories, with the proportions of males and females in each category being quite similar. Forty-five percent of each sex responded in terms of a "general orientation to life." That is, they said that the church provided the kinds of values that served as a framework for life, that gave meaning to all its aspects *including* marriage and family. This awareness regarding the function of religion in their lives is remarkable verification of Frazier's observation regarding its central role in the black community.

Comments that came under this heading included: "Without God, you can't do anything—if you're looking for success in marriage you better seek the Lord first of all." "Religion helps you prepare for everything if you do the right thing." "Because the church is the place to learn to unite ourselves together and teaches us love and things like that." "It helps when you have religion to fall back on—you get the extra strength you need." "Church taught you that marriage was a serious thing—nothing to be played with." "The principle of religion—love—the ten commandments." "Religion is supposed to be something helpful and a good way of life." In this sense of general orientation to life and marriage, the church was functional or beneficial to our respondents in much the same way as their parents had been. The church tended to reinforce parental values at this general level. Indeed, one respondent made an explicit point of this reinforcement by saying, "The basis for family life I learned at home wasn't too different from what we were taught in church."

At the same time, the church also reinforced parental emphasis on *specific role obligations* of husbands and wives. Forty-nine percent of males and fifty-three percent of females who said the church had helped, responded in this more specific sense. For example: "Went by what I read in the Bible—that a man should take care of his own." "Made me care more for my family and do the things for my kids a father should do—love them and make a nice home for them." "It teaches us to behave like fathers and mothers—to love thy neighbor—to suffer little children." "By its teaching not to commit adultery and cleave to one wife." "They told me how to be a good wife and mother." "The church taught me right and wrong—I knew it was wrong to run away and leave the girl alone with my child to raise—the church and my father helped me to see this." We discussed in Chapter 3 the crucial import to black youth of the "overstress" on marital role *duties* rather than on role *rights*. This overstress is apparently carried out by church as well as home. As one male vividly put it: "The Christian life is a narrow road to travel and to live it takes a good man. Jesus says there is only one way, and I believed every word of it when I said 'I do'—I really meant it."

Finally, a small proportion of those indicating the church had helped in this fashion (6 percent of males, and 2 percent of females) pointed to its utility for *mate selection*. On the one hand, several of these persons underscored the point that the church taught skills that enabled them to select a suitable partner. As one put it: "Well, I think that when you go to church you learn the good way to live and this helps you to choose the right kind of man." On the other hand, most of these particular persons noted that the church, in *addition* to its teachings on mate selection (its *manifest* function), also had the *latent* function of providing a social setting in which to meet "respectable" members of the opposite sex. For example: "People looked up to churchgoers— you could get a better type of girl." "At church you meet nice people—if a girl would dance I wouldn't go with her." "The girl I married was a Sunday school member and so was I." For these respondents, as Frazier observes, the church was a kind of all-encompassing institution. Not only did it provide values and norms appropriate for life and survival in general in society, it was looked to as the chief social center for one's nonwork time and activities. In this position, it tended to be the place where, if one were particularly self-conscious in his motivation to maintain the family form sanctioned by the dominant society, one could find a mate that might aid greatly in attaining this goal.

But 86 respondents, it will be remembered, replied that the church had not helped in preparation for conjugal role performance. Of these, only about 61 cases could verbalize *why* this was so. And 20 percent of this number (12 cases) replied simply they had not attended frequently enough to gain any good or help from the church. The remainder indicated that to their knowledge their church never broached the subject at all: "I never discussed marriage with the church—we had no marriage counsel in our church." In short, alongside the majority of the sample who perceived the church as beneficial to their later conjugal experiences, there is a minority who, for reasons of infrequent attendance or else nonemphasis by the church, do not see it as "functional" for that particular goal.

In addition to probing the church's perceived benefits for marriage per se, we wanted to obtain some idea of the church's impact on the success ethos discussed in Chapter 3. In response to the question, "Do you feel that the church or religion helped to prepare you for getting ahead in life," 68 percent of males and 62 percent of females said "yes," 21 and 25 percent, respectively, said "no," and 11 and 13 percent replied "don't know." The majority of these black respondents, therefore, perceived the church as aiding them in their mobility aspirations.

Sociologists generally agree that the church in America—black or white—has been historically a major bearer and purveyor of the Protestant Ethic. Although almost all our respondents were adolescents prior to the fifties, this empasis within the church itself came to a peak probably at that time in the writings and public utterances of spokesmen such as Norman Vincent Peale (*The Power of Positive Thinking*). The emphasis was that self-discipline, hard work, and diligent effort were pleasing to both God and man, and therefore "success" was almost certainly inevitable. Whether the more recent attention of black and white churches to civil rights and poverty has dimmed this traditional emphasis is not yet clear. Very likely in the vast majority of churches, it has not. Instead, notions of hard work and diligent effort are seemingly becoming fused with stress on government programs (or corporation-sponsored programs) that provide work opportunities and thus make "diligent effort" worthwhile.

Whatever trends are currently taking place, almost all the respondents who saw the church as functional in this way and who told *why*, spoke in traditional ascetic Protestant terms. Most couched it in very specific language. For example: "The church teaches you to move ahead, not to stand still—teaches you to do your best and move ahead—gives you faith in yourself and God-given motivation." "Church made me look forward to better things in life and not get them the wrong way." "I figured I had God first—you have to have Him to accomplish anything." "I get good jobs because I am a Christian." "If you believe in God you will get ahead in life." "Always the right way will help you win." "If you believe in God all things are possible." "If you live by the good book you are bound to get ahead in life."

Others who answered this question positively perceived the church as aiding them in "social adjustment." A major emphasis in the occupational world for sometime has been on "getting along with others." Employers in the modern business setting can rarely tolerate the person who frequently gets involved in clashes and altercations with fellow employees. Conversely, the worker who is reasonably personable is considered a desirable employee. These realities apply doubly to blacks who generally are the last to be hired, the most suspect while on the job, and the first to be fired. Sample comments in this vein included: "Church helped me to learn a sense of fair play—to get along with fellowmen." "Taught me how to treat my fellowman." "There I learned the golden rule—do unto others as you would be done—follow this and you will be successful." "The church helped me to learn to respect the people I came in contact with." "Church is a society where you meet all types of people in all walks of life and through associating with them you help prepare yourself for getting ahead."

Now some might argue that this emphasis on "social adjustment" is simply another means the white society utilizes to denigrate the black person and to keep him in subjection. What is needed, some might say, is *activism* not adjustment. Although no one would deny the necessity of black activism, there are certain "hard realities" in the occupational structure faced by our respondents and indeed faced by all blacks and whites. Whether palatable or not one of these is the capability of being at least moderately civil and congenial with associates. Whatever its origins it is nonetheless essential to occupational attainments in a modern milieu, and at least some of our respondents, who probably represent the bulk of American blacks, perceived the church as being beneficial toward them in this respect.

In addition to specific application of the Protestant Ethic and the social adjustment theme, the remainder of those indicating "help" from the church spoke in general terms of the utility of religious teaching for life. What they appear to have in mind is the cultural convergence in America between Christianity and the American Dream. But they apprehend the linkage in a far more amorphous sense than do the respondents noted above. For example: "Because you get the right kind of teaching and you begin to think right." "Taught me to live right." "If you don't have the love of God you still can't get nowhere in life." "It was very encouraging to me." "Church is a big help if you will just listen." "Without prayer I wouldn't be anywhere today."

Of those respondents who said the church did *not* help in getting ahead ($N = 66$), more than half ($N = 37$) stated that this was not the purpose of the church at all. "I don't think the purpose of religion is to help you get ahead with material things." "I think the church is more to teach you the right way, not to show you how to get ahead." "It wasn't supposed to—the purpose of the church was to preach and teach the gospel." The remainder reported either that they did not attend frequently enough or it simply did not help in this particular instance: "The church played no part in that matter." Thus a minority of respondents felt that the church was not an aid in achievement and success—some because it should not; others less ideological, simply because it did nothing for them personally in this regard.

It will be recalled that the prime objective in examining the role of religion and church in respondent adolescent experiences is to assess whether it was functional or beneficial to them alongside family interaction. In the great majority of cases, the conclusion appears to be affirmative. Our respondents were highly involved in the church and they perceived that it aided them to fulfill, as adults, expectations in both the occupational and conjugal spheres. Furthermore, this preparation was often an extension and reinforcement of norms and values learned in the home. At other points, the church went beyond the home in providing an arena in which the respondent could obtain the kinds of contacts, attitudes, and interpersonal skills requisite to optimal functioning within the conjugal, and particularly, the occupational systems. For certain persons the church may, in effect, have been a "structural bridge" between the family and entrance into the larger society. Therefore, it can be said with some degree of certainty that among the bulk of these respondents, the church did provide resources supplemental to their families which aided them in performance of adult roles and thus in their later marital stability.

School

In contrast with the public schools, operations of these sorts by the churches may be described as *latent* functions. As some respondents themselves noted, these were not the prime *stated* goals of religious organizations, although in fact they occurred. But for the public school, preparation for adult life, particularly for the occupational sphere, is its manifest and overt goal. In recent years, many studies and much observation have drawn attention to the difficulties encountered by blacks attempting to "make their way" through the mazes of the white middle-class school system. Perhaps the most formidable barrier is the teacher herself (usually a female).

Proshansky and Newton suggest:

We can expect the American school teacher to express . . . prejudice in her treatment of the [black] child—often in a variety of subtle ways. The issue gains increasing complexity when we realize that even a teacher who is relatively free of prejudice toward Negroes may react to class-associated differences between her own and her pupils' orientations toward learning, work, and discipline. . . . even [middle-class] Negro teachers may be hostile and resentful toward lower-class Negro children. . . . [they] may displace their own self-hatred by expressing hostility toward lower-class Negro children.[26]

In addition to the prejudices, resentments, and hostilities felt by parties on both sides of the desk toward each other, there is the question of academic performance itself. The notion of the "self-fulfilling prophecy" has been applied to the area of student performance. In an exhaustive study of the literature, Rosenthal and Jacobson conclude that "the teacher's expectation of pupil's performance may serve as an educational self-fulfilling prophecy. The teacher gets less because she expects less . . ."[27] Conversely, the teacher who expects more gets more. Teachers who feel that black children are incapable of anything but "below average" or "poor" work will, in fact, receive that level of performance. The process may be quite unconscious and not necessarily based on overt racist premises, such as "inherent Negro intellectual inferiority."

Instead, the teacher may be led to believe (consciously or not) that her black students have been deprived of "intellectual enrichment" and thus are "bound" to reveal their academic poverty in the classroom. Consequently, she expects and demands little from them and "receives" it in generous measure. Interestingly, recent studies have shown that when high expectations are pressed on underprivileged children, their performance rises accordingly.[28] Finally, both in terms of being the object of lessened hostility and of gaining higher achievements, some evidence indicates that the black female fares better in school than the black male.[29]

We have already seen that a large proportion of our respondents receiving special adult help from outside the family identified a school teacher as the source of that help. Hence, we might expect that they would not generally have perceived their school experiences in cynical or bitter fashion. To determine how our respondents viewed their school experiences we asked a series of four questions.

"How do you think your teachers, in general, felt about

you as a student? Did they think you were a good, average, fair or poor student?" The same question was asked regarding how *friends* felt, *parents* (or parent substitutes) felt, and finally how the respondents themselves felt about this same matter.

Table 4–7 shows the responses to these questions, by sex of respondent. Earlier work suggests that the black child (especially in the lower class) faces a milieu in which significant others— teachers, parents, friends—often view him as a "poor" student. Consequently, he comes to incorporate this definition of himself into his own thinking, i.e., into his own self-image. Soon he too comes to believe "I am a poor student; I can't make it in school so why try." However frequently this process may occur in the underclass, these data reveal it was not that way for our respondents.

The majority of respondents report that they perceived that their teachers, their friends, and their parents thought of them as "good" students. Interestingly, the majority of males also thought of themselves as "good" students, whereas the majority of females thought of themselves as "average" students. Most significant is the fact that while 80 percent of males and 85 percent of females define themselves as either "good" or "average" from 80–90 percent of the sample perceived that these three kinds of significant others agreed with them that they were either "good" or "average" students. Only a small minority ever indicates definitions of themselves (by self or by others) as either "fair" or only "poor" students.

The sociological dictum that "however one defines a situation to be real, to him it is real" surely applies here. That there was such a great degree of convergence in terms of these several evaluations may be construed as highly beneficial to whatever later attainments may have been gained by these persons. The black youth who thinks of himself as a good or average student in school will probably more likely think he can "make his way" in the world—even a white world—than the one who thinks otherwise. Just *thinking* this way—defining it as real for himself —is probably a boost compared to those who do not. The more

TABLE 4–7. RESPONDENTS' PERCEPTIONS OF EVALUATION AS A STUDENT

		Good Student	Average Student	Fair or Poor Student	T	N	
Teachers' Evaluations	Males	43.4%	39.7	16.9	100%	(189)	n.s.
	Females	44.4%	43.4	12.2	100%	(198)	
Friends' Evaluations	Males	40.7%	40.6	18.7	100%	(180)	$x^2 = 6.2$ $p < .05$ 2 df
	Females	47.5%	42.7	9.8	100%	(183)	
Parents' Evaluations	Males	44.9%	37.1	18.0	100%	(178)	$x^2 = 7.8$ $p < .05$ 2 df
	Females	52.6%	39.1	8.3	100%	(192)	
Self-Evaluation	Males	42.3%	37.0	20.7	100%	(189)	n.s.
	Females	39.5%	44.6	15.9	100%	(197)	

the "success" in school, the more likely it is that he will probably think that he can attain in the world "out there." Conversely, the less the perceived "success" in school the lower the likelihood he will feel that he can "make it out there."

In Table 4–7, we find there are no significant differences between males and females and what they perceived their teachers thought of them, and also in what they thought of themselves. There is, furthermore, a correlation of .57 between self and teachers' evaluations, as compared to .50 for self-parents' and .39 for self-friends' evaluations. Apparently these males did not experience the customary difficulties with school teachers that are said to face many lower-class black youths. *They were just as likely as females to be well thought of by their teachers, and just as likely as females to think of themselves in positive academic terms.* Although our data do not permit a conclusive statement regarding the self-fulfilling prophecy notion, we can at least suggest that it was operative in the following way. Respondents' teachers probably expected them to be good or at least average students, and in turn this is how the students came to think teachers felt, and also how they themselves thought they performed. There is little or no indication of the hostility and underachievement that other studies suggest takes place in the school experiences of the underclass. And it is highly meaningful that this applies equally to *both* sexes.

At the same time, there are significant differences between the sexes in how they perceived their friends and parents to evaluate them. Females were more apt than males to perceive their friends and parents to evaluate them as good or average students; whereas males were more likely than females to see these particular "others" evaluate them as fair or poor students. Why this should be is not certain but several observations can be made in terms of the consequences of these different perceptions for later attainments. We know that the correlation between self-other evaluations is strongest with teachers and weakest with peers. We know too that what the teacher thinks, rather than anyone else, is in fact what actually determines the student's objective standing in school in terms of grades. From our own data and from other observations, such as Billingsley's, we also know that academic figures have played a vital role in black attainments.

The great aura of respect and even reverence that American blacks have shown in the past to those in educational roles is well known. By comparison, others' opinions—even the family's—on academic matters are probably considered less significant. (This very likely applies whether the teacher feels good or ill toward the student.) Therefore, our male respondents were quite likely to place great premium on what teachers thought of them in terms of school performance. What teachers thought *really* mattered; what parents thought and especially what peers thought mattered less. So that even if parents and peers did not feel he was doing too well, as long as the teacher did, he too felt he was doing well and that to him was what counted most. Thus in terms of actual male attainment in school and impetus toward later attainments, the positive role of the teacher probably outweighed any negative or disparaging influence from parents, or especially from peers.[30]

Even when we examined social class of respondent, based on occupation of father (middle or working-class), we found no significant differences in teachers' evaluations of student performance. Neither were differences significant for self or for peer evaluations. Interestingly, middle-class parents were significantly more likely than working-class parents to evaluate their children as a "good" student (63 percent to 45 percent).[31] The working-class parent, in short, was more likely to underrate his child than was the child's teacher. In spite of that, it can be argued (for reasons cited above) that the parent's underrating was not as meaningful to the child as the teacher's positive rating. Furthermore, with regard to the *direct impact* on actual educational attainment, how male respondents perceived that their teachers evaluated them, and how they evaluated themselves, showed much greater influences than how either friends or parents evaluated them. The path coefficient from teacher evaluation to male's years of education is .198; from self-evaluation to education = .147; parent-evaluation = .030; peer-evaluation = .006.[32] So that in terms of

actual educational performance, measured by years of school completed, evaluations of black males by teachers and self would appear to be more critical than evaluations by either peers or parents.

There is an additional though less crucial indication that our
respondents experienced little if any of the debilitating circumstances that are known to retard academic achievements and to
inculcate strong distaste for school in general. We asked the open-
end question: "When you were a teenager, what did you like
best about school?" The question immediately following was:
"And what was the *worst* thing about school?" We wanted to give
these respondents maximum latitude to pick out *anything* in their
school experiences that stood out as particularly satisfactory or
distasteful. We were especially interested in knowing how many
if any would identify teachers as being the worst thing about
school.

The proportions of responses to both items suggest a pattern
that in all likelihood is very similar to that characteristic of children within the dominant white society. For instance, in response
to what they liked "best" 58 percent of males and 59 percent
of females named an academic subject: math, English, history,
spelling, reading, etc. Likewise, in response to what was worst 51
percent of males, and 70 percent of females named an academic
subject. In brief, what stands out in their minds as either "best"
or "worst" is a *subject* for which they had some aptitude or liking,
or one in which they probably did poorly. In addition to those
who could name a "best" thing about school, 16 percent of males
and 12 percent of females reported there was no "one thing";
they simply liked school and everything about it in general. And
in response to the second question, 27 percent of males and 15
percent of females said there was no "worst" thing at all; they
simply had a general liking for school.

Overall, therefore, most of our respondents seem to report a
"typical" school pattern. Some subjects they did not like, some
they did, but in most cases there is the absence of any identifiable
hostility toward either the "system" or its "agents," the teachers.
At the same time, like most adolescents, our respondents do not

indicate they were overjoyed with school either. It seems significant to note that of 19 males and 11 females who did report that the "worst" thing about school was the teacher, all but 3 males indicated it was due to their being in a "mixed" or "integrated" school. As one put it: "It had just been integrated and the white teachers just seemed to put up with us."

Another respondent in this grouping found white teachers and white classmates to pose a problem of a different sort: "All the white kids thought I was the white teacher's pet." Evidently the teacher was perceived by the whites as over-indulgent to this black student and that aroused their hostility. These negative experiences with teachers (and pupils) in integrated schools underscore the point made by Proshansky and Newton: "Integration is not an automatic cure for the ills caused by segregated schools."[33] But the great majority of our respondents apparently attended segregated schools, found no great tensions with teachers, and tended to evaluate school in much the same ways as do most white children.[34] We may assume that one consequence of these kinds of positive school experiences was to keep them in school longer than would otherwise have been the case. The benefits of this added education for occupational and marital stability would seem to be substantial. Both in terms of the added economic resources it brings, plus the skills it provides in resolving interpersonal tensions, education is known to be a major asset for the conjugal unit.

The Kin

One final and important set of adolescent experiences concerns the blood kin or extended family. There is a great amount of literature describing relations between the kin and the black conjugal unit, especially in the lower class.[35] Several attempts have also been made to classify anthropologically various forms of black family structure based on kinds of linkages between the several parts of the extended kinship unit.[36] Our more modest purpose is to discover how much of a "fit" there is between earlier generalizations that describe kin and conjugal unit relations, and what currently exists in a sample of blacks taken from other than the lower class.

To begin with, there is the question of sheer physical proximity. Within the black lower-class it has been quite common for several generations, or parts of the kin, to live together under one roof. Often a maternal grandmother is the acknowledged head of this type of household which has given rise to the term "matrifocal" to describe lower-class black family patterns. These patterns develop, of course, where black males are excluded from effective participation in the job market. We already know that most of those in the sample grew up with both natural parents present, and most of the remainder could identify some sort of a father or mother-substitute. Besides asking if they lived with mother and father (or substitute) we asked: "Were any of your *other* relatives living with you most of the time while you were a teen-ager?" We also probed further to find if *anyone else* besides parents and relatives lived with them.

Overwhelmingly, the results indicate that as adolescents they lived in households separate and distinct from those of the kin. Eighty-six percent responded "no" to the above question. There were no kin nor anyone else living with them and their parents during their formative teen years. Instead, they grew up in a situation quite similar to the prevailing pattern in the dominant society—husband, wife, dependent children, dwelling apart from the kin in their own house or apartment. Since they learned this pattern as youngsters, chances are good they will at least prefer to continue it as adults. To the degree the husband-father has economic opportunity, such preferences will likely be allowed to develop into reality.

Although no value-judgment is implied regarding the desirability of the matrifocal as over against the conjugal form of the household, structural kin attachments of the matrifocal type might tend to restrict "motility," which Blau and Duncan define as the capacity (psychological or economic) to migrate in order to seize better job opportunities.[37] In turn, limited motility tends to reduce levels of social and economic mobility. The independently based conjugal unit is seemingly the family form best suited to move about and to be flexible enough to take advantage of what-ever economic opportunities arise.

This does not mean, of course, that there was not extensive visiting with relatives, or that there was not continual exchanges of goods and services. On the basis of the mass of literature in this area, we assume there was, although we did not specifically in-vestigate how frequently our respondents as adolescents inter-acted with their kin.[38] Nevertheless, we obtain something perhaps more fundamental by asking first whether "any of your relatives *helped* you to get ahead in life while you were a teen-ager?" It is an unresolved issue in sociology whether the wider kin actually promotes or impedes the social mobility of some of its members.[39] As far as these blacks perceived the situation, 28 percent of them replied "yes" to the above question, 69 percent said "no," the remainder did not reply.

A separate question was asked whether "any of your rela-tives *hindered* you when you were a teen-ager as far as your getting ahead in life?" Only 2 percent replied "yes," whereas some 96 percent said "no."[40] Therefore, as far as the great majority of our respondents are concerned, their relatives had neither a positive nor negative impact on their subsequent social mobility. Of that quarter of the sample that reported the kin did help, some three-fifths indicated the aid was financial while the remainder said it consisted of advice and counsel.

Although we do not know for certain how a similar sample of whites would respond to these two questions, we might speculate that an obtained pattern of responses would suggest the same pos-sibility. That is, among black and white families above the lower class, the wider kin does not seem to exercise substantial influence one way or the other on the ultimate economic and social destinies of particular related individuals. White or black, once the husband-father has escaped the job deprivations of the lower class he is better able to hold together an independently based conjugal family. This unit then has the major influence on the child's mobility. School, church, peers, community, and wider kin tend evidently merely to reinforce the family unit.[41]

Although much more research is needed in this realm, it is

quite likely that major exceptions to the foregoing generalizations occur more frequently among certain groups of whites rather than among blacks. One example might be Gans' urban, ethnic-type, white, working-class family. Owing to strong ethnic bonds (even among second and third generation Americans), work is seen as a means whereby money is brought into a common pool to be shared by and for the benefit of *all* the relatives.

Thus the central trend of American, and all Western, education—that the student is an individual who should use his schooling to detach himself from ascribed relationships like the family circle in order to maximize his personal development and achievement in work, play, and other spheres of life—is ignored or openly rejected. . . . What matters most . . . is that there be a family circle which is wider than the nuclear family, and that all of the opportunities, temptations and pressures of the larger society be evaluated in terms of how they affect the ongoing way of life that has been built around this circle.[42]

We found no indication whatsoever of these kinds of orientations among either our working- or middle-class respondents, nor do we know of any hint of it in any other literature on the black family. A second example of a "white departure" from dominant patterns is, according to Weller, the white rural Appalachian family system. Weller contends that the description Gans uses for the white, ethnic-bound, working-class family applies to Appalachian whites as well.[43] It is significant that in connection with the wider kin, urban blacks above the lower class seem to have adopted family patterns that are closer to those of the dominant society than are those of at least two subgroups of whites.

IDENTIFICATION WITH
REFERENCE PERSONS

We began this chapter with an examination of parental identification. We then moved outside the immediate family unit to locate both persons and institutional settings that may have proved functional or beneficial to our respondents in terms of later economic and conjugal role performance. At the outset of the chapter we found a relationship between parental functionality and specific role identification with parents. After looking at various sources of nonfamilial functionality, is there any evidence that these respondents may have also identified with nonfamilial figures, such as teachers, clergy, relatives?

Theoretically, we might expect this to be so. Although Winch's model was designed to account primarily for parental identification, because its rationale is based on a general principle of reciprocity—an *exchange* of resources for identification—it might be able to be applied to these other situations as well. At the same time, Billingsley's observation that these nonfamilial figures are conceived of in the black community as parental extensions, in that they reinforce parental socialization, provides an additional reason for thinking that this notion of exchange might apply to their relations with black youth.

As we have seen, both Winch and Merton make an important distinction between what Merton calls identification with a role model and identification with a reference individual. We have also seen that many of our respondents' parents functioned as models for *specific* role behavior, i.e., either task-oriented or person-supportive. In addition, we have found that certain nonfamilial figures (school teachers, church officials) were perceived as beneficial by our respondents in both the instrumental and expressive realms. We did not, however, specifically test to see if these particular persons were actually being used as role models. That is, we do not know empirically that our respondents may have wanted to be *like* them or to be *different* from them, as compared to the specific information we have regarding parental identification. Very likely, however, some of these persons were used as models in terms of specific role behaviors.

But, as Merton notes, "Emulation may be extended to a wider array of behaviors and values of these persons who can then be described as reference individuals."[44] To use someone as a reference individual (or Winch's personal identification) is to identify with the person in general, i.e., with *many* of his roles and role behaviors. For our respondents these might include the behaviors and values of persons within the family, school, church, occupational world, community. The idea of reference individual goes beyond the notion of role model because of a larger range and scope of personal, rather than positional or specific, identification.

In a recent review of reference group theory and research, there is not much indication that sociologists have tried to test the distinction made by Merton.[45] Although it may thus be hazardous to attempt to get at the distinction empirically, an effort was made. Respondents were asked: "Who would you say was the *one man* whom you looked up to and admired more than any other, while you were a teen-ager?" The same question was asked regarding the *"one woman."* By using general terms such as "looked up to," "admired," it was hoped that we could obtain some idea of an overall or *personal* identification. By not specifying either a familial or nonfamilial context, the respondent was free to choose from a wide range of possibilities. Muzafer Sherif has used the term "reference idol" to describe the kind of total emulation or admiration that is in view here.[46]

In response to the item on *male* reference individual, among male respondents, 57 percent replied it was their father (or father substitute), 25 percent named someone else, and 18 percent said no one at all (see Table 4–8). For females, responses in the three categories were 60, 23, 17 percent, respectively. To the degree this item actually measures the notion of reference individual, the data are convincing evidence that the black father was indeed a "significant other" to the majority of our respondents. He was not simply tolerated, nor bland, nor ignored. Instead, he was identified as a reference individual—the man who, in general, was most looked up to and admired, and was almost certainly therefore someone to be emulated.

We also asked those who replied "father" whether there was "any other man you especially looked up to" at that time. Approximately 55 percent of both sexes indicated there was another reference individual; the remainder said there was not. When we

TABLE 4–8. CHOICE OF REFERENCE PERSON

	Male Respondents					Female Respondents				
	Father (or) Mother	Other	No One	T	N	Father (or) Mother	Other	No One	T	N
Man Most Admired	57.0%	25.0	18.0	100%	(196)	60.0%	23.0	17.0	100%	(202)
Woman Most Admired	77.2%	10.7	12.1	100%	(197)	72.0%	18.0	10.0	100%	(202)

Male Respondents: $x^2 = 21.19$, 2 df, $p < .001$

Female Respondents: $x^2 = 7.55$, 2 df, $p < .05$

asked those who replied "yes" to this last question, plus those who said "someone else" to the earlier question, just who this "other" reference individual might be, the replies most frequently cited were relative, teacher, minister, Sunday School teacher. So among those having the father as a reference individual, a little more than half also had another (though less salient) male reference individual, while other respondents had *only someone other* than father. Given the structure of the black community in which adult males often take an interest in children not their own, these patterns should not be unexpected. Liebow notes that a "striking" characteristic of lower-class black males is the serious responsibility they often take for *others'* children.[47] In contrast, most of our respondents' fathers who chiefly represent strata above the lower class (whether or not they were involved with others' children) had adopted the dominant pattern of being significantly involved with their *own* children (something the lower-class men on Tally's Corner did not do). In exchange, their children identified them more frequently than any other sort of figure as a reference individual.

But as frequently as fathers were identified in this way, mothers were identified still *more* frequently by both sexes, particularly by males. In response to the question regarding the woman most admired, 77 percent of males said "mother," 11 percent replied "other," and 12 percent said "no one." Among females, the proportions were 72, 18, and 10 percent, respectively.[48] There was earlier indication of greater involvement with children on the part of mothers than of fathers, and also greater choice of mothers as role models. This trend of greater mother-involvement continues in terms of comparative frequency of choice as reference individual. This situation, however, is not surprising, given the negative pressures by white society on the black male at all status levels, and thus on the black family system per se.

We likewise asked those who responded "mother" whether there was "any other woman you especially looked up to" at that time. Unlike the case with fathers, a significant difference emerged between male-female responses. Sixty-three percent of males said "no" ($N = 155$), whereas 52 percent of females said "yes."[49] While on the one hand both sexes were equally likely, as adolescents, to have had male-reference individuals besides their fathers, males were considerably less likely than females to have identified with female-reference individuals *in addition* to their mothers. Males, in other words, were less likely to identify in a *total* or *personal* sense with an adult female other than their mothers.

This information suggests an important point. It is often said that young lower-class black men find themselves dominated on every side by a plethora of female figures. By way of contrast, these male respondents did not appear to have experienced that type of situation. Although there was strong positional and personal identification with their mothers, our evidence indicated that this identification was beneficial for them. And when it came to a choice of reference individuals or "idols" beyond the family, they went much more to a male than to a female.

In short, extra-familial figures who had the most influence over them tended to be males, not females. Consequently, when it came to learning and emulating adult role-behavior that would fit them for the larger society, it was the behavior of males rather than females that "captivated" them. It is very likely, therefore, that this kind of identification with adult males and with what *males* are "supposed" to do, had positive consequences for their own later behavior as adult males. Presumably, those (lower-class) black youths who lack this type of personal identification may find it that much more difficult to enact "approved" adult roles in the larger society. For our male respondents, such role fulfillment was probably that much more feasible.

Moreover, we see from Table 4–9 that respondents who chose their own fathers or mothers as reference persons, received more benefits or resources from them than those who chose "other" or else "no one." This conclusion holds for both sexes and for both parental figures.[50] In Tables 4–4 and 4–5, we found that the greater the parental benefits, the more children use parents as their role models. Finally, in Table 4–10, we find that parental functionality is the strongest predictor of identification, both with male

TABLE 4–9. PARENTAL FUNCTIONALITY AND IDENTIFICATION WITH
REFERENCE PERSON

		Father-Functionality (Mean scores)		Mother-Functionality (Mean scores)
Male Identification	Father	14.5 (111)	Mother	15.7 (152)
	Other	10.5 (51)	Other	12.4 (22)
	No One	7.9 (35)	No One	11.4 (24)
	(F = 19.2; df = 2 & 194; p<.001)		(F = 10.2; df = 2 & 195; p<.001)	
Female Identification	Father	15.4 (121)	Mother	16.7 (146)
	Other	9.0 (47)	Other	13.3 (36)
	No One	7.9 (34)	No One	12.1 (20)
	(F = 39.1; df = 2 & 199; p<.001)		(F = 14.6; df = 2 & 199; p< .001)	

and female reference persons, and holds for respondents of both
sexes. It would thus appear that resource-provision by their parents
was the single most critical factor leading those in the sample to
identify with them, at both the specific and general levels. The
weight of much consistent evidence, therefore, leads to the inescapable conclusion that there are strong bonds between fathers
and children, and between mothers and children in the black
family above the underclass, just as there are in white society.
These bonds, moreover, consist of an exchange of parental rewards
for child identification—both specific and general. There simply is
no indication whatsoever of the minimal cohesiveness that is alleged to exist between parents and children (males, especially) in
the black lower-class.

A related point, which is vital both theoretically and practically, is the connection between choice of role model and choice
of reference individual. Merton speculates that emulating *specific*
aspects of someone's behavior might later lead also to emulation
of that person in *general*. From Table 4–11, it would appear that

TABLE 4–10. INFLUENCE OF PARENTAL FUNCTIONALITY ON CHOICE OF
REFERENCE PERSON, CONTROLLING FOR OTHER INFLUENCES

	Male Reference Person				Female Reference Person			
	Males		Females		Males		Females	
	p	r	p	r	p	r	p	r
Father-Functionality	.201	.07	.305	.03	—	—	—	—
Mother-Functionality	—	—	—	—	.225	.03	.239	.06
Occupation of Father	.044	.20	.016	.01	.079	.13	.098	.09
Family Wholeness	.117	.23	.046	.11	.005	.20	.209	.04
Education of Father	.060	.35	.087	.20	—	—	—	—
Education of Mother	—	—	—	—	.073	.27	.086	.27
Father as Role Model	.124	.26	.084	.33	—	—	—	—
Mother as Role Model	—	—	—	—	.061	.26	.073	.28
R^2	.30		.35		.28		.40	
N	(125)		(127)		(130)		(142)	

his speculation is valid insofar as these black respondents are concerned. Those persons who chose the parent as a *positive* role
model ("be like father" or "be like mother") are also most likely
to choose that parent as a reference person, i.e., "admire father"
or "admire mother" more than anyone else. As Merton suggests,
there exists a definite relationship between positive "positional"
or specific identification, and a "general" or personal identification.

TABLE 4-11. RELATIONSHIPS BETWEEN CHOICES OF ROLE MODEL AND REFERENCE PERSON

		Person Most Admired By Male Respondents					Person Most Admired By Female Respondents				
		Father	Other	No One	T	N	Father	Other	No One	T	N
Father as Role Model	Like	79.0%	13.1	7.9	100%	(61)	84.0%	12.0	4.0	100%	(51)
	Different	52.0%	32.0	16.0	100%	(60)	53.0%	32.0	15.0	100%	(67)
	Neither	59.0%	26.0	15.0	100%	(47)	70.0%	8.0	22.0	100%	(59)
		$x^2 = 10.0$; 4 df, p<.05					$x^2 = 21.0$; 4 df, p<.001				
		Mother					_Mother_				
Mother as Role Model	Like	85.0%	9.0	6.0	100%	(81)	85.0%	8.0	7.0	100%	(105)
	Different	71.1%	18.4	10.5	100%	(38)	62.0%	28.0	10.0	100%	(58)
	Neither	81.3%	3.1	15.6	100%	(64)	60.0%	23.3	16.7	100%	(30)
		$x^2 = 10.1$; 4 df, p<.05					$x^2 = 15.9$; 4 df, p<.01				

We can refine and extend Merton's theorizing in at least two senses. First, we note that those who wanted to be *different* from father or from mother are also least likely to "look up to or admire" either father or mother. In three or four instances in Table 4–11, those who use the parent as a *negative* role-model in a specific or positional sense, are also most likely to reject him (her) as a reference individual in a more general or personal sense. This is the logical obverse of Merton's notion that maximum specific identification is linked to maximum general identification: it seems that minimum specific identification is likewise linked to minimum general identification.

Second, in between those polar extremes are those respondents who were *neutral* toward their parents as far as using them as a role-model was concerned. These particular persons (wanting "neither to be like nor different" from parents in a *specific* sense) are more likely to identify with their parents in a general or personal sense (reference individual) than those who use their parents as a negative role-model. Nevertheless, they are also less likely to use their parents as a reference person than those who use their parents as a positive role model. Persons in this middle situation apparently choose neither to emulate nor to reject their parents in any specific sense, yet at the same time they tended to "look up to" and "admire" them. Therefore, in addition to Merton's original hypothesis and its obverse cited above, we may also say that (for these black respondents) a neutral *specific* identification with parents is linked to relatively moderate amounts of *general* identification with parents.

SUMMARY

In view of negative pressures imposed historically and currently on blacks by whites, two specific points stand out: (1) that there is as much father-identification (including negative-type) by both sexes as there is; (2) that the overwhelming bulk of identification by black children (both positional and personal) found its locus within the confines of the conjugal unit itself. One might have predicted that the families of these blacks would have been so lacking in rewards and resources that almost all the children would have turned outward and elsewhere to receive rewards and to extend their identification. But this was not the case. To be sure, there were resources "elsewhere." School teachers, church figures, and others provided valued and important rewards and these kinds of persons were undoubtedly used as specific role-models. But the crucial point to keep in mind is that for most respondents these resources were provided in *conjunction* with those provided by the conjugal family as part of a process to *reinforce* the family unit.

Within the dominant society, it is evident that school, church, and community stand in *this same type of symbiotic relation* to the family. They are supportive, and they also aid in the process of gradual weaning of offspring *from* ascriptive familial ties towards assimilation into achievement-oriented society. These black respondents came, therefore, from situations that closely approximate those within the dominant society. These situations involved resources provided by "significant" adults, and reciprocally, identification with these adults, especially parents.

It will be recalled that Winch defines identification as "more or less lasting influence on attitudes and behavior." Thus far we have shown adult influence on the attitudes of these respondents when they were adolescents. This influence was evidently such as to motivate many of them to want to carry out educational, occupational, and conjugal expectations of the dominant society. Since their "significant others" (role models, reference persons) accepted the legitimacy and value of dominant patterns, consequently so did these black respondents. This type of process within both white and black family systems may be said to be *sine qua non* to facilitate the gradual transition of the child into the web of the larger society. And the majority of these blacks seem to have experienced this process.

But it is one thing to influence attitudes and quite another to be able to manipulate behavior. Lipset and Bendix, in describing the conditions faced by youth in general when they attempt to carry out mobility aspirations, aptly comment that "intention is one thing, action another."[51] The white child, having identified with significant adults and thus in turn the dominant society, finds his "road of transition" paved with many chances to mine the opportunity structure to the full. On the other side, the black child, in spite of resource-provision and degree of identification, finds his path into the opportunity structure "booby-trapped" at almost every conceivable point. It is much more problematic, in short, whether the highly motivated black youth who does identify with dominant occupational and conjugal patterns can actually fulfill these patterns. We already know, however, that our respondents are able to maintain ongoing family units, so we would therefore suspect that, relatively speaking, they are likewise experiencing certain amounts of economic benefits. This situation we shall consider in Chapter 5. In Chapter 6, we shall examine in detail husband-wife interaction within these conjugal units.

One point must be made regarding the identification of black youth with *any* pattern within the dominant society. Some black and white militants contend that almost all dominant patterns and values should be rejected by all youth—more succinctly, "burn it down." However, these militants themselves admit they have not yet devised (nor are they yet concerned about) alternatives in any of these areas. Furthermore, what evidence exists reveals that those who are most extreme constitute only a tiny minority of the black or white communities.[52]

The point is that *currently* the vast majority of blacks appear to value dominant society patterns, but see themselves limited in their access to them. What this majority strongly desires is *change* that will bring about greater access to these patterns, not their destruction. According to Billingsley, a vital "imperative is for changes in the economic system of the society in order to enhance the economic viability of Negro families."[53] We shall have more to say about policy implications of the study in Chapter 8. For now, let us turn directly to the matter of the "economic viability" of families in the sample.

NOTES

1. Winch, *Identification*, p. 53.

2. Winch says little about the troublesome issue of "rational calculus" in terms of these family processes, see *Identification*, p. 29; and since we have considered the matter at length elsewhere, there is no need to repeat the discussion here. See Scanzoni, *Opportunity and the Family*.

3. Winch, *Identification*, p. 29.

4. Robert K. Merton, *Social Theory and Social Structure* (New York: The Free Press, 1957 rev.), p. 300; Theodore M. Newcomb, *Social Psychology* (New York: Dryden Press, 1950), p. 227; Herbert H. Hyman and Eleanor Singer, *Readings in Reference Group Theory and Research* (New York: The Free Press, 1968), pp. 9–10.

5. Merton, *Social Theory*, p. 300.

6. Ibid., p. 302.

7. Ibid., p. 303.

8. Ibid.

9. See, for example, Peter M. Blau and Otis Dudley Duncan, *The American Occupational Structure* (New York: John Wiley and Sons, Inc., 1967), ch. 9; also Seymour M. Lipset and Reinhard Bendix, *Social Mobility in Industrial Society* (Berkeley, Calif.: University of California Press, 1960), chs. 7–9.

10. While there may be certain problems of accurate recall in this type of retrospective question, it was the only avenue open to us. More important, the distributions shown in Table 4–1 suggest no undue skewing or bias. Respondents appear to have answered as accurately and thoughtfully as possible. See Hill and Rodgers, "The Developmental Approach."

11. Hyman and Singer imply that one need not always be found at the "polar opposites" of identification with an object, i.e., clearly positive or negative toward it. They hypothesize that such individuals "may well show the consequences in terms of diffuseness, lack of crystallization, inconsistency. . . ." Respondents in our sample who were "neutral" toward using parents as role models substantiate this notion that identification is not always polarized. As to their hypothesis regarding "diffuseness," there is data in Chapter 5 to show such persons were *least likely* to be upwardly mobile. See Hyman and Singer, *Readings in Reference Group Theory and Research*, pp. 10–11.

12. Merton, *Social Theory*.

13. The middle-class $N = 75$; working-class $N = 270$; $x^2 = .95$, 2 df, n.s.

14. Middle-class $N = 74$; working-class $N = 281$; $x^2 = .02$, 2 df, n.s.

15. Whole-family $N = 233$; other $= 112$; $x^2 = .11$; 2 df, n.s.

16. Whole-family $N = 222$; other $= 133$; $x^2 = 7.4$; 2 df; $p < .05$.

17. In Chapter 5, we discuss these contrasting generalizations in greater detail. See Lipset and Bendix, *Social Mobility*, p. 250, for a seminal discussion of this discrepancy.

18. Blau and Duncan, *The American Occupational Structure*, p. 296.

19. In Chapter 5 we shall see that negative identification is related to upward mobility.

20. See Morris Rosenberg, *Society and the Adolescent Self-Image* (Princeton, N.J.: Princeton University Press, 1965), pp. 128–146, where he concludes that parental disinterest in the child is more deleterious to the development of self-esteem than even harsh parental reactions, which at least indicate some interest in the child.

21. In the middle class, those wanting to be "like" their fathers report a mean "father-functionality" score of 16.8, those wanting to be "different" show 14.9, those who want "neither" reveal a score of 13.1; $F = 4.3$, df $= 2$ & 72, $p < .05$, N's $= 26, 24, 25$, respectively. In the *working class*, the three mean scores are 15.8, 13.5, and 7.4, respectively. $F = 60.3$; df $= 2$ & 306, $p < .001$; N's $= 86, 103, 120$ respectively. Middle class, *mother-functionality:* Like $= 17.2$; different $= 16.5$; neither $= 13.4$; $F = 5.25$, df $= 2$ & 74; $p < .01$; N's $= 39, 19, 19$. *Working class*, mother-functionality: 16.8, 15.2, 11.3; $F = 34.2$, df $= 2$ & 298; $p < .001$; N's $= 147, 77, 77$.

22. *Father-identification, Whole family:* Like $= 34.1$, different $= 29.5$; neither $= 28.4$; $F = 12.2$; df $= 2$ & 223, $p < .001$, N's $= 77, 85, 64$. *Father-other:* $\bar{x} = 29.6, 29.6, 29.6, 17.4$; $F = 32.9$, df $= 2$ & 155, $p < .001$, N's $= 35, 42, 81$. *Mother-Whole:* $\bar{x} = 32.0, 28.8, 27.4$; $F = 6.92$, df $= 2$ & 222, $p < .001$, N's $= 124, 49, 52$. *Mother-other:* $\bar{x} = 28.0, 25.1, 16.5$; $F = 16.7$; df $= 2$ & 150; $p < .001$, N's $= 62, 47, 44$.

23. Billingsley, *Black Families in White America*, p. 98.

24. Ibid., p. 99.

25. Chester M. Pierce, "Problems of the Negro Adolescent in the Next Decade," in Eugene B. Brody, ed., *Minority Group Adolescents in the United States* (Baltimore: Williams and Wilkins Co., 1968), p. 22.

26. Harold Proshansky and Peggy Newton, "The Nature and Meaning of Negro Self-Identity," in Martin Deutsch, Irwin Katz, Arthur R. Jensen,

eds., *Social Class, Race, and Psychological Development* (New York: Holt, Rinehart and Winston, 1968), p. 209.

27. Robert Rosenthal and Lenore Jacobson, "Self-Fulfilling Prophecies in the Classroom: Teachers' Expectations as Unintended Determinants of Pupils' Intellectual Competence," in Deutsch, et al., ibid., p. 220.

28. Ibid., pp. 226–243.

29. Proshansky and Newton, *Negro Self-Identity*, pp. 207–208. See also "Teachers of the Poor," S. M. Miller and Frank Riessman, *Social Class and Social Policy* (New York: Basic Books, 1968), Chapter 9; Price, *Changing Characteristics of the Negro Population*.

30. Lipset and Bendix, *Social Mobility*, note that lower status children who are mobile tend "to identify themselves with a school culture," p. 229. Likewise they note a tendency on the part of upwardly mobile children to identify with adults and their values, *rather than with other children*, p. 238.

31. $x^2 = 7.9$, 2 df; $p < .02$.

32. The fifth independent variable in the equation was father's occupation which showed the strongest Beta weight (.440); $R^2 = .48$; $N = 149$. We delay until Chapter 5 a fuller discussion of the generalization that father's occupation is the single best predictor of the educational level of those in the sample.

33. Proshansky and Newton, *Negro Self-Identity*, p. 209.

34. These data should in no way be used to support segregated education. As Miller and Riessman remark, "The Coleman Study's report is striking: disadvantaged Negro pupils in schools with white youngsters with a strong educational background did better in educational improvement than Negro students in non-integrated settings." *Social Class and Social Policy*, p. 144.

35. See Frazier, *The Negro Family*, 1966 edition; Allison Davis and John Dollard, *Children of Bondage* (New York: Harper and Row, 1964 edition); St. Clair Drake and Horace R. Cayton, *Black Metropolis* (New York: Harper and Row, 1962 edition).

36. See Billingsley, *Black Families in White America*, Chapter 1; Jessie Bernard, *Marriage and Family Among Negroes* (Englewood Cliffs, N.J.: Prentice-Hall, 1966), Chapter 2; Stuart A. Queen and Robert W. Habenstein, *The Family in Various Cultures* (New York: J. B. Lippincott Co., 1967 edition), Chapter 15; Rainwater, "Crucible of Identity."

37. Blau and Duncan, *The American Occupational Structure*, p. 250.

38. See Marvin B. Sussman and Lee Burchinal, "Kin Family Network: Unheralded Structure in Current Conceptualizations of Family Functioning," *Marriage and Family Living* 24 (1962): 231–40.

39. See Eugene Litwak, "The Use of Extended Family Groups in the Achievement of Social Goals: Some Policy Implications," *Social Problems* 7 (1959–60): 177–87.

40. Two percent did not reply.

41. See Bert N. Adams, *Kinship in an Urban Setting* (Chicago: Markham Publishing Co., 1968), pp. 170–71; Denise B. Kandel and Gerald S. Lesser, "Parental and Peer Influences on Educational Plans of Adolescents," *American Sociological Review* 34 (April 1969): 212–21.

42. Herbert J. Gans, *The Urban Villagers* (New York: The Free Press, 1962), p. 245.

43. Jack E. Weller, *Yesterday's People: Life in Contemporary Appalachia* (Lexington, Ky.: University of Kentucky Press, 1965), pp. 4–5; also see Richard A. Ball, "A Poverty Case: The Analgesic Subculture of the Southern Appalachians," *American Sociological Review* 33 (December 1968): 891–94.

44. Merton, *Social Theory*, p. 303.

45. Hyman and Singer, *Readings in Research Group Theory and Research*, p. 9.

46. Ibid.

47. Liebow, *Tally's Corner*, p. 84.

48. As in Table 4–1, the pattern of Table 4–8 continues to hold separately among respondents from working-class and from middle-class backgrounds; and also among those from "whole" as well as from "other" types of family composition.

49. $x^2 = 6.2$, 1 df, $p < .02$; $N = 145$.

50. As in Table 4–4, the relationships in Table 4–9 continue to hold separately among those from working and from middle-class backgrounds, and among those from "whole" and from "other" family situations.

51. Lipset and Bendix, *Social Mobility*, p. 230.

52. Among college students, who are generally more extreme than post-college age adults, black or white, the proportion of black students who can truly be called "revolutionaries" is around one percent. Among white students, the proportion is about three percent. These data were compiled from a nationwide probability sample of college students, as part of a study commissioned by CBS News, and executed by Daniel Yan-Kelovich, Inc. See *Generations Apart* (New York: Columbia Broadcasting System, Inc., 1969).

53. Billingsley, *Black Families in White America*, p. 167.

5

Achievement
and Mobility

Implicit in the minds of many whites, especially since the press popularizations of the Moynihan report, is the feeling that the black family is a phenomenon quite distinct from the dominant family system. Some sociologists use the term, "middle-class family model" or the "normal American family" to describe those conjugal patterns that are most widely diffused throughout society.[1] Others criticize this assertion and argue there is no such thing as "the normal American family," but rather several varied types of family patterns.

Actually both conceptions are valid. To the degree our society can be broadly classified as a "middle-class" society, there are certain *general* family patterns that predominate. On the other hand, there are clear variations chiefly by social class, ethnicity, and region. With regard to the family system that predominates among blacks, our evidence so far suggests that it is basically more similar than dissimilar to the dominant family form. There is, of course, that twenty-five to thirty percent of black families that differ from those in our sample and from the dominant pattern. But that proportion is part of the lower (lower-lower) or underclass, and social class is precisely the key to the question of identifying and classifying family forms. Family forms may be said to be mainly a consequence of social class, not of skin color or of "race." As seen in Chapter 1, however, the unique historical experiences of black people (slavery, legal segregation, and economic discrimination) have been largely responsible for the emergence of a black ethnic subsociety or *ethclass*. There is a kind of "intersection," says Gordon, between the black's economic or class position and his ethnic position.[2] For example, we saw in Chapters 1 and 3 that blacks with education (a class factor) equal to whites, receive fewer rewards (discrimination—an ethnic factor) than whites. Consequently in the remaining chapters, when we refer to social class in connection with blacks, even above the underclass, we must keep in mind the "ethnic factor," i.e., the built-in economic discrimination and deprivation that blacks at all status levels tend to experience. Individual achievement does not carry for blacks the same measure of benefits and rewards that it does for whites.

The relationship between class and family structure is multi-faceted and is based primarily on the husband's dual position in both the economic and conjugal settings.[3] The class level of the family (as measured by husband's occupation) largely determines the level of material and nonmaterial resources funneled to the child. In large measure, therefore, the ultimate class position of the child rests with his family of origin. When the child forms his own family of procreation, he tends to provide his children with approximately the same level of resources he received. The result is a recurring cycle: class position, family resources, class position, etc. This cycle is altered when a person is able to supply fewer or greater resources to his children than he received. The capability to provide greater resources almost necessitates that the person has been socially mobile, i.e., he has a higher class position than his father.

In Chapter 2, we learned that most respondents in the sample came from *relatively* advantaged class backgrounds. The question here is: Have they maintained or increased their class position? Since for blacks and whites social status is positively related to marital stability, we would expect that our respondents have experienced a certain degree of upward mobility or at least maintenance of class position. This expectation is based primarily on the positive kinds of background experiences discussed in Chapters 2, 3, and 4. Occupational and dominant conjugal goals are closely intertwined, whether parents or children are conscious of this or not. Hence, benefits which accrue to the attainment of one goal, do the same for the other. So far we have seen that status advantage has influenced parental functionality which, in turn, has influenced identification with parents. In this chapter, we shall try to discover if there are relationships between any of these earlier influences and the current class position of those in the sample. Specifically, Chapter 5 consists of three questions: Have our respondents been socially mobile? What background factors can account for their general levels of mobility? What factors account for differences in degree of mobility? In Chapter 6, we shall examine how class position substantially affects husband-wife interaction.

GAINS IN OCCUPATION, EDUCATION, INCOME

Blau and Duncan, in their investigation of American mobility patterns, write:

. . . we had expected that Negroes, given their much lower socio-economic origins, would be less likely to be downwardly and more likely to be upwardly mobile than whites. The findings, however, contradict this expectation; nonwhites are more likely to be downwardly and less likely to be upwardly mobile than whites . . .[4]

Ginzberg and Hiestand note that the "Negro labor force [1960] is substantially concentrated [over 70 percent] in the semi-skilled, unskilled, service and farm occupations."[5] They conclude that "the occupational position of Negroes relative to whites has improved very slightly over the long run" (from 1910 to 1960).[6] However, more recent indications reveal that disparate parts of the black community are moving in opposite directions economically. On the one hand, there is the familiar description of black disadvantage. "Compared to whites, Negroes still are more than three times as likely to be in poverty, twice as likely to be unemployed, and three times as likely to die in infancy or childbirth. In large cities, more than half of all Negroes live in poor neighborhoods."[7]

Yet for the other group of blacks, that segment of which our sample is probably more representative, a far different picture emerges.

". . . the new [1967–68 census] data show important gains in the level of living for Negroes in the United States. Typically, Negroes are more likely than ever before to be earning decent incomes, holding good jobs, living in better neighborhoods, and completing their education."[8]

Andrew F. Brimmer contends, moreover, that a "substantial proportion of [Negro] families enjoy a standard of living thoroughly comparable to that enjoyed by the white middle class . . ."[9] The literature, in sum, presents a mixed picture of trends in black mobility and economic equality. Overall, there has been considerable black advance, but there has been substantial white advance too. Hence, *compared to whites*, many blacks still remain *relatively* deprived. Yet compared to lower-class blacks, there are trends that suggest that working and middle-class blacks are making many *absolute* gains.

Occupation

In the light of these descriptions of certain national increases in black advantage, how does our own sample compare with the larger black society in general? Table 5–1 shows the occupational levels held by (1) fathers of respondents, compared with (2) present occupation of the husband in each household within our sample, (3) the occupational distribution of the heads of nonwhite (black) "whole" families living in the Indianapolis area in 1960, and (4) the occupations of *all* employed male blacks in the North and West in 1966.[10]

To simplify comparisons, we have combined professional-technical-managerial, clerical-sales, and foremen-craftsmen (skilled workers) into the middle class; operatives and related jobs (semi-skilled workers) constitute the upper working-class, and all other

TABLE 5–1. OCCUPATIONAL DISTRIBUTION OF MALE HEAD OF HOUSEHOLDS
IN SAMPLE COMPARED WITH SELECTED INFORMATION

	Fathers of Respondents	Whole Black* Families Indianapolis, 1960	Employed Black Males, North and West 1966	Households in 1968 Sample
Middle-Class	19.6%	27.8%	32.0%	33.8%
Upper Working- Class	17.5	26.7	35.9	34.0
Lower Working- Class	48.9	36.3	32.1	31.2
N. A.	14.0	9.2	**	1.0
T	100%	100%	100%	100%
N	(400)	(14814)	**	(400)

* Synonymous with "Nonwhite" since "less than one percent of the Nonwhite
population in Indianapolis is other than Negro," p. 10, *The Negro in Indianapolis*,
1967.
** Figure not given in original source: *Current Population Reports*, P. 20, No. 168.

occupations make up the lower working-class. Looking first at
respondents' fathers and also at occupations represented by husbands in the sample, we find there has been some upward movement.[11] While only 20 percent of our respondents came from
middle-class backgrounds, almost 34 percent of them are now
located in the middle-class. Likewise, whereas only 18 percent of
them came originally from upper working-class homes, 33 percent
are currently found at that point. There has been a drop in those
found in the lower working-class from 49 to 31 percent.

In short, one-fifth of the sample came from the middle class,
and now one-third of the sample is located there. Slightly better
than one-third of the sample came from the upper working-class or
above, and now about two-thirds are found within this broad range.
That there has been general upward occupational achievement

seems therefore evident. Whether these proportions of upward mobility would fall short of those within a comparable sample of whites is not certain, though likely. Nevertheless, the fact that there is at least some mobility among these blacks lends credence to the theoretical notion we have been following: background resources influence later valued outcomes in black as well as in white society. Later in this chapter, we shall explore in detail some of the connections between these background factors and movement upward. At this point, we need to focus primarily on the phenomenon of mobility per se.

In Chapter 1, the severe limitations of our sample were discussed insofar as we may generalize from it to the larger black society. Conclusions drawn from this sample should be considered initial (though testable) *hypotheses* with regard to black family patterns in general above the underclass. Viewed in this light, the data in Table 5–1 may provide some additional help in evaluating the scope, usefulness, and validity of these conclusions.

For example, compared with whole (husband-wife present) nonwhite families in the Indianapolis area in 1960, our sample (husband-wife present) appears to be skewed upward in the direction of the middle- and upper-working classes. It seems to be overrepresented there and underrepresented in the lower working-class. But more recent census data indicate that during the decade of the sixties there has been a significant upgrading of the occupational levels of all employed blacks. Specifically, the proportion of national increase among black workers found at the professional-technical level between the years 1960 to 1967 has been 80 percent; at the level of managers and officials it is 17 percent; at the clerical level, 77 percent; at the sales level, 22 percent; at the craftsmen-foremen level, 49 percent; for operatives, 33 percent; and for nonhousehold service workers, 23 percent.[12] These substantial upgradings *exceed changes for whites at all levels* except the last where there is parity.

These dramatic upward changes among blacks probably help to account for the occupational distribution (shown in Table 5–1) of employed black males in the north and west regions of the

United States (of which Indianapolis is obviously a part) by 1966. Blau and Duncan note that blacks in the North (and West) have substantially higher job status than their southern counterparts.[13] Almost all (91 percent) northern blacks live in urban areas, so that the 1966 census data tend to be representative of an urban population, relatively more advantaged than any other cohort of blacks in American history. Interestingly, there is remarkable similarity between the national data and our sample of ongoing marriages. Approximately one-third of each sample contains respondents of current middle-class status; one-third of each sample may be described as upper working-class, and one-third of each sample is composed of those from the lower working-class. The similarity in class distribution between the national and the 1968 Indianapolis samples, in spite of the severe limitations inherent in both (especially the latter), is perhaps a measure of the validity in the generalizations drawn from the Indianapolis sample. That is, if the conclusions are treated as hypotheses and tested on a national (strict) probability sample, there is that much more reason to believe that perhaps they might hold there as well.

Furthermore, besides evidence in Table 5–1 for upward occupational mobility on the part of the sample as a whole, we have additional, more specific evidence for this statement. The Census Bureau, alongside of and based on its gross occupational categories, has devised a more precise and refined method of measuring "socioeconomic status" (or what they call S.E.S.).[14] By utilizing their technique, it is possible to rank occupations on a scale from 00 (low) to 98 (high). Once this is done it is a straightforward matter to measure degree of occupational mobility, simply by subtracting the father's S.E.S. score from the son's S.E.S. score. If the result is positive, the son's rank is higher; if negative, the father's rank is higher; if the result is zero, there has been no change.

This procedure was followed in the case of male respondents. For females, their fathers' occupations were subtracted from the occupations of their husbands. The question of the mobility of married females (white or black) has not been explored much. Generally, however, it is assumed that at marriage she takes the status of her husband. More will be said about this assumption later.

Making use of the above procedure, we found that 58 percent of persons in the sample had experienced *upward* occupational mobility, compared to father's occupational status. About 5 percent experienced no change at all. Some 23 percent had been downwardly mobile, and for 14 percent mobility could not be determined in this precise fashion, because information on fathers' occupation was incomplete.

These are gross characterizations, however, and do not tell us *how far* offspring may have moved beyond their fathers, nor how high they stand on the S.E.S. scale. By comparing mean S.E.S. scores of fathers and offspring, we obtained some information on both matters. For instance, the mean S.E.S. score for all males in the sample is 45.4. Conversely, their fathers had a mean S.E.S. score of only 30.9. Females had experienced a similar degree of upward mobility, for their own fathers' mean S.E.S. score was 33.0, as compared to 44.7 for their own husbands. (In both instances, the *t* test reveals a .001 level of significance.)[15] Hence, based on these several procedures and comparisons the theoretical expectation that upward movement in the class structure would be the lot of the *majority* of our respondents seems to be verified. Furthermore, their occupational mobility has occurred in the context of definite trends toward upward mobility within black society (above the underclass) as a whole. Besides occupational achievement, we need to look briefly at two related indicators of movement upward through the American class structure, i.e., education and income.

Education

Table 5–2 compares education separately for male and female respondents with their fathers and with northern and western black people in general.[16] Both sexes have advanced far beyond their fathers in years of school completed, particularly in the three top categories: some high school, high school graduates, and some college or beyond. Although only about 16 percent of their fathers completed the ninth grade or beyond, 56 percent of males and 68 percent of females are found within this upper educational range. In addition, the proportion of females in each category closely ap-

TABLE 5-2. EDUCATIONAL ATTAINMENTS OF RESPONDENTS, THEIR FATHERS, AND THE BLACK POPULATION IN THE NORTH AND WEST

Years of School Completed	Male Respondents			Female Respondents		
	Their Fathers	Themselves	1966 North & West Black Males	Their Fathers	Themselves	1966 North & West Black Females
None	12.1%	1.5%	1.2%	2.5%	1.0%	1.0%
1–4	14.1	13.1	7.6	17.8	3.0	4.4
5–8	25.2	29.3	27.3	34.7	28.2	26.2
9–11	6.6	21.7	31.1	6.9	32.1	31.6
High School Graduate	5.2	18.3	23.1	5.0	25.7	26.8
Some College or Beyond	4.0	16.1	9.7	3.4	10.0	10.0
N. A.	32.8	—	—	29.7	—	—
T	100% (198)	100% (198)	100%	100% (202)	100% (202)	100%
N			*			*

* Figure not given in original source: *Current Population Reports,* P. 20, No. 168.

proximates that found within the national sample. Males fall somewhat below national figures in the high school categories, but *more* of them have been to college than is true of black males generally within the North and West. In short, our sample does reveal considerable educational mobility, and in so doing, tends to be somewhat similar to the levels of education attained by the nonsouthern (nonrural) black population.

Earlier, under occupational mobility, we subtracted father's S.E.S. score from his son's in order to determine precise rates of occupational change. We also did the same for years of education: subtracted father's years from son's; and father's years of education from daughter's *own* years of education. We found that about 50 percent of the sample exceeded their fathers in years of education attained; 12 percent stayed at the *same* educational level as their fathers; 7 percent dropped *below* their father; and for 31 percent, change could not be calculated due to insufficient information regarding their fathers. Hence from this perspective also, it seems clear that the majority of our respondents have experienced educational mobility compared to their *own* fathers, or at least have been able to attain the same level he had. This last point is particularly relevant in those cases where the father was a high-school graduate or beyond. In such cases, the child has been able to maintain a certain "cycle of attainment," instead of the cycle of "defeat and poverty" so often observed among lower-class blacks.

One should not be misled, however, into thinking that education is the same guarantee of occupational status and income to blacks that it is to whites. In fact, Blau and Duncan maintain that the *more education* the black male receives, the *more disadvantaged* he becomes when compared to whites with equal education.[17] The only exception is what they term the "minority" of blacks who actually complete college. For example, in Table 5–3 we show the relationships between years of education and occupational status for males in our sample, as compared to whites and also nonwhites in the 1962 Blau-Duncan national sample. The comparisons are in terms of the *mean* occupational status score for males in each educational category.[18]

TABLE 5–3.　COLOR, EDUCATION, AND MALE OCCUPATIONAL STATUS

Years of Education	Mean 1962 Occupational Status*		Mean 1968 Occupational Status of Black Males in Sample
	White	Black	
0–8	23.6	16.8	14.8 (87)
9–11	29.7	18.6	23.0 (43)
12	37.8	22.8	21.8 (36)
13 +	56.8	41.1	38.6 (32)

* Source: Blau and Duncan, 1967, p. 208.
　　N (in thousands) for whites is 7286, 5420, 8855, and 7534, respectively, low to high education. For nonwhites (or blacks, for all practical purposes) it is 2243, 1032, 827, 477, respectively.

At every educational level, black males fall far behind whites in occupational attainment. This condition is particularly significant in view of the place that education holds in the "American Dream" syndrome. Ideally, those who "make it" in school are "supposed" to have the way paved for them to "make it" in the occupational world. But both the national and local samples show that blacks who have been to college, for instance, attain a job level *barely* above that attained by whites who have merely graduated from high school. Thus while today's blacks have gone considerably beyond their fathers in educational attainment, this important "means" has not brought them "ends" comparable to whites. In spite of "relative success" in school, black males still experience considerable (ethnic-related) discrimination in obtaining, holding, and being advanced with respect to higher status jobs.

The same investment of time and resources in education does not yield Negroes as much return in their careers as it does whites. Negroes, as an underprivileged group, must make greater sacrifices to remain in school, but they have less incentives than whites to make these sacrifices, which may well be a major reason why Negroes often exhibit little motivation to continue in school and advance their education. . . . Since acquiring an education is not very profitable for Negroes, they are inclined to drop out of school relatively early. The consequent low level of education of most Negroes reinforces the stereotype of the un-educated Negro that helps to justify occupational discrimination against the entire group, thus further depressing the returns Negroes get for the educational investment they do make, which again lessens their incentives to make such investments.[19]

Later in the chapter, we shall have more to say regarding the phenomenon, among blacks, of the relationship between restricted incentives and achievement-striving.

Income

Since we have no data on income of the families in which these respondents grew up, we cannot ascertain precise differences in income gains. Nonetheless, based on observed changes in occupational status and in education, we may safely assume they almost certainly experience more family income now than was true during childhood. We can, however, compare their current incomes with those reported through national census data, to obtain some idea of how they reflect national trends in this sector. Initially, Table 5–4 seems to suggest that our sample is *less* represented in the lower (poor and fair) income brackets than the national sample of blacks, and *more* represented in the "good" and "high" income brackets.[20] Instead, however, it will be seen that our sample does tend to reflect the very latest in income trends among urban blacks.

First, we must realize that the *national* data include blacks who reside in the South. The median income in 1965 of all black families (including husband-absent) in the South was $3,033, compared to $5,271 for black families (including husband-absent) in the North and West.[21] Furthermore, this last figure inevitably climbs when we exclude husband-absent families. For example, in 1967 the median income of central city black families headed by a woman was $3,270, less than half the income when urban black families were headed by a male ($6,778).[22] Finally, it can be seen that this

TABLE 5–4. INCOME OF BLACK HUSBAND-WIFE FAMILIES IN THE UNITED STATES, AND IN SAMPLE, BY WIFE EMPLOYMENT

Total Income	U.S., 1965— Male Head— Married, Wife Present*			Indianapolis Sample—1968		
	Wife Employed	Wife Not Employed	Total	Wife Employed	Wife Not Employed	Total
$00–3999 (poor)	30.5%	53.2%	42.6%	15.3%	32.0%	22.3%
4000–6999 (fair)	32.0	31.1	31.5	21.8	33.5	26.1
7000–9999 (good)	21.6	11.7	16.3	32.4	24.9	26.4
10,000–over (high)	15.9	4.0	9.6	30.5	9.6	18.1
N. A.						7.1
T	100%	100%	100%	100%	100%	100%
N	1,499,000	1,665,000	3,164,000	(170)	(197)	(400)
Median Income			$4616			$6660

* Source: Current Population Reports, P. 20, No. 168.

last figure closely approximates the median income of $6,660 reported by families in our sample.

In short, just as the sample appears to reflect the stable, urban, black family with regard to occupational status and education, it likewise seems to mirror national trends in terms of black family income. Moreover, Table 5–4 makes clear that wife employment substantially boosts total family income among American black families. Here too our sample reflects the national pattern since, out of 400 households, 181 or 45 percent contain a wife who is currently working. The national figure among "whole" black families is 47 percent.[23] The phenomenon of wife employment, although becoming increasingly significant in white families, has traditionally been crucial among blacks, and we shall examine its consequences in greater detail in the next chapter.

Furthermore, just as blacks with comparable education to whites are disadvantaged in terms of job status, they are also disadvantaged with regard to income. The national median income for urban, whole, white families in 1967 was $8,741, two thousand dollars more than the $6,778 for urban, whole, black families.[24] The reason for this substantial discrepancy can be readily explained when we examine census data showing differences between black and white males with regard to 1967 median incomes *at the same job level*.[25] Whites who were professionals and managers earned $9,542, while blacks at this same job level earned only $6,208. White clerks and sales workers, earned $6,878; blacks, $5,515. White craftsmen and foremen earned $7,545; blacks earned $5,962. White factory workers received $6,475; blacks, $5,414. White nonfarm laborers earned $5,335, blacks, $4,492; and white service workers (janitors, etc.) received $5,536, blacks, $4,159.

To be sure, since 1959 when the median income for whole black families was $4,959, many blacks have made considerable monetary gains using *other blacks* as a reference point. But since this is a white-dominated society, blacks inevitably tend to use whites for at least some comparison or reference points. And when they do, they find that the "American Dream" does not apply equally to them. First, they find that education comparable to whites fails to bring them comparable job status. Second, even when they somehow manage to attain comparable job status, they discover inequities in income.

The cumulative effect of the discrepancies in annual median incomes is predictable in terms of lifetime earnings. For instance, the white male with four years of college can expect to earn $395,000 throughout his lifetime; the nonwhite male with four years of college can expect only $185,000, less than half (47 percent) of white earnings.[26] Once more it is those who have conformed *most strenuously* to the "demands" of the American Dream, (i.e., "getting through college") who are most severely disillusioned in terms of expected rewards. (The nonwhite elementary school graduate earns 61 percent as much as comparably educated whites.)

Consequently, we have the paradox of blacks making genuine gains occupationally, educationally, and monetarily; nonetheless *relatively* they continue to remain deprived compared to whites. There has been substantial achievement and mobility, yet considerable social distance persists. But in spite of the distance, and perhaps because there has been *some* participation in the "Dream," we found, in earlier chapters, significant similarity in the patterns of black and white family systems. In the remainder of this chapter, we will consider both additional similarities and differences. Our focus will be on certain relationships between family background and experiences, and present position within the occupational structure.

FAMILY INFLUENCES AND MOBILITY

In describing the optimum family conditions that give rise to mobility, Blau and Duncan refer precisely to the kinds of situations that many persons in the sample encountered (see Chapters 3 and 4). These include "economic support," plus "diverse forms of social support, which range from such subtle factors as furnishing thought patterns and role models . . . to such explicit ones as encouraging children to study and helping them if they have trouble. . . . The achievement orientation that disposes the man to strive to better himself is acquired by the child largely in his parental family."[27] This description applies with equal force to blacks and whites for as Billingsley remarks: "Prominent in the background of Negro men and women of achievement is a strong family life."[28]

Having demonstrated both that our respondents experienced the "strong family life" characterized by Billingsley, and by Blau and Duncan, and also, that most of these black Americans have become upwardly mobile, the next task is to try to see what, if any, actual relationship exists between the two phenomena of family background and mobility. Blau and Duncan conclude that the males' current occupation is influenced by *at least* four different variables. Father's *educational* level and father's *occupational* level both influence directly the son's *education*. The father's occupation influences the *first job* the son ever holds. Finally, father's occupation, son's first job, and son's education directly influence son's current occupation, with son's education having the greatest impact of all.[29] In short, within the larger society, a male's education is the *single best* predictor of his present job status. We have measures of all these variables except respondent's first job. Following essentially the same procedures as Blau and Duncan, we look first at Table 5–5. When we examine the joint effects of father's education and occupation on respondent's education, we find that father's

TABLE 5–5. INFLUENCE OF FATHER'S EDUCATION AND OCCUPATION ON EDUCATION OF RESPONDENTS

	Males		*Females*	
	p	*r*	*p*	*r*
Father's Occupation	.478	.52	.249	.38
Father's Education	.056	.51	.089	.28
R^2	.51		.30	
N	(130)		(133)	

occupation has by far the stronger path of influence. This is true for both sexes, though the relationships are more pronounced for males than for females. Although there has been little research on female mobility (black or white), this bit of evidence suggests that for black females as well as males (above the underclass) the occupational level attained by fathers will strongly influence the educational level that they eventually attain. This conclusion corroborates the Blau and Duncan finding in terms of their national sample, though their results also showed greater causal influence of father's education than ours do.

Looking next at Table 5–6, we found in our sample of blacks, as did Blau and Duncan, that a male's education is a better predictor of his own job status than is his father's occupation. For a female, in comparison, both path coefficients are quite weak, and the influence of her father's occupation is slightly stronger than the influence of her own education. It must be remembered, of course, that the dependent variable is not wife's own occupation but the occupation of her husband. Females (black or white) in American society have far less control over their "status destiny" than do males, because female mobility is almost always measured in terms of her husband's occupation. Her social status is ascribed to her through marriage and not usually achieved through independent educational or occupational achievements of her own.

TABLE 5–6. INFLUENCE OF FATHER'S OCCUPATION AND RESPONDENT'S EDUCATION ON SON'S OCCUPATION (OR FAMILY SOCIAL STATUS)

	Job Status of Males		Job Status of Husbands of Wives in Sample	
	p	r	p	r
Father's Occupation	.109	.41	.151	.33
Respondent's Education	.432	.29	.135	.20
R^2		.49		.23
N		(170)		(172)

Consequently, between her family background and her own education, and her subsequent social status, there intervenes an enormous factor which, prior to marriage, operated totally outside her control, i.e., the interplay of her potential husband with the opportunity structure. After marriage, the foundation for additional male attainments has largely been shaped (through his education) and forces in the system of opportunity continue to function *apart from her direct sphere of influence.* Nationally, for instance, Blau and Duncan report the influence of the wife on her husband's mobility is very slight indeed.[30] We found the same thing in that wife's education has virtually no impact on husband's occupational level.[31] Theoretically, therefore, the association between individual attainments and subsequent status is less clear and certain for married females in our society than it is for males, black or white. This situation is chiefly due to the fact that her status depends on social forces that exist above and beyond her own family of orientation. In effect, it lies ultimately with the family from whence her husband—not she—came.

Besides this general pattern, moreover, the black female faces additional uncertainty and lack of control over her "status destiny." Her status is almost inevitably linked to a "pool of eligibles" who continually experience severe occupational discrimination within the white-dominated opportunity structure. One outcome of these oft-capricious forces is to reduce the number of available black males with higher status, which in turn applies greater pressures on black females (particularly from the middle class) to select mates more randomly with regard to job position than would otherwise be the case (i.e., of lower status than they might prefer).

For example, males in the sample who came from a middle-class background have a mean S.E.S. score of 57.0 compared with 42.1 for males who came from a working-class family.[32] Such strongly significant differences do not emerge for black females. Among wives who came from the middle-class, the mean S.E.S. score for their husbands is 47.1; for husbands of wives who came from the working-class, it is 45.2.[33] Thus while the black male from a higher status background has a reasonably good chance of maintaining that status, the higher status black female has far less certainty of doing so. Due to pervasive job discrimination against black males, black girls in general (and those from the middle-class in particular) encounter great difficulty in finding black males with middle-class job status. Consequently, as Pettigrew observes, many black girls are very often forced to marry "downward" in terms of social status.[34] For instance, in this sample, only 28 percent of women coming from a middle-class background were able to wed males with similar status. The remaining 72 percent of these women married working-class men, i.e., married "downward."

Conversely, black males with higher job status can have their "pick" of the "relative abundance" of black females with comparable status, in addition to attractive or intelligent females with lower status. Therefore, although for black males individual educational attainment exercises considerable influence on his job position and thus on his social standing in society, such paths of influence are far more tenuous for black females.

Nevertheless, in Table 5–7, we see that among those females who are employed, their *own* education is the strongest predictor

TABLE 5–7. INFLUENCES ON JOB POSITION OF EMPLOYED WIVES, OF FATHER'S OCCUPATION AND EDUCATION, AND MOTHER'S EDUCATION

	p	r
Father's Occupation	.060	.39
Father's Education	.025	.30
Mother's Education	.092	.29
Respondent's Education	.492	.16
R²	.51	
N	(106)	

of their *own* job position. On this basis we may therefore say that
for both sexes educational level determines job level. Yet in spite
of far-reaching changes that may be stirring with respect to the role
of the American female, and within our family structure (further
discussed in Chapters 6 and 8), the class position of the American
family (black or white) still rests chiefly on the occupation of the
male. It is obligatory for the male to work, to make participation
in the opportunity structure his chief life endeavor. For females,
work remains largely optional and dependent on freedom from
pressing home responsibilities. Unless and until the more casual
work participation of most females begins to alter, the source of
family social status will continue to lie chiefly with the husband's
job.[35]

In Chapter 3, we found that interpersonal stress on and help
toward education was one of the fundamental resources provided
by parents to our respondents. While Blau and Duncan strongly
underscore the critical nature of the social psychological processes
involved in that type of resource-provision, they unfortunately had
no attitudinal data of that sort.[36] However, since we do, we shall
explore just how parental resources and parental identification
might, in addition to the factors just considered, also influence
educational and occupational attainments of our respondents.

In Table 5-8, we show the direct impact on respondent's education of the several functionality and identification variables discussed in earlier chapters. We also include father's education as a
control factor, because it was the variable that most influenced parental functionality (Chapter 3). Looking first at males, we find that
father's education is a more powerful predictor of *son's* education
than are any of the interpersonal variables. This seems especially
interesting since in Table 5-5 it exhibited almost no direct influence
at all. At the same time there are relatively meaningful paths of
influence from choice of *father* as role model, choice of a *male*
reference person (most frequently the father) and functionality of
father. In contrast, the three "mother-type" influences are virtually
nil. Add this evidence to what we already know about the impact
of father's occupation, and it appears that fathers of these black

TABLE 5–8. INFLUENCE OF FUNCTIONALITY, IDENTIFICATION, AND FATHER'S EDUCATION ON RESPONDENT'S EDUCATION

	Males		Females	
	p	r	p	r
Father as Role Model	.113	.58	.068	.12
Mother as Role Model	.001	.21	.088	.14
Male Reference Person	.172	.02	.192	.03
Female Reference Person	.032	.32	.191	.24
Father-Functionality	.190	.36	.278	.03
Mother-Functionality	.008	.06	.094	.07
Father's Education	.262	.07	.125	.04
R^2	.38		.44	
N	(118)		(123)	

males had considerably greater impact on their educational attainments than did mothers.

What is more, fathers also seemed to have had more of a direct influence on females' education than did mothers. Only for females it was not through father's education as much as through his resource-provision or level of functionality. Of all the influences shown in Table 5–8 on females' education, father-functionality is by far the strongest, followed by choice of reference persons both male and female. Continuing indication that among blacks above the underclass there is a "strong father-figure" (and not the stereotype of the overpowering and domineering female) emerges when we examine Table 5–9, influence on respondent's own occupation.

TABLE 5–9. INFLUENCE ON RESPONDENT'S OWN OCCUPATION OF FUNCTIONALITY, IDENTIFICATION, FATHER'S OCCUPATION, SPOUSE'S AND OWN EDUCATION

	Males		Employed Females	
	p	r	p	r
Father-Role Model	.028	.51	−.014	.25
Mother-Role Model	.003	.18	.015	.20
Male Reference Person	.165	.02	.039	.03
Female Reference Person	−.135	−.30	−.028	−.27
Father-Functionality	.015	.33	.015	.04
Mother-Functionality	.050	.00	.050	.10
Father's Occupation	.145	.05	.006	.04
Respondent's Education	.367	.12	.387	.16
Spouse Education	.057	.03	.288	.01
$R^2 =$	.52		.57	
$N =$	(148)		(131)	

For males, the strongest impact remains his own education, followed by choice of male reference person, then father's occupation. Aside from his own education, it is identification with his *father* (or some other male) that provides the greatest impetus toward occupational attainments.

However, when we examine influences on the occupational level of employed wives, we find that their own education (and their husbands') exercises considerable influence, whereas identification or functionality have almost none.[37] Why, for these black females, identification should have as little impact as it does on occupational achievement is not totally clear. Possibly, for most females adolescent identification is directed more toward domestic than toward occupational activities. They patterned themselves after certain adults with the intent of becoming "good wives and mothers," in contrast with males for whom identification is pointed primarily toward the occupational world. It follows, therefore, that in the absence of direct impetus by "significant" adults toward female occupational achievement, there should be little linkage between identification with them and subsequent job position. We shall return to the complex problem of black female employment in Chapter 6.

Figure 5–1 presents a simplified diagram illustrating some of the paths of influence discussed in the last few chapters. It deals primarily with conclusions pertinent to male respondents, and the reader should be alert to similarities and deviations that apply to females. The main feature of the diagram is that it helps us to see that within the black family system (above the underclass), as within the white, there are significant forces operating that tend to move young males into the opportunity structure.[38] The diagram also shows how interpersonal factors, such as parental functionality and identification, actually parallel "material" factors such as father's occupation. It shows how father's education operates not only directly on son's education, but also through functionality and identification. Hence, in spite of severe deprivations experienced by blacks even beyond the lower class, we find a viable and functioning family structure. Insofar as a modern society makes demands upon family systems to prepare its offspring to operate effectively in the larger milieu, the more advantaged black family has been able to meet these demands. It has been able to do this at the same time that the larger society has paradoxically exerted pressures to keep it from doing so. In the remainder of this chapter, we shall con-

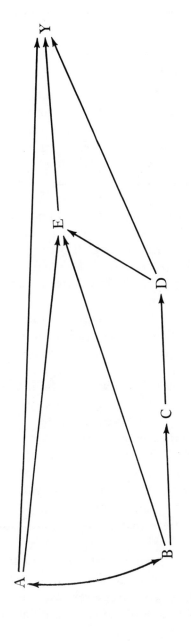

A = Father's Occupation
B = Father's Education
C = Parental Functionality
D = Identification with Parents
E = Son's Education
Y = Son's Occupation (Family Social Status)

Fig. 5-1. Chain of influences on son's occupation (or family's social status).

sider some of the negative consequences that these kinds of pressures may have on black achievement.

IDENTIFICATION AND DEGREE
OF OCCUPATIONAL ATTAINMENT

So far we have examined the phenomenon of upward socioeconomic movement per se on the part of these blacks, plus the background factors that are most significant in general in accounting for this mobility. An equally crucial question has to do with the relationship between differences in parental identification and differences in actual occupational level achieved by our respondents. Recall that we have confirmed Winch's prediction that parental resources result in identification by the child. These resources were presumably of the type that would enable the child to operate with relative efficiency in the opportunity structure. We have also seen that indeed they do have a direct bearing on the child's (black or white) educational and occupational attainments.

An hypothesis, which flows from the resource-identification conclusion, is that positive identification leads to higher occupational achievement than either negative or neutral identification. Presumably, the child who receives most resources from his parents will not only identify most positively with them, but will also be most capable of achievement within the opportunity structure. This achievement is owing not only to the resources per se, but also to the process of identification. Using the parent as *positive* role model, i.e., wanting to be *like* him, should be a motivational spur to attain valued goals espoused by the favored role model. In short, the influence of optimum resources operating in conjunction with positive identification should result in optimum attainments. Surprisingly, however, this is not the pattern that emerges from Tables 5–10, 5–11, and 5–12.

In Table 5–10, males who rejected their fathers, and those who rejected their mothers ("wanted to be different," or chose someone besides parent, or else chose *no one* as a reference person) *consistently* reveal the *highest* occupational scores. The differences

Table 5-10. Male Identification and Present Male Occupational Position

		S.E.S. Score		S.E.S. Score
Parental Role Model	Like Father	44.7 (61)	Like Mother	45.1 (81)
	Different from Father	50.2 (60)	Different from Mother	51.0 (38)
	Neither	39.2 (47) F = 3.84 p<.05 df = 2&165	Neither	40.8 (64) F = 2.89 df = 2&180, n.s.
Reference Person	Father	42.4 (111)	Mother	43.9 (152)
	Other	50.9 (51)	Other	52.1 (22)
	No One	44.5 (35) F = 2.79 df = 2&194, n.s.	No One	46.2 (24) F = 1.47 df = 2&195, n.s.

in these mean scores are statistically significant in the instance of *father* as role model, and come close to being so with regard to mother as role model and also male reference person. However, males who wanted to be *like* their fathers or mothers rank higher than those who did *not* use parents as role models in either a positive or negative sense. Yet, at the same time, males who chose parents as reference persons rank *below* those who could identify *no* reference person whatsoever. Overall, it would thus appear that black adolescents who rejected their parents, i.e., who identified with them negatively, attain higher occupational position than black youth who do otherwise.

This result is not to imply that other studies of black mobility might not reveal a relationship between positive identification and occupational achievement. For instance, some reports of whites within the dominant society stress the significance of a positive identification while others underscore the precise opposite. In commenting on this divergence, Lipset and Bendix state, "the characteristic family experiences in childhood of the upward mobile . . . remain still a relatively unexplored area. The contrast among the findings of the studies on these subjects is striking."[39] The "striking contrast" they refer to is based on the differing findings of those reports which claim that *positive* identification with parents leads to optimum mobility, versus those that maintain the import of *negative* identification.

Of course, if we recall the mean occupational score of their fathers (30.9), it is obvious that in general these males have moved upward, indicating that within the black family (above the underclass) positive or even neutral parental identification is also linked to occupational achievement. Hence within black and white family systems, there are contrasting patterns of identification which, nonetheless, lead to similar ends. The point here, however, is that these data suggest that those blacks who move furthest up the occupational ladder are consistently those who reject their parents as role models or reference persons. Even when we look *separately* at males from middle-class or from working-class backgrounds, the basic conclusion remains the same: those who achieve the *highest* occupational status are still those who *reject* their parents.

Middle-class males who wanted to be *like* their fathers have a mean S.E.S. score of 47.1; different, 65.1; neither, 54.1.[40] For working-class males, the S.E.S. scores were 43.9, 45.7, and 37.4, respectively.[41] When it came to choice of a *reference person*, middle-class males who chose their fathers had a mean S.E.S. score of 50.0; those choosing someone else had a score of 72.7; no one, 61.7.[42] For working-class husbands, the S.E.S. scores were father, 40.2; other, 45.6; no one, 42.4.[43] Identical patterns also emerged in *both* social classes when we looked at identification with *mother* as role model and as reference person.[44]

In Chapter 4, we found that although social class was directly related to level of benefits provided to the child, basic processes of identification were the same in each class: maximum rewards were linked to positive identification, lesser rewards to a negative identification, and least rewards to a neutral stance toward parents. Here we find that while social class is definitely linked to ultimate achievement, the kind of parental identification that is conducive to the greatest occupational achievement in both classes can be described as a negative one.

As we saw in Chapter 2, Blau and Duncan conclude that coming from a "broken family is a handicap for subsequent status achievement." They claim, however, this is due almost entirely to the *educational* handicaps that ensue from a broken family. For instance, in the case of black families headed by females (the poorest of the poor), severely reduced finances impose critical hardships on school attendance and subsequent occupational attainment. In spite of this seeming handicap, family composition among our sample resulted in only minimal, nonsignificant differences for male occupational achievement. Those males from whole families have an S.E.S. score of 46.5; for males from "other" families, 42.8.[45] Evidently these latter blacks were able to overcome at least some of the "educational handicaps" that ensue from a broken home. As we saw in Chapter 4, processes of rewards and identification were basically similar in whole and in "other" families, as they had been in the middle and working classes. Even more important, when we compare men from whole and "other" backgrounds, we find no basic difference in the relationships between identification and achievement. As was true for social class, so it appears for both types of family composition, i.e., *rejection* of parents consistently results in *greater* male occupational achievement than either a positive or a neutral identification with them.[46]

Even beyond class background or family wholeness, the respondent's own education is clearly most critical to his occupation. To discover whether or not education would destroy the consistency of the pattern that has emerged so far, we divided male respondents into *low* education (11 years of school or less, below a high-school diploma) and into *high* education (12 or more years, high school diploma or better). In spite of this dichotomy, the pattern remains. Males with low education who wanted to be *different* from their fathers had a mean S.E.S. score of 45.0 that was significantly greater than the mean of 39.3 for males (low education) who wanted to be *like* their fathers, and the score of 32.2 for those remaining neutral.[47] The same pattern emerged for those with *high* education in terms of father as role model; and the pattern continued for both educational categories with respect to mother as role model and to choices of male and female reference persons.[48]

The indication that neither class background, family composition, nor respondent's education alters the recurring identification-achievement pattern gives rise to a very important question. In the light of the earlier theoretical discussion, we had expected that *positive* identification would lead to highest achievement levels. Positive identification, it is recalled, was associated with greater resources provided for children by parents. Presumably with greater resources should come greater capabilities for achievement and mobility. But such does not appear to be the case. Instead, those males provided with *lower* (but not lowest) levels of resources seem capable of greater attainment than those given somewhat more benefits as adolescents. This pattern may have several implications for upward mobility among blacks. But before considering this issue in detail, we must look at how parental identification influenced *female* social status.

From Table 5–11, we learn that how black females related to their *own* parents makes less difference in their subsequent status

TABLE 5–11. FEMALE IDENTIFICATION AND PRESENT FEMALE SOCIAL STATUS

		Mean S.E.S. Scores of Their Husbands		Mean S.E.S. Scores of Their Husbands
Parental Role Model	Like Father	44.4 (51)	Like Mother	45.8 (104)
	Different from Father	44.5 (67)	Different from Mother	48.3 (57)
	Neither	45.4 (57)	Neither	39.8 (28)
		$F = .03$; n.s.		$F = 1.5$; df = 2&186; n.s.
Reference Person	Father	43.8 (119)	Mother	44.4 (143)
	Other	47.5 (46)	Other	47.5 (36)
	No One	49.4 (33)	No One	50.7 (19)
		$F = 1.2$; n.s. df = 2&195		$F = .09$; n.s.

than it does for males. In spite of a consistent pattern suggesting that rejection helps choose a husband with higher status, the S.E.S. scores in each of the four comparisons are not far apart and never significantly different. This, of course, is related to our earlier discussion of the crucial factors that intrude for females (particularly the black) between identification and subsequent adult status.

As was the case with males, whether these wives came from a whole or "other" type of family made little difference in present social status. Wives from whole backgrounds were married to husbands whose mean S.E.S. score was 44.4, while wives from "other" situations had husbands whose mean S.E.S. score was 46.5.[49] Likewise, among females from both middle- and working-class backgrounds, from both whole and "other" families, the pattern of Table 5–11 tends to maintain itself. That is, there is still the persistent hint that female rejection of parents results in greater social status than does positive identification.[50] But since the differences in their husbands' occupational position are not great, we must still conclude that whatever impact female identification has on mobility, the relationship becomes blurred because she must take on the status of her husband.

However, when we examine Table 5–12 (the S.E.S. scores of the wife's own occupation, and hence the extent of her own individual achievements), a much sharper image emerges. For these black wives, as for males in the sample, *rejection* of parents (especially father as reference person and mother as role model) leads to higher individual occupational achievement than either a positive or neutral identification. So while her husband's experiences (past and present) may intervene and thus blur the connection between her parental identification and her *ascribed* social status, they apparently do not interfere as strongly with her identification and her own *achieved* occupational position, even when her education is controlled.[51]

It is important to note that the S.E.S. scores, and thus the occupational levels of these wives, are substantially below the levels of their husbands. More specifically, the mean S.E.S. score of working wives is 36.2 compared to 45.8 for husbands.[52] Thus there

TABLE 5-12. FEMALE IDENTIFICATION AND FEMALE'S OWN OCCUPATIONAL POSITION

		Wife's Own S.E.S Mean Score			Wife's Own S.E.S Mean Score
Parental Role Model	Like Father	30.8 (41)	Like Mother	32.7 (90)	
	Different From Father	40.2 (61)	Different From Mother	43.8 (51)	
	Neither	29.8 (42) $F = 2.2$; df = 2&141; n.s.	Neither	25.2 (16) $F = 3.90$; df = 2&154; $p < .05$	
Reference Person	Father	32.7 (103)	Mother	33.7 (122)	
	Other	46.5 (39)	Other	43.5 (29)	
	No One	32.0 (29) $F = 3.88$ df = 2&168 $p < .05$	No One	37.2 (20) $F = 1.4$ df = 2&168 n.s.	

is no evidence of occupational or status rivalry in those households with an employed wife. Although more shall be said about potential rivalry in Chapter 6, the major point here is that as individuals, black males and females attain the *highest* occupational position when they identify *negatively* with (reject) their parents. This point returns us to the question raised earlier as to *why* this should be so, given the fact that *positive* identification was associated with the *maximum* amounts or resources useful for achievement.

Undoubtedly, the key is that we are talking about people who are *black*, which is synonymous with being *disadvantaged* compared to whites with the *same class* background. For example, our respondents not only started out behind comparably situated *white* adolescents, but also faced the additional burden of having to migrate into a *foreign* milieu, i.e., an opportunity structure dominated by whites. Whites started out ahead and faced the prospect of a relatively nonhostile milieu. Given that the goals of maximum achievement within the opportunity system are uniformly distributed throughout the society (at least above the underclass), it is therefore obvious that for blacks these goals are *ipso facto* more difficult to attain.

We have seen that black families do provide substantial resources and rewards to their children, and where these are optimal, positive identification is greatest. In exchange theory terms, valued rewards reinforce group (parent-child) cohesion. Yet is it precisely those feelings of solidarity with one's family of orientation that impede *degree* of occupational achievement among some blacks? This is not to say that receiving optimal rewards from parents does not result in upward mobility. We have seen that it has, and so has a neutral identification with parents.

But, say Lipset and Bendix, "The process of social mobility requires . . . the capacity to leave behind an early environment and to adapt to a new one."[53] So the question becomes what generates *optimum* mobility within either a high or low educational or social class category? Let us speculate that whether parents were viewed positively or negatively, attempts by blacks to penetrate the opportunity structure were relatively equal at first. That is, at the outset of their serious occupational experiences, and regardless of the type of parental identification, almost all these blacks held strongly to the American Dream, and sought to share in the abundance supplied by a modern society. Using Merton's notion of "anticipatory socialization," let us assume they had all more or less equally absorbed the norms and behaviors of more advantaged social positions before having actually entered them. If anything, those respondents provided with greater resources may have had greater confidence and thus perhaps exhibited greater efforts than their counterparts.

A recent government investigation supports the contention of this study that many black families do in fact supply their youth with both motivation and success goals sufficient to enable them to believe that it is worthwhile at least to *try* to achieve. However, the report concludes: "The Negro youth starts out with determination to do a good job, but experience with a number of menial, low-paying and insecure jobs quickly produces an erosion of his commitment to work."[54] This conclusion is a variation on the theme suggested earlier that restricted educational incentives reduce educational striving. Here, it may be that blocked job rewards, plus minimal job security and advancement reduce job striving. The difference between this situation and that of white immigrants who, in years previous, also had to take "menial, low-paying and insecure jobs," is a simple one: realistic *hope* for oneself and for one's children.

. . . the sons of immigrants have lower social origins and less education than the majority group of northern whites with native parents, yet their occupational achievements are on the average as high as those of the majority group, not only if initial differences are controlled but also without such controls.[55]

Contrary to actual substantial fulfillment of the American Dream on the part of formerly deprived whites, black youth knows that blacks have been doing the menial work in America for generations. Hope for anything better often seems dim, and thus sustained effort often appears futile. For in spite of having internalized dominant success goals, and after a certain period of striving with the vagaries of the white occupational system, those blacks who had identified positively with their parents may have begun to exhibit less "push," impetus, or desire to engage in the myriad of strenuous behaviors that would blend them into that system, and perhaps move them away from their parents socially. Instead, since the white milieu was hostile anyway, it may often have been simpler to "retreat" to the "cordial warmth" and "good comfort" of one's family (of orientation), rather than to try to continue to do battle against external hostility.

But if, conversely, one's parents are *not* defined in such positive terms, then one cannot retreat from external hostility back to the family quite so easily. The more viable alternative may simply be to keep on striving within the white-dominated opportunity structure. This more persistent striving may be an attempt to compensate for relatively negative parental relationships, at the same time that these negative definitions impede the establishment of rewarding interaction with parents. Maximum rewards, in short, are defined as coming from the external world, not the family. Hence, it is interaction with the outside world that is primarily cultivated.

There may, in other words, be two patterns operating within the black family system within the working and middle classes. First, optimum resources provided by parents and parent-figures with the clear and genuine intent of "helping" their children to become socially more advantaged than they were. This condition leads to identification with parents and a warm, cohesive bond between them. During adolescence and young adulthood, when the foundations of subsequent career patterns are laid, these offspring had their first serious encounters with the white-dominated opportunity structure. They found it tough and unyielding. Perhaps the cohesiveness of parental ties provided a compensation for the cold rebuffs of the larger society. In turn, perhaps these kinds of sure rewards may have (unconsciously) reduced *somewhat* the impetus to continue the risk of seeking uncertain rewards from the intractible opportunity system.[56]

Second is a pattern in which rewards and identification between parents and children are somewhat less, but the white-dominated opportunity system remains the same. Only in this situation there are fewer compensations *from* and less cohesiveness *with* one's family of orientation. The lack of these kinds of rewards may, in reaction, result in *more persistent* efforts to glean rewards from the occupational system. Needless to say, in neither situation is there any "rational calculus" by either parents or offspring in terms of means or ends. It is an *unintended consequence* that maximum rewards should actually result in lower social status, and that fewer rewards should eventuate in greater status. As in so many sectors of the black man's life, his destiny here seems largely influenced by white cupidity. Whether or not these dual patterns operate similarly within white family structure is unclear, largely because whites simply do not face so hostile an opportunity system.

In a study of black adolescent achievement in high school, Lott and Lott describe an analogous situation that can be explained by the same theoretical stance.[57] They found that compared to white students, black students possess similarly high educational ideals, yet rank below whites in actual academic achievement. The authors dismiss inherent inferior "academic aptitude" as an explanation for the black-white discrepancy. Instead, they argue that black students find it difficult to "withstand the temptations of the *immediate rewards* that are attainable through social life, sports, and other activities that inevitably interfere with good intentions regarding studies" (italics supplied). And why do they find it difficult to resist the lure of "immediate rewards"? Once again, it is because of the fickleness and outright discrimination blacks experience within the opportunity structure.

While white students . . . may take for granted that their efforts in school will be somehow rewarded by society, Negro students cannot. . . . academic achievement requires hard work and study. . . . for white students with ability, the promise of eventual reward, in terms of high social status for example, is assumed to outweigh the negative aspects [of hard work and study]; for Negro students with ability, this same assumption cannot be made as readily.[58]

From Census Data plus our own data (Table 5–3) it is clear that the gloomy perceptions of black adolescents regarding limited future rewards, in spite of educational attainments, are largely accurate when blacks compare themselves to whites. According to Lott and Lott, blacks are *forced* to make a painful choice between sure and immediate rewards versus highly uncertain and tentative future rewards. The result is (naturally enough, as S. M. Miller et al. note) that many of them do not defer gratifications—they respond instead to those situations that provide immediate gratifications.[59]

It is likely that one of the several situations that provides immediate gratifications to adolescents and young adults is one's own family. This situation would be particularly true in those cases where one identifies *positively* with either his father or mother or both, in response to gratifications provided by them. And just as some black adolescents achieve below their capacity in high school, because they respond to obvious *immediate* rewards instead of vague *future* rewards, some blacks may actually achieve below their capacity in the white-dominated occupational structure. On the one hand, because immediate rewards in the form of warm interpersonal relations with one's family that produce feelings of solidarity and cohesion are so easily accessible and obtainable, the motivation to strive for uncertain occupational rewards is undercut. On the other hand, when there are fewer family rewards and less positive parental identification, the black youth is more apt to look elsewhere for gratifications. "Elsewhere" may include the opportunity structure. Failure to find immediate familial rewards may spur motivation to achieve occupational rewards, even though they may also be dimly perceived and also limited vis-à-vis whites. Nonetheless, the result of persistently seeking these kinds of rewards is a higher level of occupational attainment than blacks (from the same class background) who do not seek these particular rewards quite as diligently. In both situations, parents and youth are equally sincere toward each other and in their desire for a generous share of the "Dream." *What may differentiate these situations is a non-*

conscious reaction to varying levels of parental rewards in conjunction with a fundamentally hostile milieu.

We should emphasize that parental rewards cannot be *so meagre* as to limit occupational achievements in extremely severe fashion. Nor can experiences in the white-dominated job market be so debilitating as to make all effort seem meaningless. Himes points out that in the black lower-class both situations pertain to a great degree.[60] It seems clear, however, that neither situation applies with much force above the underclass. But even within more advantaged strata, there would appear to be a kind of reward-continuum among black families. At the top level of this continuum, rewards are great enough to stimulate positive parental identification. Moderate reward levels stimulate negative parental identification, and yet this "reward zone," as we saw empirically in Chapter 4, is not radically removed from the top zone. However, when rewards drop substantially beneath the "second zone," and consequently adolescents neither accept nor reject parents, then as revealed in the tables, this neutral type of identification usually results in the lowest degree of occupational achievement. The issue of "how much of a good thing" may have negative consequences, whereas "less" of it is more positive, and "least" of a good thing is most negative of all, is thorny indeed and deserves much more investigation both in black and white families.

These conclusions are, of course, part of the more general issue of the impact of the family of orientation on social mobility. In terms of the class level of the family and its subsequent influence on the child's education and job level, its impact seems well documented. However, at the social-psychological level, the question may not be as clear cut, especially among blacks. The association discovered here between parental rejection and occupational achievement tends to support those social pychologists who argue that it is the "less satisfactory childhood" that gives rise to greater achievement and mobility.[61] Occupational striving, they contend, is a form of *compensation* for certain unsatisfactory child and adolescent relationships. Further research is needed into the obviously related consequences of resource-provision by the family, feelings of solidarity with family members, and subsequent direction and degree of mobility.

SUMMARY

The urban black population above the underclass has made substantial economic gains during the decade of the sixties. Our sample seems to be fairly representative of these major trends (in occupation, education, income) within this large (two-thirds) segment of black society. More specifically, we found that blacks both in the sample and nationally have advanced (become socially mobile) beyond their parents in terms of occupational and social status, and education, and very often income. Yet in spite of all of these absolute gains, the paradox is that blacks (in the sample and nationally) remain significantly deprived when compared to whites at the same status level.

There was evidence, nonetheless, of a basic similarity with the dominant family system in terms of the processes whereby achievement and mobility are fostered. Father's occupation and education, plus parental resources and indentification by respondents, directly influenced their educational attainments. More than any other single factor, the years of education attained by males and females had the greatest direct impact on their own current occupational position. When we examined differences in *degree* of occupational achievement, one conclusion emerged consistently and seemed inescapable: males who *reject* their parents are more likely to attain higher social status than males who identified positively, or who were neutral toward their parents. For females, the relationship between parental identification and present social status is more blurred, chiefly because their actual status depends on the attainments of their husbands. Yet among *employed* females, their own job status is highest when they, like males, choose *not* to use parents as role models or reference persons.

It was suggested that the maximum parental rewards that lead to positive identification by children (see Chapter 4) may actually have the *unintended* consequence of cementing parent-child ties to such an extent that mobility by blacks is unconsciously impeded. Where rewards are fewer, there is less identification and less cohesion and thus, perhaps, greater pressure to seek rewards elsewhere, e.g., in the white opportunity system. To the degree these processes actually occur within black society, they underscore the pervasive influence and the dominance of white society on the black man's destiny. Black families that conform most fully to dominant society "ideals" regarding parent-child interaction may find, strangely enough, that their children are subsequently less advantaged than children from black families who conform somewhat less fully. This irony, of course, is part of the larger (ethnic-based) syndrome evidenced throughout the chapter—even when blacks amply demonstrate that they have shaken stereotypes of "laziness and indifference," and actually fulfill their part of the American Dream (hard work, diligence, education), white society neglects its part and, instead, denies them fullest possible access to the "promised rewards" of the "Dream."

NOTES

1. Gerald R. Leslie, *The Family in Social Context* (New York: Oxford University Press, 1967), chapter 9; see also Talcott Parsons, "The Normal American Family," in S. M. Farber, P. Mustacchi, Roger H. L. Wilson, *The Family's Search for Survival* (New York: McGraw-Hill, 1965), pp. 31–59.
2. Gordon, *Assimilation in American Life*, op. cit.
3. Sidney M. Greenfield, *English Rustics in Black Skin* (New Haven: College and University Press, 1966), pp. 24–29 and 155ff; Scanzoni, *Opportunity and the Family*; see also Blau and Duncan, *The American Occupational Structure*, p. 205; see chapter 6 of this book.
4. Blau and Duncan, *The American Occupational Structure*, p. 209.
5. Ginzberg and Hiestand, *Employment Patterns*, p. 209.
6. Ibid., p. 224.

7. "Recent Trends in Social and Economic Conditions of Negroes in the United States," *Current Population Reports* (Washington, D.C.: U.S. Dept. of Labor, Series P-23, No. 26, BLS #347, July 1968), p. v.

8. Ibid.

9. Andrew F. Brimmer, "The Negro in the National Economy," p. 261, Davis, 1966.

10. Source for Indianapolis Data: U.S. Bureau of the Census. *U.S. Census of Population: 1960*. Detailed Characteristics. Indiana. Final Report PC (1)–16D., p. 382. For National Data: U.S. Bureau of the Census, *Current Population Reports*, Series P-20, #168, "Negro Population: March 1966," (Washington, D.C.: U.S. Government Printing Office, 1957), p. 33.

11. The assessment of social mobility is always and inevitably a complex issue. However, we have followed Duncan in using "father's occupation [as a] time point proximate to the opening of the son's career, [hence] this origin status provides a natural base line against which one can measure the son's subsequent occupational achievement." See Otis Dudley Duncan, "Methodological Issues in the Analysis of Social Mobility," in Neil J. Smelser and Seymour M. Lipset, *Social Structure and Mobility in Economic Development* (Chicago: Aldine, 1966), p. 62.

12. *Current Population Reports*, July 1968, p. 16; Series P-23, No. 26.

13. Blau and Duncan, *The American Occupational Structure*, p. 220.

14. See Census Working Paper #15, "Methodology and Scores of Socio-economic Status" (Washington, D.C., Population Division, Bureau of the Census, 1963).

15. The "n" for father-son comparison = 170, df = 169, t = 7.03. Wives' husbands and their own fathers: n = 172, df = 171, t = 5.81.

16. Source for Data: *Current Population Reports*, Series P-20, #168, p. 22.

17. Blau and Duncan, *The American Occupational Structure*, p. 239. See also Rashi Fein, "An Economic and Social Profile."

18. The national data are from Blau and Duncan, op. cit. The measure of occupational position in Table 5–3, though related, is not the same as the Census Bureau Index used in the other tables. It is the *Duncan* index of socioeconomic status. See Ibid., p. 118ff for its description. Since the data from the Blau and Duncan report used the Duncan index, we did the same for this table in order to enhance comparability.

19. Blau and Duncan, Ibid., pp. 405–406.

20. Source for National Data: *Current Population Reports*, series P-20, #168, March 1966, p. 34.

21. Ibid.

22. U.S. Bureau of the Census, *Current Population Reports*, series P-23, Special Studies #27, "Trends in Social and Economic Conditions in Metropolitan Areas," Washington, D.C., 1959, p. 38.

23. *Current Population Reports*, series P-20, March 1966.

24. *Current Population Reports*, series P-23, #27, p. 38.

25. Ibid., p. 49. The median incomes of black males in the sample are quite similar to those reported in the text for black males nationally. Thus our sample is representative of the larger black population in terms of the amount of money earned at each major job status level.

26. Brimmer, "The Negro in the National Economy"; p. 250, see also Melvin Borland and Donald E. Yett, "The Cash Value of College—For Negroes and for Whites," *Trans-action*, 5 (November 1967), 44–49. A statistical measure has just become available to measure overlap of income distributions of white and black families. *Technical Paper 22*, U.S. Bureau of the Census, 1970.

27. Blau and Duncan, *The American Occupational Structure*, p. 296.

28. Billingsley, *Black Families in White America*, p. 97.

29. Blau and Duncan, *The American Occupational Structure*, p. 170.

30. Ibid., p. 359.

31. See Table 5–9.

32. Middle-class $N = 39$; working-class $= 159$; $df = 1$ & 196; $F = 16.0$, $p < .001$.

33. Middle-class $N = 38$; working-class $= 160$; $df = 1$ & 196; $F = 0.26$; n.s.

34. Thomas F. Pettigrew, *A Profile of the Negro American* (Princeton, N.J.: D. Van Nostrand Co., Inc., 1964), pp. 16ff.

35. An excellent summary of unique factors influencing historical and current patterns of black female employment is found in Jeanne L. Noble, "The American Negro Woman," in Davis, 1964, pp. 522ff.

36. Blau and Duncan, *The American Occupational Structure*, p. 316.

37. Background influences on wives' status in society (in contrast to their occupation) are omitted from the text owing to the weak relationships attributable to factors discussed earlier in the chapter.

38. The curved arrow between A and B represents a correlation ($r = .19$) rather than a path of influence.

39. Lipset and Bendix, *Social Mobility*, p. 250.

40. N's $= 15, 14, 6$, respectively; $df = 2$ & 32, $F = 2.18$; n.s.

41. N's $= 46, 46, 34$, respectively; $df = 2$ & 123; $F = 2.06$; n.s.

42. N's $= 25, 10, 4$, respectively; $df = 2$ & 36; $F = 4.02$; $p < .05$.

43. N's = 86, 41, 31, respectively; df = 2 & 155; F = 1.0; n.s.

44. *Middle-class,* "Like" mother, S.E.S. = 46.5; different = 60.2; neither = 52.1. N's = 14, 12, 10 respectively; df = 2 & 33, F = .33, n.s. Middle-class, "Mother as reference person," S.E.S. = 56.9; other = 69.3; no one = 50.4. N's = 31, 3, 5, respectively; df = 2 & 36; F = .60; n.s. *Working-class,* "like mother," S.E.S. = 42.0; different = 48.5; neither = 38.1. N's = 67, 26, 40, respectively; df = 2 & 130; F = 2.36; n.s. Working-class, "mother as reference person," S.E.S. = 40.5; other = 49.4; no one = 45.1. N's = 121, 19, 19, respectively; df = 2 & 156; F = 1.9, n.s.

45. "Whole" N = 122; "Other" = 76; df = 1 & 196; F = 1.4; n.s.

46. *Whole. Family Background:* "Like Father" S.E.S. = 44.0, different = 52.3; neither = 42.0; N's = 47, 43, 28; df = 2 & 115; F = 2.76; n.s. "Like mother," S.E.S. = 45.9; different = 54.0; neither = 43.1; N's = 54, 23, 44; df = 2 & 118; F = 2.20; n.s. Father as "reference person," S.E.S. = 44.3; other = 53.7; no one = 48.1; N's = 85, 23, 14; df = 2 & 119; F = 1.99; n.s. Mother as "reference person," S.E.S. = 46.1; other = 51.4; no one = 44.5. N's = 100, 12, 10; df = 2 & 119; F = .39; n.s. *Other Family Background:* "Like Father," S.E.S. = 45.1; different = 47.0; neither = 35.0. N's = 14, 17, 12; df = 2 & 40; F = 1.2; n.s. "Like Mother," S.E.S. = 43.7; different = 46.4; neither = 36.0. N's = 27, 15, 20; df = 2 & 59; F = 1.2; n.s. Father as "reference person," S.E.S. = 36.5; other = 48.5; no one = 42.0; df = 2 & 72; F = 2.0; n.s. N's = 26, 28, 21. Mother as "reference person," S.E.S. = 39.6; other = 53.0; no one = 47.5. N's = 52, 10, 14; df = 2 & 73; F = 1.9, n.s.

47. N's = 37, 4, 22, respectively. F = 3.76; df = 2 & 97, p < .05.

48. High education, father as role model: like = 55.7 (N = 20); different = 58.7 (23); neither = 49.3 (18); F = .96, n.s. Low education, mother-role model: 40.0 (54); 44.4 (21); 36.9 (32); F = .98, n.s. High education: mother-role model: 55.5 (27); 59.3 (17); 48.0 (18); F = 1.29, n.s. Low education: male reference-person: father = 37.2 (76); other = 43.7 (30); no one = 42.4 (23); F = 1.51, n.s. High education: male reference person: 53.8 (35); 61.2 (21); 48.5 (12); F = 1.48, n.s. Low education: female reference person: 38.6 (102); 46.8 (13); 42.1 (15); F = 1.16, n.s. High education: female reference person: 54.7 (50); 60.0 (9); 53.1 (9); F = .25, n.s.

49. "Whole" N = 112; "other" N = 86; df = 1 & 196; F = 0.9; n.s.

50. *Middle-class:* Like Father = 35.3; different = 60.4; neither = 47.0; N's = 11, 10, 15; df = 2 & 33; F = 3.82, p < .05. Like mother = 45.8; different = 59.0; neither = 46.1; N's = 25, 6, 6; df = 2 &

34; $F = .89$; n.s. Father as reference person $= 44.0$; other $= 60.4$; no one $= 36.7$; N's $= 25, 9, 4$; df $= 2$ & 35; $F = 2.48$; n.s. Mother as reference person $= 44.5$; other $= 62.0$; no one $= 54.2$; N's $= 30, 3, 5$; df $= 2$ & 35; $F = 1.1$; n.s. *Working-class:* (father) $= 41.7$; 46.9; 44.1; N $= 40, 57, 33$; df $= 2$ & 127; $F = 0.7$; n.s. (Mother) $= 45.9$; 47.0; 40.8; N $= 79, 51, 16$; df $= 2$ & 143; $F = 0.5$; n.s. (father) $= 43.8$; 44.3; 51.2; N $= 94, 37, 29$; df $= 2$ & 157; $F = 1.5$; n.s. (mother) $= 44.4$; 46.2; 49.5; N $= 113, 33, 14$; df $= 2$ & 157; $F = 0.4$; n.s. *Whole Background:* (father) $= 43.5, 44.3, 44.8$; N $= 30, 42, 33$; df $= 2$ & 102; $F = 0.0$, n.s. (Mother) $= 43.4$; 52.2; 38.0; N $= 70$; 25, 15; df $= 2$ & 107; $F = 2.57$; n.s. (father) $= 43.3$; 44.1; 50.6; N $= 77, 21, 14$; df $= 2$ & 109; $F = 0.7$; n.s. (mother) $= 43.4$; 47.4; 52.0; N $= 92, 15, 5$; df $= 2$ & 109; $F = 0.5$; n.s. *Other Background:* (father) $= 44.7$; 45.7; 45.5; N $= 21, 25, 15$; df $= 2$ & 58; $F = 0.0$; n.s. (Mother) $= 45.2$; 5.10; 42.0; N $= 34, 32, 13$; df $= 2$ & 76; $F = 1.1$; n.s. (father) $= 44.8$; 50.3; 48.6; N $= 42, 25, 19$; df $= 2$ & 83; $F = 0.6$; n.s. (mother) $= 46.2$; 47.6; 50.3; N $= 51, 21, 14$; df $= 2$ & 83; $F = 0.2$; n.s.

51. Low education: father-role model: like $= 24.4$ (30); different $= 33.0$ (38); neither $= 28.4$ (28); $F = .97$, n.s. High education: father-role model: 53.4 (10); 56.5 (20); 36.1 (12); $F = 1.9$, n.s. Low education: mother-role model: 27.0 (65); 34.8 (30); 21.7 (9); $F = 1.48$, n.s. High education: mother-role model: 51.5 (22); 59.8 (20); 29.0 (6); $F = 2.60$, N.S. Low education: male-reference person: father $= 26.8$ (69); other $= 37.7$ (25); no one $= 27.7$ (18); $F = 1.84$, n.s. High education: male-reference person: 47.5 (30); 57.2 (13); 42.1 (8); $F = 2.69$, N.S. Low Education: female-reference person: 28.0 (83); 39.3 (17); 25.0 (12); $F = 1.72$, n.s. High education: female-reference person: 50.1 (32); 53.5 (11); 55.5 (8); $F = .12$, n.s.

52. See Billingsley, *Black Families in White America*, pp. 79–87, where he argues that traditional superiority in educational and occupational achievements of the black female over the black male is diminishing in the urban north and west.

53. Lipset and Bendix, *Social Mobility*, p. 249.

54. Cited in *Manpower Report of the President*, U.S. Dept. of Labor, April 1968, p. 88; see also Theodore L. Cross, *Black Capitalism* (New York: Atheneum, 1969), pp. 22 ff.

55. Blau and Duncan, *The American Occupational Structure*, pp. 406–407.

56. A pattern of this type may partially account for the high rates of *downward* mobility discovered among Negro sons of white-collar fathers, in the data collected by Blau and Duncan, and reported by S. M. Miller, Martin

Rein, Pamela Roby, and Bertram M. Gross, "Poverty, Inequality, and Conflict," in Bertram M. Gross, ed., *Social Intelligence for America's Future* (Boston: Allyn and Bacon, Inc., 1969), pp. 315–16.

57. The discussion in the text is based on Albert J. Lott and Bernice E. Lott, *Negro and White Youth* (New York: Holt, Rinehart and Winston, 1963), pp. 132 ff.

58. Ibid., p. 134.

59. See S. M. Miller, Frank Riessman, Arthur A. Seagull, "A Critique of the Non-Deferred Gratification Pattern," in Louis A. Ferman, Joyce L. Kornbluh, Alan Haber, *Poverty in America* (Ann Arbor: The University of Michigan Press, 1965), pp. 285–301. They point out that gratifications can be deferred only if there is a reasonable certainty that "payoffs" will eventually be forthcoming. Blacks possess far less certainty of this than whites. Consequently, gratifications are that much more difficult to put off.

60. Joseph S. Himes, "Some Work-Related Cultural Deprivations of Lower-Class Negro Youths," *Journal of Marriage and the Family*, 26 (November 1964): 447–49.

61. Lipset and Bendix, *Social Mobility*.

6

Husband-Wife Relationships

This chapter is the focus of all that has gone before; but because it rests on the foregoing, it cannot stand alone. Full understanding of what goes on between husbands and wives requires knowledge of what occurred to them prior to marriage. Every conjugal family is part of an ongoing, cyclical or developmental process. Each partner brings to his (her) family of *procreation* the stream of events experienced in his background family of *orientation*. When these streams "merge" to form a new conjugal family, they contribute significantly to the "flow" of interaction within that unit. Among many American blacks, the "stream and flow" has been seriously hampered by economic deprivation. Up to this point, we have looked primarily at "streams." What about the resultant "flow" in the modern black family?

As far as occupation, education, and income are concerned it would appear that those blacks in the sample are fairly representative of the majority of urban blacks. This majority is found above the lower class and is made up of households with *both* spouses present. At the least what emerges in the sample regarding marital interaction ought to be regarded as hypotheses which might apply to this larger segment of black society as well. The majority of blacks in America have escaped (or are escaping) the "vicious cycle of poverty and disorganization" that many have referred to in describing lower-class family patterns. Likewise, most blacks seem to be adopting family forms of the dominant society. Although we shall have more to say about this question in Chapter 8, there is no indication whatsoever that American blacks are devising new or unique conjugal patterns to meet the particular exigencies of living in white America. On the contrary, other research suggests that while the matriarchate is indeed an adaptation for survival, it is not considered permanent nor desirable even by lower-class blacks.

To underscore the idea that some blacks are escaping the traditional "vicious cycle," we found that many in our sample had background advantages in terms of long-time urban residence and social-class position equal to or better than blacks in general. In trying to grasp the kinds of relationships these blacks as adolescents had with their parents, we followed Winch's ideas based on exchange theory. It seemed that most of their parents did provide ample resources to their children to enable them to fulfill economic and conjugal patterns held out to them by the dominant society. Then, in turn, we saw that most black youths do identify (either positively or negatively) with their parents. This identification then seemed to influence the degree of occupational achievement of the offspring. If occupational position is the single best indicator of social status, then it would appear that most blacks both in the sample and nationally have increased their status level compared to their parents. And, as in the dominant society, the father's occuppation was found to be a strong determinant of son's education which, in turn, was the most powerful determinant of the son's occupation.

The upshot is that most married blacks today seem to have greater objective economic and social resources *than their parents had*. The next step in examining the ongoing cycle of the black family is to discover how these resources influence husband-wife relationships. We shall continue to draw on exchange theory, although we shall now investigate husband-wife relations rather than parent-child relationships.

SOCIAL EXCHANGE AND
HUSBAND-WIFE INTERACTION

In another place we have spelled out in considerable detail the ways in which exchange theory applies to husband-wife relations.[1] Several notions are basic to this approach.

1. The economic-opportunity-structure, or the network of means and ends that results in achievement and success in American society, can also be thought of as a system of rewards or resources—both material (money) and nonmaterial (status, prestige, self-worth).

2. The conjugal family is linked to the opportunity structure through the occupation of the husband-father. He occupies a role in both systems. In the opportunity system he is a bricklayer, physician, truck-driver, or salesman, i.e., he is some sort of a *worker*. At the same time in the family, he occupies the role of *provider*, or "production-agent."

3. The conjugal family is, in American society, the basic unit of consumption. It is primarily through visible consumption patterns that status is assigned to a family by other members of the community. But consumption requires resources. These resources come chiefly via the occupant of the *provider* role, i.e., the husband.

4. Every role has both *duties* and *rights* that correspond to the rights and duties of a particular reciprocal role. In this case, the *right* of the occupant of the *wife* role to receive economic and status resources corresponds to the *duty* of the husband to meet these rights. *In exchange*, she is then obliged to provide her husband with expressive rewards and also, to some extent, deference to his authority, both of which correspond to his *rights* to receive them.

In sum, the relationship between husband and wife in modern society can be thought of in terms of a reciprocal exchange of role duties and rights. The more fully the husband fulfills his chief role obligations as *provider*, the more fully the wife is motivated to

fulfill her chief obligations as "expressive agent," or "socioemotional hub" of the conjugal family. The key to this ongoing series
of mutual (and basically nonconscious, nonrationally calculated)
exchange processes is the extent to which the husband carries out
his role as provider.

In white society, almost all available evidence shows the
greater the occupational status, or education, or income of the husband—

1. The more satisfactorily and positively do both spouses evaluate
   the expressive elements (primary relations) of ongoing marriage;
2. The lower the rates of marital dissolution.[2]

These propositions may be explained by thinking of occupational
status, education, and income as representing degrees of integration
with the opportunity structure. The *more* reward elements a male
provider has, the more integrated, or articulated he may be said
to be with the opportunity system. And the more articulated (the
more he is part of the opportunity structure), the more rewards he
provides to his wife (and children, usually via her), and the more
positively both spouses evaluate primary relations. Since both
spouses experience greater feelings of solidarity about their relationship, greater cohesion of the family as a social system exists, reduc-
ing the likelihood of marital dissolution.

Obviously many questions have not been touched on in this
brief summary. However, a fuller elaboration is available elsewhere,[3] and additional points will be clarified when we look at the
following data. The core question here is: To what extent does this
social exchange model apply to black as well as to white families?
We already know that numerous studies in the United States and
elsewhere in the hemisphere trace the dissolution of the lower-class
black family to "failure" of the male to function as provider. Therefore, because economic-status factors play such a crucial role in
families at all levels of white society and at the bottom of black
society, we would expect them to carry considerable weight too
among black families above the lower class.

HUSBAND-WIFE PRIMARY RELATIONS

The total gamut of husband-wife relationships can be divided into several broad areas. The first and perhaps most vital of these might be called "primary relations" or "expressive gratifications."[4] These are the kinds of behaviors played up so forcefully in the mass media. Although they are given so much attention, often only superficially, this does not diminish their importance. The fact remains that modern black and white Americans seek these kinds of expressive gratifications from marriage: someone to *do things* with (companionship); someone to love (physical affection); someone to talk to (empathy). These several aspects of husband-wife primary relations can also be labeled "affiliative," "cathectic," and "cognitive" gratifications, in that order. While in reality there is sometimes overlap between these kinds of behaviors, they are nevertheless distinct dimensions of marital primary relations and should not be confounded.

Companionship

Companionship has to do with shared leisure or nonworktime activities, e.g., movies, picnics, parties, dancing. Each respondent was asked to evaluate the companionship he (she) experienced with his (her) spouse.[5] Seventy-eight percent of males replied it was "very good," 21 percent said it was "ok," and only 1 percent said it was "not so good." But wives were not quite as satisfied with their companionship. Only 50 percent replied in the most affirmative fashion, while 32 percent said it was merely "ok," and 18 percent indicated "not so good."[6] In short, while black husbands feel they spend "enough" time with their wives, and that this time is "worthwhile," black wives tend to see things quite differently.

Significantly, the same contrast emerged in a study of whites within the dominant society.[7] Wives in general—black or white— are considerably less euphoric than husbands (black or white) over the expressive gratifications they experience in marriage. *Why* this might be so will be considered shortly. The point is that this represents an additional convergence between the dominant white family and the more advantaged black family. Moreover, for blacks (as for whites) the same kind of contrast in husband-wife perceptions appears when we look at the remaining aspects of primary relations.

Physical Affection

Cathectic interaction has to do with feelings and emotions pertaining to the physical aspects of marriage. These may range from the most innocent to the most intimate demonstrations of affection. When asked to evaluate these kinds of behaviors, 77 percent of husbands replied "very good," whereas only 60 percent of wives replied this positively.[8] Twenty percent of husbands, and 30 percent of wives said it was "ok," and only 3 percent of husbands indicated it was "not so good," compared with 10 percent of wives who were this negative.

Empathy

Empathy, or "communication and understanding" is the third highly valued expressive goal sought after in modern marriage. Empathy can be defined as "the intellectual identification with or vicarious experiencing of the feelings, thoughts, or attitudes of another." Communication is essential to empathy. We measured communication by asking respondents to evaluate how they felt they could "confide, talk things over, discuss anything" with their spouse.[9] When "channels of communication" are open (whether between husband-wife, parent-child, university administration-students), the sender feels few inhibitions in "transmitting" any message he so desires. And the reason he feels free to "transmit" or communicate is because he perceives that the "other" readily "receives" or understands what he is trying to say. So empathy is a two-way street consisting of mutually interdependent processes of communication *and* understanding—sending *and* receiving verbal messages.

In response to the question on communication, 74, 21, and 5 percent of husbands, respectively, said "very good," "ok," "not so good." For wives the responses were 55, 26 and 19 percent, respectively.[10] When we asked them to evaluate the *understanding* half of the process, husbands reported 77, 18, and 5 percent, respectively. In contrast, wives reported 49, 33, and 18 percent, respectively.[11] Thus the pattern is consistent over all three forms of husband-wife primary interaction among blacks above the lowest stratum: *husbands perceive these gratifications in more positive terms than wives.*

One reason this generalization holds for white families is that the wife plays the role of the "socioemotional hub," or "expressive leader" of the conjugal family.[12] It would appear that she does the same within the black family. Women (black and white) are socialized (as girls) to focus on marriage as their central life-interest, and especially on its expressive components. Hence, they grow up expecting far more of these kinds of gratifications from marriage than do males. Expecting more than males it takes more to satisfy them.

To be sure, males also desire these kinds of goals from marriage, but their central life-interest is not as much the family as the sphere of production, i.e., the job. Given this dichotomy of interests, they tend to be less absorbed by and thus more easily satisfied with what they define as "reasonable" amounts of expressive conjugal behaviors. But for wives, the conjugal sphere still evidently remains their central focus or interest. Hence, they are more absorbed by and demand more of these kinds of behaviors. In short, the husband and wife from the *same* marriage might *define* their identical situation in different terms. He might perceive it quite positively; she, far less so. And it is how one *defines* a situation that actually matters to *him*, not at all how *someone else* may perceive it.

That this kind of "role specialization" appears true for blacks as well as whites is particularly significant given the long history of black female employment and her extensive activity in the production of family resources. However, in Chapter 3 we found no indication that females in the sample had been socialized to fulfill the role of provider. Instead, we saw that they were being influenced more or less toward the "traditional wife-role" as conceived of in our society. There was no explicit preparation, in short, to play anything but her prime role as expressive leader within the family.

This result implies that since someone must play the role of provider, black females expect their husbands to do so. There would appear to be, in short, the same basic role specialization in black families (above the lower class) as found in white families. In this regard, therefore, the long history of "forced" female employment has not fundamentally altered black family structure in a direction diametrically opposite dominant patterns. Where she assumed the role of provider, it was because she had to, not because she necessarily wanted to.

This is obviously the situation among whites as well. Irrespective then of historic exigencies impinging on the black female, she basically desires to play the same role in the family as the white female. In this role as "socioemotional hub," American wives come to expect maximum amounts of expressive gratifications. But precisely because these expectations are so very high, they are almost impossible of complete fulfillment. The result is that wives in general (black or white) evaluate these gratifications less positively than husbands, who usually expect and are satisfied with less.

Social Position and
Primary Relations

Having established these several major convergences between white and black family patterns, we consider next the matter of *variations* in levels of expressing gratifications. We recall that within white family structure, expressive satisfactions vary directly with the social status of the husband. To what extent does this generalization likewise hold for blacks?

To try to answer this question, let us look first at three widely used indicators of social position (or integration with the opportunity system): occupational status, education, income. It became clear in Chapter 5 that the majority of black families in America have experienced considerable gains over their parents in all three areas. Nonetheless, Pettigrew argues that these gains are accompanied by what he calls "psychological losses."

. . . the frame of reference for many Negro Americans has shifted during the past few decades. . . . formerly most Negroes judged how well off they were by their own previous conditions, [now] the rising expectations of the present are increasingly framed in terms of the wider [white] society.[13]

As we saw in Chapter 5, though the majority of blacks possess more rewards from the opportunity structure than ever before, they still lag far behind compared to whites at the same educational level. And whites have evidently become a *major reference group* for aspiring blacks. The results, according to Pettigrew, are extremely intense feelings of relative deprivation on the part of blacks. Their aspirations, once temperate vis-a-vis whites, are now virtually the same. But what they actually possess relative to whites remains severely limited. These painful and powerful feelings of relative deprivation are the "fundamental basis of mass Negro dissatisfaction today . . . [they are] the stuff out of which revolutions are made."[14]

It may very well be that this notion of relative deprivation is the basis for the results that appear in Table 6–1. For there we do not find what almost always appears in studies of white families. Increases in occupational status, education, and income among blacks do not correspond with increases in positive evaluation of (satisfaction with) husband-wife primary relations. (To measure satisfaction with primary relations, we have taken the four items discussed above and combined them into a single index. The mean scores in Table 6–1 represent joint degree of satisfaction with companionship, physical affect, and empathy: the higher the score the more positive the evaluation.)[15]

TABLE 6–1.   OBJECTIVE ARTICULATION WITH THE OPPORTUNITY SYSTEM
AND SATISFACTION WITH PRIMARY RELATIONS

		Husband Evaluation of Expressiveness (mean scores)	Wife Evaluation of Expressiveness (mean scores)
Husband's	Low	18.1 (66)	15.8 (63)
Occupational	Medium	18.3 (67)	15.3 (68)
Ranking	High	17.3 (65)	15.6 (67)
		(df = 2 & 195, n.s. F = 2.3)	(df = 2 & 195, n.s. F = .17)
Education of	0–8	18.0 (87)	15.9 (65)
Respondent	9–11	17.9 (43)	15.4 (65)
(in years	12	18.3 (36)	14.8 (52)
completed)	13 +	17.2 (32)	16.6 (20)
		(df = 3 & 194, n.s. F = .83)	(df = 3 & 198, n.s. F = 1.1)
Family	$0–3 (poor)	18.4 (41)	16.4 (48)
Income	4–6 (fair)	17.6 (49)	14.5 (55)
(in thousands	7–9 (good)	18.2 (52)	16.3 (53)
of dollars)	10 + (high)	17.4 (35)	15.0 (36)
		(df = 3 & 173, n.s. F = .94)	(df = 3 & 188, F = 3.1; p < .05)

Consider first the occupational ranking of the husband.[16] Husbands who hold "low" and "medium" status jobs actually evaluate expressive relations with their wives somewhat higher than do husbands with "high" status jobs. Likewise, husbands who have merely a grade-school education feel their primary relations are slightly more satisfactory than husbands who have gone *beyond* high school (some in this category having completed college). Finally, husbands with family incomes of $3,000 or less evaluate expressiveness somewhat more positively than husbands whose family incomes are $10,000 or more. However, in none of the three dimensions are the mean differences statistically significant, which suggests the following basic conclusion. Among black husbands, neither differences in occupational status, education, nor income *meaningfully* influence their satisfactions with the expressive components of marriage.

The same conclusion applies to black wives as well. Insofar as their husbands' occupational status or their own education are concerned, differences in their evaluation of primary relations are very slight. When it comes to family income, differences are larger and significant, however the pattern is cloudy since wives with "high" incomes rank below those with "good" and "poor" incomes. As we saw earlier, exchange theory supplies an explanation for the linkage (among white families) between these three elements and expressiveness. In his role as provider, the husband supplies "rewards" to his wife in the form of material and nonmaterial (prestige, status) benefits. The more the rewards, the more positively she responds on the expressive level, and the more positively he feels rewarded at that level. He in turn, also responds more positively to her at the expressive level, and what is generated is a series of ongoing, mutually reinforcing and reciprocal processes that serve to bind the married pair.

But among black families, these "objective" rewards ("objective" in the sense that occupational status, years of education, and dollars, exist more independently and "out there" than certain other kinds of "subjective" rewards discussed below) fail to generate these ongoing processes of reciprocity and exchange. It may be that the reason for this situation is the intense strain of *relative deprivation* that Pettigrew (and others) claim exists among blacks at all status levels. If the information supplied by Blau and Duncan is any indication, the higher the status of blacks, the greater the feelings of relative deprivation.[17] This conclusion may account for indications in Table 6–1 that higher status blacks are no more satisfied expressively than blacks with less status.

For example, the higher status black wife may receive more absolute objective rewards from her husband than the lower status black wife. But instead of being therefore situationally motivated to respond more positively to him in "gratitude and rectitude,"[18] the element of relative deprivation—not compared to other black wives, but compared to *white* wives at the same social position—intervenes to influence the process. It must be strongly emphasized that processes involved in social exchange need be neither rational nor conscious. As Merton remarks:

. . . exchange is (not) necessarily the result of an explicit utilitarian calculus in which the contractants deliberately weigh the economic and social returns to be gained. . . . the event may be experienced by them as simply an affectional relationship, but this psychic reaction is manifestly structured by the social organization.[19]

There is no more "rational calculus" here than in Chapter 5 when we looked at processes of parental rejection in occupational achievement. It is simply that by denying equal benefits (either monetarily or in terms of worth and respect) to blacks who have "achieved" the same position as whites, white society engenders feeling amongst blacks of being relatively deprived. These socially structured feelings may act to prevent the kind of positive response by black wives to their husbands, in return for objective rewards, that white wives emit to theirs. Higher status white wives use other white wives as a reference group and consequently feel relatively satisfied with husbands' objective rewards. But since higher status black wives probably also use white wives as a reference group, it may be exceedingly difficult for the black wives to view their husbands' objective rewards in the same manner.

Black wives do not consciously "blame" their husbands for fewer tangible or intangible rewards, since most are undoubtedly aware that white control of the opportunity structure is at the root of their deprivation. Yet they have apparently adopted the dominant conjugal pattern in which the husband is the one who mediates rewards from the opportunity system into the family. Since the wife cannot react directly to the "system," she must react in some fashion to her husband, the "occupant" of the provider role. And her reaction is structured in such a way that generally she responds no more positively to him than black wives with fewer absolute rewards.

To the degree this reasoning is valid, it represents a fundamental difference with white family structure and deserves careful attention. Turner remarks that ". . . pride and self-respect rather than economic opportunity constitute the problem of today's middle-class Negroes. . . ."[20] Billingsley, in referring to middle- and upper-income black families, asserts that "money has not given them the sense of mastery over the conditions of their life *that is available to white families of similar economic status*"[21] (Italics supplied.)

Hence, Billingsley too underscores blacks' feelings of relative deprivation. Blacks at the same social level as whites receive fewer actual dollars, as well as less admiration, status, respect, prestige, etc. This insight regarding limited pride and self-respect can be traced back at least as far as the fifties—to Frazier's comments on the black bourgeoisie.[22] Just how blacks go about gaining both comparable dollars (for Turner's point is most salient in conjunction with equal dollars) *and* a sense of worth comparable to that ascribed to whites for similar achievements is currently a matter of great public debate.[23] This volume adds to the controversy insofar as it suggests consequences of this deprivation for black family structure above the underclass.

The major implication is that this relative deprivation weakens the bond of marital cohesiveness among blacks—even those with higher social status. Udry for instance, in an extensive analysis of 1960 census data, concludes that although status and divorce are inversely related among blacks as among whites, blacks have higher divorce rates than whites at comparable status levels. In an even more extensive and detailed analysis of 1960 census data, Bernard arrives at similar conclusions.[24] Although higher status black families have escaped the great rates of divorce and desertion that characterize the lower class, nonetheless they exceed the rates for whites at similar occupational and educational positions. In his earlier works on the black family, Frazier saw economic advances as the key to its greater stability. In a very real sense this has proved to be true. But once again because of white cupidity, his prediction is limited to advances *within* the scope of the black community per se. Because middle-class black families are denied the dollars, prestige and respect accorded middle-class whites, feelings of solidarity and cohesion are less, and the probability of dissolution higher.

Economic Alienation
and Primary Relations

Nevertheless, all the families in the sample are currently stable, as are the majority of black families in urban America. Most black husbands in American society are present and functioning in the role of provider. They may not be able to supply *objective* reward levels equal to those of whites, but the three "objective" elements discussed above by no means exhaust the range of rewards that husbands may supply their wives. Elsewhere, it was pointed out that there are certain *subjective* rewards that may be equally, if perhaps not more, important than objective factors.[25] These rewards consist of feeling-states or attitudes toward the opportunity structure. One of these is a feeling of alienation from this economic system.

Although the term "alienation" has often been used loosely and carelessly, we have employed it as a general construct, defined carefully (a feeling of separation, gulf, distance, or separatedness) and consisting of several very specific dimensions each of which can be measured independently. It may be argued that in our society it is the husband's duty to "provide" reduced feelings of alienation from the economic opportunity system. Within the dominant white society it has been shown that to the degree husbands reward their wives by allaying feelings of economic alienation, wives tend to respond more positively on the expressive level.[26] In other words, given that expressive gratifications are a major goal of the modern conjugal unit, these gratifications may be generated not only by *objective* rewards that the husband mediates into the family, but also by *subjective* rewards.

Job Satisfaction. Discontent with husband's fulltime job is one important dimension of alienation from the opportunity structure. Respondents were asked how satisfied they were with their own (their husbands') "job overall, i.e., with the security, chances for advancement, and money." These three items cover the most crucial tangible and intangible aspects of the husband's job. Satisfaction or contentment with these items (hence, with the job) represent *feelings of articulation or integration* with the opportunity structure, in the same sense that differences in occupational rank, education, and income represent *actual* articulation.

In Table 6–2 we find that the greater the discontent with husband's job, the less the satisfaction with husband-wife primary relations. This finding is true for both husbands and especially wives; and as job satisfaction or *contentment* increases, so does the level of expressive gratifications. This is a significant convergence with what we know about white family structure. For in terms of social exchange we may say that by providing feelings of job contentment, the husband (black or white) is rewarded by increased expressiveness gratifications that lead him to reciprocate in kind, and so the process continues, thus contributing to marital cohesion.

It is readily apparent that reduced feelings of economic alienation supply a kind of "antidote" to relative deprivation with respect to the three objective elements discussed above. The black person (above the lower class) may in fact feel deprived compared to whites, yet *simultaneously* feel "very" or "fairly" "satisfied" with

TABLE 6–2. DISCONTENT WITH HUSBAND'S JOB AND SATISFACTION WITH PRIMARY RELATIONS

		Husband Evaluation of Expressiveness (*mean scores*)	Wife Evaluation of Expressiveness (*mean scores*)
Satisfaction with husband's job	Very satisfied	18.6 (109)	16.8 (107)
	Fairly satisfied	17.6 (70)	14.4 (74)
	Dissatisfied	16.9 (19)	13.5 (19)
		(df = 2 & 195, F = 8.28; p < .001)	(df = 2 & 197, F = 11.11; p < .001)

several basic reward elements of his (her husband's) fulltime job. (We note, for instance, from Table 6–2 that only about 10 percent of the sample report they are actually "dissatisfied" with job rewards.) And the reason for this seeming paradox may lie with the reference group used by blacks to assess elements of *job satisfaction* (money, security, advancement).

It may very well be that when it comes to job prestige, and education or income levels, blacks do compare themselves to the white community and feel severely deprived. Blacks learn early in life that these particular elements are all products and offshoots of white society. They were created and are controlled by whites, and often, chiefly for whites. It is little wonder then that blacks aspiring to these dominant goals within the white opportunity structure must inevitably feel relatively deprived and denied of just rewards. At this point, the notion of *multiple* reference groups becomes useful. Hyman and Singer remark:

In forming their total constellation of attitudes, several reference groups may be employed, each accorded a limited jurisdiction over some specialized attitude sphere. . . . multiple reference groups impinge simultaneously on the same sphere of comparison or the same realm of attitude, and then they may either reinforce the same outcome or produce conflicting consequences for the individual.[27]

As applied here it may be that, on the one hand, blacks use whites for comparison of "objective" elements directly related to the production of resources (money, education, status). On the other hand, they may use other blacks for comparison of subjective factors related to the consumption of resources.

To most segments of the population below the white, "career-oriented," upper middle-class, job satisfaction rests precisely on the factors of money, security, and advancement (usually thought of in terms of better pay). The white upper middle-class is free to focus on innate or intrinsic job fulfillment, primarily because these three "baser elements" are already met. *And these elements are important precisely because they can be readily translated into "conspicuous consumption" symbols.* In American society, tangible symbols are used to assign status, and also as indicators of the "worth" or "goodness" of the individual. Black Americans (like whites) are socialized to assess their own self-worth on the basis of how they perceive they are viewed by others. Their own sense of worth is thus heightened if they perceive that others view them positively in connection with certain symbols of achievement and success. In this regard, research into consumption patterns of blacks shows that there exists a "Negro market" within a distinct black subculture.[28]

Once again, because whites have structured it that way, blacks buy and display consumption symbols almost exclusively for other blacks. At times they may adapt certain kinds of white patterns currently in vogue simply because there are no others around. Still, their consumption patterns, like black religion and black art and music, are unique and distinctive because they represent areas where white society—after having excluded blacks—permitted them to evolve unmolested within these sealed-off perimeters. Moreover *de facto* segregation in housing (as well as in most voluntary associations) forces most blacks to interact almost exclusively with other blacks during nonwork time—precisely those periods when material symbols function to accord status and worth.

In short, because they have been "forced" to do it, most blacks probably use other blacks as their "consumption reference group." And unlike comparisons with whites, in which blacks almost always see themselves "second best," when blacks compare themselves to other blacks, they may sometimes see themselves as relatively more advantaged.[29] Hence, when blacks use other blacks as a reference group for job rewards that are translatable into consumption symbols, many can say they are "very" or "fairly" satisfied. It is not likely they could make this assessment if they were using whites as a basis for comparison. This view is further supported by Tables 6–3, 6–4, and 6–5.

Status-Estrangement. Table 6–3, for instance, presents another dimension of opportunity alienation, *status-estrangement,* in which the respondent identifies the social class he himself thinks he belongs in.[30] In the table "high" social class means the respondent placed himself (herself) in either the upper class or upper middle-

TABLE 6–3. STATUS-ESTRANGEMENT AND SATISFACTION WITH PRIMARY RELATIONS

Social class in which respondent places himself		Husband Evaluation of Expressiveness (mean scores)	Wife Evaluation of Expressiveness (mean scores)
	High	18.6 (61)	17.2 (53)
	Medium	17.8 (23)	15.0 (28)
	Low	17.6 (112)	14.8 (121)
		(df = 2 & 193; F = 2.3, n.s.)	(df = 2 & 199; F = 6.0; p < .01)

TABLE 6–4. SATISFACTION WITH FAMILY LIVING STANDARD AND PRIMARY RELATIONS

Satisfaction with family life-style		Husband Evaluation of Expressiveness (mean scores)	Wife Evaluation of Expressiveness (mean scores)
	Very satisfied	18.5 (76)	17.4 (71)
	Fairly satisfied	17.6 (92)	15.1 (94)
	Dissatisfied	17.5 (30)	12.9 (37)
		(df = 2 & 195, F = 2.5, n.s.)	(df = 2 & 199, F = 18.2; p < .001)

class. If he replied "lower-middle" he was put in the "medium" category. "Low" means he placed himself in either the working or lower classes.

Those in the "high" grouping may be described as sensing less status-estrangement than those in the "medium" grouping who, in turn, perceive less status-estrangement than those in the "low" category. Thus the higher the class self-placement, the less the sense

TABLE 6–5. FUTURE SUCCESS EXPECTATIONS AND SATISFACTION WITH PRIMARY RELATIONS

How good are your chances to reach your success goals?		Husband Evaluation of Expressiveness (mean scores)	Wife Evaluation of Expressiveness (mean scores)
	Excellent	18.3 (36)	17.4 (31)
	Good	18.1 (56)	15.3 (67)
	Fair	17.1 (40)	15.1 (59)
	Poor	18.1 (14)	13.5 (23)
		(df = 3 & 142; F = 1.3; n.s.)	(df = 3 & 176; F = 4.4; p < .01)

of status-estrangement. This condition is because social class is generally signified to others by the display of tangible symbols. Thus the higher the class one places himself in, the more of these symbols he likely perceives himself to possess. The more of these symbols he possesses, the less he may be said to feel estranged form the status order of society. Conversely, the fewer of these symbols possessed, the more likely it is that he feels estranged from this same status order. Display of visible success symbols represents an important goal which is part of what it means to be part of or integrated with the opportunity structure. And as was the case with *discontent*, it is the husband's "duty" to his wife to allay these feelings of status-estrangement, through provision of status symbols.

Within white society, it appears that the more of this kind of reward the husband provides his wife, the more positively both spouses evaluate marital primary relations.[31] From Table 6–3, we learn that this same pattern emerges strongly for black wives, but only weakly for black husbands. We may conclude, therefore, that the higher the social class the black wife places herself in, the more satisfied she is with marital expressiveness.

Especially in black families, but also in white society, the wife plays the role of "chief consumption agent." In this role, she receives resources from her husband and translates them into certain consumption symbols that will accord status to herself, her children, and her family in the eyes of the particular neighborhood or social network of which she is a part. This emphasis on family life-style by the female is part of the overall syndrome in which she is also the "expressive leader" of the family. In short, the family unit is her chief milieu, both in its expressive and consumptive aspects. For the black wife, this micro-milieu exists within her larger milieu of other blacks—"significant others," neighbors, friends, kin—who constitute a reference group to assess her worth and assign her respect based on visible consumption symbols.

To the extent this analysis is correct, the wife who defines her husband as providing the kinds of symbols that enable her to rank herself at a higher class level, will respond to him with greater gratitude and rectitude. This is not to suggest that the husband (black or white) does not consume, for he obviously does. But the meaning of family consumption is not the same to both sexes in American society.[32] For men, consumption is a "byproduct" (inevitable and desired) of the status he achieves in the occupational sphere. His focus must be chiefly on the latter if the former is to be meaningfully carried out. Therefore, it is his occupational achievement that is probably the ultimate source of his sense of worth. But to the wife, it is the "byproduct" of her husband's efforts that accords her status and worth in the eyes of her social network. It is this, therefore, with which she is primarily concerned.

Life-Style Evaluation. Another way we probed the same issue was to ask respondents how they felt about their "family's standard of living—the kind of house, clothing, car, opportunities for the children and so on."[33] From Table 6–4, we learn that for *wives* there is a very strong relationship between family life-style (living standard) and marital expressiveness, i.e., the more satisfied with consumption patterns, the more satisfied with expressiveness, and vice versa. For husbands, consumption satisfaction is less related to marital expressiveness. The life-style of a family is exhibited within the scope of its own neighborhood and social network. For black families, this situation almost always means exclusive contact and comparison with other black families. The wife, as chief consumption agent, is thus usually more involved than her husband in display of family life-style. Her status and sense of worth are almost totally dependent on the factors that make it up.

Therefore, the more her husband can provide resources that enable her to maintain a life-style with which she is satisfied, the more positively she rewards him on the expressive level, and in turn defines herself as so rewarded. And the comparison to determine life-style satisfaction is not made with whites, for if that were done there would inevitably be little satisfaction due to ongoing relative deprivation. More likely, the comparison is made with blacks against whom more realistic comparison is possible.

Success Expectations. Discontent, status-estrangement, and life-style satisfaction all represent feelings of present alienation i.e., *currently* being "cut off" from the opportunity system. But what about *future* economic prospects in a society that is essentially future-oriented? In white society, it was found that the more promising the future economic prospects, the more positively husbands and wives evaluate marital expressiveness.[34]

To discover these same notions within black families, we assumed that these blacks had certain *aspirations* for "success" (usually defined in American society by means of tangible symbols). We then determined how strongly they actually *expect* these future goals to be attained.[35] The more strongly they expected these goals to be realized, the less of a *gap* may be said to exist between their future aspirations and expectations. This kind of gap can also be described as a sense of alienation. In Table 6–5, we see that the *less* the alienation (the smaller the gap between aspiration and expectations of future success goals), the *more* positively black wives evaluate marital expressiveness. For black husbands, once again, little if any relationship appears.

Black wives, like white wives, define feelings of expected future benefits from the opportunity structure as a reward which is the husband's "duty" to provide. The more of this reward he provides, the more positively she responds at the expressive level, and likewise defines her husband to respond to her. And as with prior alienation dimensions, her comparison level or reference group for future success goals is almost certainly found among other blacks, rather than among whites. Although there is strong convergence between black and white *wives* over the impact of subjective opportunity articulation on marital expressiveness, it is not totally clear why black *husbands* do not approximate white husbands over most of these patterns.

One reason may lie in what we saw earlier, i.e., the great majority of husbands in the sample seem in general to evaluate the several aspects of marital primary relations very positively. Given this uniformity of responses by almost all these males, it is difficult to find many variables that might discriminate in degrees of positive expressiveness. A second and more significant reason may lie in the matter of choice of reference group. Because the role of wife results in a greater focus on family consumption and its meaning, her reference group in this regard tends to be other black families and their consumption patterns. So while the black wife uses whites as a reference group to compare absolute *objective* rewards such as occupational prestige, education and income, she also uses blacks to compare relative *subjective* rewards and their meanings and implications for consumption behavior.

But it may be that black husbands do not dichotomize their choice of reference groups quite so readily.[36] Instead, because (in the role of provider) they have more extensive and intensive contact with the white-controlled occupational system, they may be more likely than wives to use whites as a reference group in both objective *and* subjective senses. (The only exception to this situation is "satisfaction with job rewards" in which they evidently do use other black males as a reference group.) If so, they are more prone to experience a greater overall breadth of relative deprivation than their wives. Black husbands at all status levels may feel they are providing "inadequate" economic rewards to their wives when compared to whites. Whether or not their perceptions are accurate, they may define their wives to feel the same way.

Consequently, regardless of the objective or subjective reward levels provided, these rewards do not (except for job satisfaction, Table 6–2) systematically generate greater male satisfaction with expressiveness. Since the comparison is evidently chiefly with whites, the black male is consistently forced to think of himself as "behind," or "deprived." If he perceives his wife to feel likewise, then the possibility of meaningful social exchange is limited. The structural situation of the *white* husband often permits him to *think of himself* as a *good provider* compared to at least certain other whites. His attainments, moreover, give him a sense of "self-respect" that he perceives his wife shares. This situation permits meaningful exchange between his economic rewards and her expressive rectitude and gratitude.

In contrast, the job situation of the black husband limits how well he can think of himself—and how positively he thinks his wife feels about him—as a "good provider." Whether consciously or not, he may rarely perceive that greater absolute resources earn him greater respect or positive expressiveness. The result is that from the standpoint of some black husbands, there is little if any bargaining or exchange between the economic and expressive dimensions of marriage.

The validity of this kind of perspective is reinforced by the findings of a recent study in which the authors were investigating the "family role performance" of black males. They suggest:

that those Negro males who perceive themselves as relative failures, i.e., low achievers, with little hope of success, are also more prone to feel that they are failing in their family role performance. . . . The problems encountered by the Negro male in the areas of employment, housing, and general social discrimination result in feelings of failure and inadequacy and an inability to perform his family role adequately.[37]

Wife Definitions
and Family Cohesion

Nevertheless, as perceived and defined by the black wife (above the underclass) certain meaningful processes of economic-expressive exchange may be occurring. And it has been argued that how the wife (white or black) defines the total marital situation may be more crucial to cohesion and stability than how the husband perceives it.[38] Historically and traditionally, marriage has meant an abundance of rights for the husband, and a plethora of duties for the wife. A most significant change in family structure over the last century has been one in which women have gained rights and privileges at the expense of men.[39] Nonetheless, Goode maintains, and is probably correct, that in the "ancient struggle" between the sexes, men remain a kind of "ruling status group."[40] As such, they are more likely than women to be content with the marital *status quo*. We saw evidence of this earlier when we compared husbands and wives over satisfaction with aspects of marital expressiveness. Being more content, males are thus less apt to push for change in existing patterns. It is wives who seek for greater rights for themselves and greater satisfaction of these rights by husbands.

Hence, black wives (and white wives) expect their husbands to meet their economic rights (in terms of status and consumption) as well as their expressive rights. We have seen that the more the wife defines her husband as meeting her economic rights, the more she defines him as meeting her expressive rights. Since both types of gratifications represent twin (and vital) goals of modern marriage, we may suggest that *the cohesion of the black conjugal unit rests strongly on the wife's subjective sense of articulation* with, or feeling a part of, the opportunity structure. We have seen that "objective" rewards do not generate systematic increases in marital expressiveness and that this probably contributes to the greater dissolution among higher status blacks when compared to whites. Thus, the burden of cohesion falls almost totally on the subjective definition of the family's economic situation—and chiefly the wife's at that. For the wife, in general, seems to be the key to family cohesion in American society. And within the black family, what seems to matter is *her* definition of the family's consumption potential in comparison to other blacks.

In this same regard, it is helpful to try to follow some "causal paths" between "objective" rewards, feelings of alienation, and feelings of expressiveness. First we combine the four indicators of alienation into a single index.[41] Table 6–6 shows that for husbands none of the four "objective" factors listed has any direct path of influence (p, or Beta weight) on their feelings of economic alienation. For wives, on the other hand, family income is the single most powerful predictor (followed by husband's education) of her sense of integration with the opportunity structure: as income (and his education) decreases, the wife's sense of alienation appears to rise; as income (and his education) increases, her alienation decreases. In Table 6–7, columns 1 and 2, we find that alienation does have a certain amount of influence on male feelings of expressiveness, but that number of years married is a slightly better predictor.[42] For wives, however, as expected, alienation has a very marked impact

TABLE 6–6. INFLUENCE OF OBJECTIVE INDICATORS OF SOCIAL POSITION ON INDEX OF ECONOMIC ALIENATION

	Husbands		Wives	
	p	r	p	r
Husband's Job Status	− .037	.43	− .065	.16
Respondent's Education	− .005	.22	.074	.27
Spouse Education	.000	.21	− .110	.35
Family Income	.004	− .04	− .348	− .15
R^2	.04		.35	
N	(139)		(164)	

TABLE 6-7. PATHS OF INFLUENCE (p) ON ELEMENTS OF HUSBAND-WIFE INTERACTION

	Primary Relations		Hostility		Authority Participation		Fertility		Spouse's Consumption Rationality	
	Hu	Wi	Hu	Wi	Hu	Wi	Hu	Wi	Hu	Wi
Economic Alienation	-.128	-.436	.126	.280	-.062	-.032	.203	.293	-.057	-.181
Husband's Job Status	.078	.08	.031	-.075	.057	-.091	.076	-.064	.093	.123
Respondent's Education	.011	.06	.057	.043	.012	-.034	-.092	-.090	.057	-.034
Spouse Education	.005	.00	-.067	.083	.028	-.147	-.125	-.071	.026	.064
Family Income	.025	.04	.073	.041	.227	.129	.073	.115	.006	.062
Wife Employment	.106	-.023	.155	.044	-.083	.138	-.184	-.161	.020	.010
Length of Marriage	.143	-.043	.068	.093	-.120	.027	.187	.185	.027	.096
R^2	.28	.42	.27	.36	.33	.26	.33	.36	.12	.31
N	(136)	(163)	(135)	(162)	(127)	(154)	(136)	(163)	(136)	(162)

on expressive satisfactions, or primary relations. Its influence is by far greater than *any* other single factor.

These additional data underscore the critical nature (for conjugal cohesion) of the wife's "definition of her family situation." The family is her main focus in life. The more objective rewards (specifically, income) her husband "funnels" into the family, the more allayed are her feelings of economic alienation; and the more these feelings are reduced, the more positively she evaluates primary interaction with her husband. For black husbands, though there is some influence of alienation on expressiveness, the sources of male alienation are less clear, owing probably to systematic discrimination. Nevertheless, precisely because the family is generally less his central life interest than hers, his evaluation of family processes is probably less critical to their maintenance than is hers.

Comparison Levels
and Family Cohesion

Thibaut and Kelley employ the term "comparison level" (CL) to describe the standard against which a person (in this instance, the black wife) evaluates the attractiveness (of the rewards) of an exchange-type relationship.[43] This construct is akin to the notion of reference group. But they carry their idea a step further through what they call "comparison level for alternatives" (CL alt.). This idea "represents the reference point employed in deciding whether or not to remain in the interaction. . . . it can be looked at as the lowest level of reward which the individual will accept in order to continue in the relationship."[44] Applied to the family, it can be said that most often wives (though husbands also) define a certain level of rewards (economic and/or expressive) as "too low" and "want out" of the marriage. Although the notion of *Cl alt.* is obviously a slippery one, we do have some indication of the extent to which respondents "wanted out" of their current marriage.

Each respondent was asked, "In all the time you have been married to your (husband-wife), have you ever thought of the possibility of separation or divorce?"[45] Only 21 percent of husbands replied "yes," 79 percent said "no." But among wives, 41 percent had considered these alternatives and only 59 percent had not.[46] These strongly significant differences underscore the point that black wives are much more likely than black husbands to have at least thought about ending their marriages, to be less content with existing conditions.

Without following these marriages over a period of years, we cannot be certain how many (if any) will actually experience separation or divorce. But given differences between the sexes in attitudes toward dissolution of their marriages, we would expect that actual dissolution would occur more often due to wife's rather than husband's agitation. We do in fact have some indication for this in that we asked those who had ever *thought* about dissolution if they had "ever been separated" from their spouse. We then inquired of these particular persons whether "either you or your spouse had ever filed a suit for legal separation or divorce." Among husbands responding *yes* to this last question, 86 percent indicated it was their wives who had done the actual filing, while 88 percent of wives admitted the same thing.[47] In all these cases, of course, the suit was eventually dropped and the couple went on living together.

In any event, the initial question probing whether they had considered separation or divorce does measure *feelings of solidarity* between husbands and wives. Those who ever "wanted out" presumably feel or at least felt less solidarity toward their marriages than those who never considered such a possibility. And to the degree that individuals in a social system perceive feelings of solidarity, to that extent is the system cohesive. And the more cohesive the system, the greater is the likelihood of its stability, its maintenance. Conversely, where solidarity is less (i.e., the person has considered "getting out") cohesion and stability are more problematic.

For example, if Thibaut and Kelley are correct in asserting that people "want out" of a relationship when rewards become "too low," then we should expect to find that blacks who have considered separation or divorce experience fewer expressive rewards in their marriages than those who have *not* considered dissolution. From Table 6–8, we learn that this is indeed the case. Using the same

TABLE 6–8. SOLIDARITY FEELINGS AND SATISFACTION WITH PRIMARY RELATIONS

		Husband Expressiveness (mean scores)	Wife Expressiveness (mean scores)
Have you ever considered separation or divorce?	Yes	16.5 (41)	13.6 (82)
	No	18.3 (156)	16.9 (120)
		(df = 1 & 195; F = 12.5; p < .001)	(df = 1 & 200; F = 37.2; p < .001)

index of expressive gratifications described previously, we see that those who replied "yes," they had "considered" ending their marriages, score significantly lower in expressiveness than those who had replied "no." In other words, the less satisfied black wives (and husbands) feel about the kind of primary relations experienced with their spouses, the more likely they are to consider ending their marriages. Conversely, a more positive evaluation of primary relations (as rewards) is associated with a desire to maintain the relationship.

Yet we also know that the more positively wives *define* their economic situation, the more satisfied they are with expressive gratifications. So that black (and white) wives who are most satisfied with *both* types of rewards are the ones most likely to want to maintain their rewarding relationships. Conversely, those least satisfied with both types of rewards are least likely to want to maintain their conjugal relationships. For black husbands, there is at least some evidence that alienation influences their satisfaction with primary relations, and it is clear that black husbands *most* satisfied with expressive gratifications are *most* likely to want to maintain their rewarding relationships, and vice-versa.

In this regard, perhaps the clearest bit of evidence we found was reported in Table 6–2 where variation in male job satisfaction is positively related to expressive satisfaction. For black males, this may be the *one* element that significantly influences how they see themselves and also how they think their wives see them in the role of provider. Job satisfaction may be the single area where they use other blacks rather than whites as a reference group. If so, then perhaps it is possible to apply the above generalization in a much more limited sense to black husbands as well as to black wives. That is, black husbands most satisfied *specifically* with job rewards *plus* expressive rewards (which hinge on job rewards) are most likely to want to maintain their marriages. The converse should also be true. Later in this chapter, after considering other factors besides economic and expressive-type variables, we shall look at the combined effects of all these elements on feelings of marital solidarity.

WIFE EMPLOYMENT

Repeated reference has been made here and elsewhere to the long tradition of black female employment and its consequences for the family. Among blacks (and especially among whites), the incidence of employment among married females is increasing rapidly. Employment for only a minority of employed females, however, holds the same meaning as it holds for males.[48] Few females, it appears, define individual achievement in a *career* as a major life-interest *equal* in importance to family roles. Yet because ever more women are working, research has begun to focus on its impact for husband-wife interaction.[49]

For the lower-status husband, one question has been: Does wife-employment undercut his role as provider and thus threaten primary relations? And when their wives work, do high-status husbands experience fewer expressive satisfactions because they define her work as an unnecessary incursion into time already limited and constrained by his career demands? In white society, there is evidence for both propositions, at least from the perspective of husbands. Wives, in contrast, generally tended to define primary relations more positively when they did work, than when they did not. We have suggested elsewhere that white women are increasingly coming to define employment as a viable role option that they feel ought to be exercised independently by them.[50] It has certainly moved out of the realm of a role *prohibition,* though female employment is not yet often defined as a right, inherent in the role of the white married female.[51] Many working wives perceive employment as an enactment or fulfillment of their role options, and the result seems to be enhanced marital expressiveness on the part of these wives. White husbands, however, often apparently prefer their wives not to exercise this option, for when they do, male satisfaction with expressiveness generally declines.[52]

Effect on Primary Relations

The tension, however, within white family structure over the nature of the female role, may not exist with the same intensity within the black family. First of all, contrary to our expectations, there was no evidence that employment-nonemployment makes any significant difference in male or female evaluation of primary relations. Wives who work report a mean expressiveness score of 15.4 vs. 15.6 for those who do not. Husbands of employed wives reported a mean expressiveness score of 17.6 vs. 18.2 for husbands of nonemployed wives, but this difference is too slight to be statistically meaningful.[53]

Furthermore, wife-employment produced no meaningful differences when used as a control or "intervening" variable to any of the dimensions presented in Tables 6–1 through 6–5, e.g., "contentment with husband's job" (Table 6–2). When we compare husbands who have employed wives with husbands who do not, in neither instance are there any meaningful changes from the "husband pattern" shown in Table 6–2. Specifically, the mean expressiveness scores for husbands in each category do not consistently rise when wife is nonemployed nor drop when she is employed. The scores remain about what they were in Table 6–2.[54] Similarly, wives' expressiveness scores remain about the same regardless of whether they work or not. Finally, recalling Table 6–7, we found that wife-employment had virtually no direct influence whatsoever on the expressiveness evaluations of females, and only very slight influence on male expressiveness. It is these several empirical findings that give rise to the notion that the tension over female-role definitions is less pronounced in black families than in white families.

Another set of data suggesting the same conclusion emerges from a study of black male and female college students.[55] For some sixteen years, these researchers have been investigating definitions of the role of woman in modern society. Their consistent finding for *whites* has been that women see themselves "as balanced" between fulfilling family obligations and enacting "self-oriented" activities, e.g., employment. They find that white women, however, perceive that (white) men prefer a "family-oriented," not a "balanced" woman. Yet (white) men themselves "deny this saying they actually prefer the balanced woman." Significantly, the investigators did not find this clash of perceptions within their black sample. Instead, they found that black men and women possess remarkable agreement regarding the "balanced-woman" definition of the female role. That is, black women perceived that black men prefer a "balanced" rather than a primarily "family-oriented" woman. Black men, the researchers say, concur in terms of their own stated preferences. So that although there is considerable dissensus between white males and females over the role of woman, among blacks there is apparently far greater consensus.

The Black Woman as Worker

The theoretical rationale for this absence of role tension has historical roots in what Jeanne L. Noble calls the "Negro woman's role as a working citizen."[56] Noble points out that the major role of the earliest American black woman was that of slave-worker. And ever since Emancipation, black women have worked in greater proportions than white women at all stages of the family life-cycle. "The typical white woman follows a different work pattern from that of the Negro. She may work a few years, marry, and then stay home to raise her children, seeking part or full-time work when her children are older."[57]

Traditional patterns of white female employment reflect the

dominant definition of this behavior as an option, to be exercised "at best" whenever it does not interfere with motherly obligations to children, or conflict with her husband's job or career interests. This last item includes the idea of "threat" to the traditional white male provider-role. We would suggest, however, that within black society, wife employment is defined (unconsciously perhaps) as more of a *right* than merely an option. This condition is what is implied by Noble's characterization of the "Negro woman as a working citizen." White (married) women are almost never described in that fashion.

This description is quite different, however, from describing employment by the black female as an obligation. Being obliged to work explicitly means that one takes on the role of provider. Evidence presented earlier in this study, plus that from many other sources, make clear the black female is not socialized to accept the obligation to work once she is married. Nor do black males or females want the wife to be a provider, although in fact she must often assume that role, particularly within the lower class. Yet precisely because of historical circumstances that have involved her extensively in the occupational world, the female work-role within black society may be defined differently from her counterpart in white society.

Generations of black people have grown up in situations where it has been "normal" or "typical" for women to work. Nationally, in fact, black females exceed black males in educational attainments, whether the indicator be literacy, median years of school completed, or high school or college graduation.[58] Noble claims this situation is due to the great impetus placed on teaching as the "ideal career" for black women. This particular impetus on schoolteaching has also resulted in twice as many black females as males being located within the professions.[59] (At the same time, of course, black males have been effectively excluded from higher status positions generally.) One upshot of these historical patterns may be that wife employment has, to a certain extent, become established or "institutionalized" within black subsociety. Black males and females have come to define employment as more or less normative—as a right

—that is part of the female role, but not institutionalized enough to take on the character of an obligation. The black wife may choose not to work if she wishes. It also follows that if she does work, its meaning is not the same as it is for males in our society. Individual achievement in her occupation is not necessarily a central life-interest superior or even equal to family interests.

Because employment of the black wife appears to be "normal," "accepted," "taken for granted," etc., employed, working-class black husbands (above the lower class) may feel their provider-role less threatened by a working wife than whites with similar status. Like-wise, middle-status black husbands may be less apt than whites to define wife employment as an "unnecessary incursion" into family routines. In neither instance, therefore, is marital expressiveness reduced. And from the wife's standpoint, her husband is not "al-lowing" her to work in the sense that the white husband does. Con-sequently, there is not generated any special feeling of rectitude toward him that might give rise to increased expressiveness. Simply because wife employment is perhaps so much an integral part of black family structure—because it is normative and accepted—it does not have the same kinds of either positive or negative conse-quences that it does among whites where traditionally it has been far less institutionalized.

We should not overlook the possibility that because black men are discriminated against economically, wife employment may help to boost the family's living standard substantially. Thus, her work-ing may be defined as a "positive good" by both partners, and although this condition may not necessarily enhance marital expres-siveness, at least it does not threaten it. The earning potential of black females, particularly the well-educated, cannot be underrated. For example, in 1967, the median earnings of black female profes-sionals was $6209 compared to $5910 for white female professionals and $6208 for black male professionals.[60] The higher earnings of the black over the white female may reflect greater consistency of career efforts. That is, while the white female may actually move "in and out" of a position (e.g., teaching) in order to fulfill family roles, the black female may be less prone to do that. "Staying with" a job over a longer, uninterrupted time span may result in greater advancement and salary increments.

The realm of female employment represents perhaps the one area where white patterns are moving in the direction of black family patterns, especially in view of the ever increasing proportion of white females attending college. Yet some sociologists have suggested that one reason white wife employment has remained at the level of option rather than right is because of the spouse rivalry that might otherwise ensue.[61] Among higher status occupations and professions, for instance, geographical and social mobility demands of the husband's job require "sacrifices" and "adjustments" by the wife. If she is working, these are often harder to make. Because in the past black husbands have generally been excluded from these kinds of "highly mobile" occupational positions, such "adjustments" have rarely faced their wives.

For example, a recent government report suggests that "the low migration rate of nonwhite workers is probably associated with the fact that relatively few of them have had a chance to qualify for the higher skilled occupations. Also, nonwhites less often receive offers of employment in other areas."[62]

The effects of the black wife's employment is summarized in the same report as follows:

. . . contrary to the situation among white families, Negro families at the higher income levels are no more likely to migrate than those with lower incomes. A move by an upper-income Negro family usually involves the displacement of several wage earners who would have to find jobs at their new location in order to maintain the family income.[63]

It continues, "Negroes had less geographic mobility than whites in every age and educational category [and] in every major occupational category including professional and technical workers."[64] Present trends, however, reveal that increasing numbers of black men are entering higher status occupational positions. If their salaries and chances for advancement begin to approximate those of whites, it is possible that the "potential rivalry" that is alleged to exist among white families may become more prevalent among black families too. This is obviously a matter for *future* observation and research. Currently, the limits placed on the black male provider, plus the definition of female employment as a right, seem to mitigate threats to husband-wife primary relations within the black family.

At the beginning of this chapter, we indicated several major areas of interaction between husbands and wives in the modern conjugal family. So far we have gone into some detail on the first and probably most important of these—expressive or primary relations. We have also considered wife-employment. In the remainder of this chapter, we shall give brief attention to complementary areas.

HOSTILITY

The area of hostility, defined as tensions, or "negative affect" or "negative expressiveness" between husbands and wives has lately been given increased attention by sociologists. As within any social system, a certain amount of hostility may exist within marriage without its *necessarily* threatening the very existence of that system. Like primary relations, husband-wife hostility can be explained in terms of exchange theory. Homans, for example, points out that just as supplied rewards generate solidarity, so withheld rewards generate feelings of resentment and hostility.[65] If, in *any* relationship, X is supposed to reward Y in some fashion and yet fails to meet Y's expectations, then Y will feel "cheated'" or resentful toward X. In turn, X will probably sense this reaction and respond similarly toward Y, and so the cycle continues.

There is indication that in white society the more articulated, or the more a part of, the opportunity structure the husband is, the lower the level of husband-wife hostility.[66] In other words, the more economic-status rewards the husband supplies to his wife in his role as provider, the more she feels these kinds of "rights" being met, and the less likely she is to feel resentful or hostile toward him. But the opposite is also true: the fewer of these kinds of rewards, the more deprived she feels, and thus the more likely she is to feel resentful or hostile. In turn, her behavior generates reciprocal hostility back toward her on the part of her husband. This is not to say that this approach explains all husband-wife hostility, any more than the exchange model could account for all husband-wife expressiveness. But it is a plausible way to explain the data described below, and it continues our use of exchange theory as a vehicle to help understand what goes on within the black (or white) family.

Our indicator of hostility was an item in which respondents were asked: "How often would you say you and your (wife-husband) really have a big 'blow-up' with each other—really get angry with each other?" Among husbands, 39 percent replied "never," 50 percent said "seldom," 11 percent said "sometimes," and none of them replied "often" or "very often." These responses were significantly different from those of wives, who as in white society reported a greater frequency of perceived hostility than husbands. Four percent replied "very often," 7 percent said "often," 19 percent "sometimes," 41 percent "seldom," and only 29 percent said "never."[67]

Unless the reply was "never" the respondent was also asked: "What is this usually about?" The one category of answers that was proportionally the greatest had to do with occupational and financial matters, including amount of money available and how it should be spent.[68] And, of course, "blow-ups" over matters other than economic may be ignited if there are basic feelings of reward-deprivation by the wife. For the exchange model to apply here, it is not necessary that all hostile behavior center overtly on economic matters.

More important, in Table 6–9 we find, as expected, an inverse relationship between certain indicators of perceived articulation with the opportunity system and husband-wife hostility.[69] First, for instance, the more satisfied husband and wife are with his job rewards, the less the reported hostility, and vice versa. Likewise, the more the satisfaction with family living standard, the less the perceived hostility by both sexes. Finally, the higher the social class one places himself in, the less the husband-wife hostility. Referring to the discussion earlier in the chapter, these three elements may be thought

TABLE 6–9.   SUBJECTIVE ARTICULATION WITH THE OPPORTUNITY
STRUCTURE AND HOSTILITY

		Husbands' Mean Hostility Scores	Wives' Mean Hostility Scores
Satisfaction with Husband's Job	Very satisfied	1.79 (107)	2.23 (105)
	Fairly satisfied	2.40 (69)	3.00 (71)
	Dissatisfied	2.63 (16) (df = 2 & 192 F = 3.5; p < .05)	3.32 (15) (df = 2 & 188 F = 6.11; p < .01)
Satisfaction with family life-style	Very satisfied	1.56 (76)	2.01 (70)
	Fairly satisfied	2.30 (89)	2.91 (91)
	Dissatisfied	2.80 (30) (df = 2 & 192 F = 6.65; p < .01)	3.87 (32) (df = 2 & 190 F = 9.61; p < .001)
Social class self-placement	High	2.31 (111)	3.09 (116)
	Medium	2.22 (22)	2.84 (25)
	Low	1.75 (60) (df = 2 & 190 F = 1.6; n.s.)	1.92 (52) (df = 2 & 190 F = 5.67; p < .01)

of as "rewards" or "resources" which the husband is "obligated" to provide to his wife. Let us assume, as we did before, that blacks—especially wives—use other blacks as a reference group to assess consumption patterns. To the degree the husband fails to provide these resources, relative to other blacks, the wife feels deprived, resentful, and hostile towards him. These feelings are then "acted out" toward her husband and help account for the hostility levels reported in Table 6–9.

It is likely that many husbands perceive their own wives as

defining job discontent, life-style satisfaction, and status-estrangement in approximately the same way that they do. For example, husbands who are "very satisfied" with family life-style believe perhaps their wives are too. If so, these wives are perceived (by their husbands) as least likely to exhibit hostility. In reciprocal fashion, these husbands report the lowest levels of hostility behaviors toward their wives. However, an alternative but related way to explain husband hostility is to make use of the "frustration-aggression" hypothesis.[70] The fewer the rewards the husband gleans from the opportunity structure, the more frustrated he feels. To relieve the frustration, he expends aggression on his wife in the form of hostile behavior. Hence, the less he feels he is part of the opportunity structure, the more the frustration, and the greater the perceived hostility with his wife.

Regardless of whether one prefers exchange theory or the frustration-aggression notion to explain male hostility, it is clear that within black, as well as white families, degree of perceived economic opportunity is inversely related to husband-wife hostility. Wives may react negatively to husbands, because they feel certain reward-obligations are not being met satisfactorily. Husbands may then reciprocate to wives' hostility in kind, or else behave negatively toward them primarily because of their own frustration over relative economic disadvantage. Whatever the exact processes involved, that point is that defining one's opportunity position (vis-à-vis other blacks) in optimistic terms tends to reduce husband-wife hostility. If we look moreover at Column 4 in Table 6–7, we find that wife's alienation level is a strong and the single best predictor of her feelings of perceived hostility: as alienation rises so does hostility. Likewise, in Column 3, we find a path of influence for males from alienation to hostility, but not as strong as the impact of wife-employment, to be discussed below.

As was the case with expressiveness, the "objective" indicators of economic well-being (husband's occupation, education, income) do not differentiate between hostility levels in the same fashion as they do in white society. Increases in these three indicators do not systematically reduce husband-wife hostility. If anything, there is a slight tendency for hostility to increase with rises in "objective status." For example, husbands with lowest occupational ranking report a hostility score of 2.0; medium, 2.04; high, 2.23. Wives whose husbands rank lowest in occupation reveal a mean hostility score of 2.45; medium, 3.14; high, 2.46.[71] Similar patterns emerge when we examine the effects of education and income on hostility.

As before, two points are especially salient. One, that these "objective" factors fail to increase expressiveness *and* reduce hostility among blacks as they do among whites can probably be traced to the notion of relative deprivation. Blacks evidently use whites as a reference point when it comes to education, income, and job status. As a result, comparison over these kinds of attainments are almost inevitably bound to reveal that blacks are on the "short end." Hence, within their marriages, painful and powerful feelings of relative deprivation undermine the type of bargaining process that probably goes on in white families. Objective rewards do not assuage hostility simply because they are almost never deemed "sufficient" compared to white families at the same objective status level. This condition is apparently true for both husbands and wives.

Second, therefore, these factors suggest an added way in which relative deprivation weakens the bonds of marital cohesion among blacks. We saw earlier that divorce rates are higher among middle-class blacks than among whites, due in part to the lack of systematic increases in expressive rewards among higher-status blacks. At the same time, it would seem that lack of systematic decreases in hostility also probably contributes to the greater frequency of black dissolution. Since compared to whites even higher-status blacks are relatively deprived in job status, etc., they also find themselves at a disadvantage in trying to obtain two janus-like goals of the modern conjugal family, i.e., expressive gratifications and a minimum level of husband-wife tensions or hostilities.

Effects of Wife-Employment

Whether the wife worked or not seemed to make no substantial difference in level of husband or wife expressiveness. Similarly, it makes no meaningful difference in wives' perceived hostility levels

(Table 6–10). But husbands whose wives do work report significantly more hostility than husbands whose wives are not employed. It was argued above that because of the long tradition of black wife employment, this behavior poses less of a threat to primary relations within black families than in white families. Nevertheless, from the black husband's perspective, although her working does not pose a threat to expressive gratifications, it does tend to increase hostility.

Because of discrimination resulting in lower-job status and lower income for the black male provider, the wife's income is often a vital and important supplement to family resources. Yet in view of the economic deprivation sensed by some black husbands, a wife who works to supplement family income may actually accentuate feelings of male deprivation. Certain husbands in this situation could define their provider role as being undercut by her employment. The result may be (although unconsciously) greater feelings of resentment and hostility toward their wives, when compared to husbands whose wives do not work and thus do not face the same kind of threat.

Nonetheless, black working wives perceive the same situation quite differently. On the one hand they may define the financial supplement as something "good" which they themselves can contribute to family well-being. On the other hand, black females may define employment as a "role right" even more strongly than black males. Although black males are likely to hold this definition more strongly than white males, it nevertheless seems plausible to argue that they are somewhat less committed to it than black

TABLE 6–10. WIFE EMPLOYMENT AND HOSTILITY

		Husbands' Mean Hostility Scores	Wives' Mean Hostility Scores
Does Wife Work?	Yes	2.39 (98)	2.87 (80)
	No	1.82 (95)	2.65 (113)
		(df = 1 & 191	(df = 1 & 191
		F = 5.16; p < .05)	F = .4; n.s.)

females. (If they are more committed to it than white males, this helps to account for why it does not threaten primary relations.) For these reasons, employed black wives are quite likely to define employment as a desirable situation, and what is more, not to perceive that their husbands may resent them, or that their working generates increased male hostility. This line of reasoning seems to be borne out by the comparative impact of wife-employment on hostility as seen in Columns 3 and 4, Table 6–7. For wives, it is quite weak; for husbands, wife-employment is the single factor that has the most to do with increasing their hostility levels.

Just as satisfaction with expressiveness was directly related to feelings of marital solidarity, so is degree of hostility, as we see in Table 6–11. Husbands and wives who have ever "thought about separation or divorce" report a significantly greater level of hostility than those who have not "wanted out." This is to be expected because if the criterion for staying in a situation is that the positive rewards are not "too low," then it follows that on balance, certain negative outcomes cannot be too high. And since we know that negative outcomes are linked to the level of perceived economic-status rewards, we may say that for black husbands and wives, the greater the perceived economic rewards, the less the hostility, and the greater is the solidarity and cohesion of the conjugal unit. Hence, the less is the probability of its dissolution. Conversely, with fewer rewards and greater hostility, there is less solidarity and greater likelihood of dissolution.

So far, we have seen that solidarity of the black family above

TABLE 6–11. SOLIDARITY FEELINGS AND HOSTILITY

		Husbands' Mean Hostility Scores	Wives' Mean Hostility Scores
Have you ever considered separation or divorce?	Yes	2.82 (40)	3.57 (75)
	No	1.91 (154)	2.22 (118)
		(df = 1 & 192	(df = 1 & 191
		F = 8.57; p < .01)	F = 20.1; p < .001)

the lower class depends largely on the subjective definitions of husbands and (especially) wives with regard to the opportunity structure, and their place in it compared to other blacks. These positive definitions are perhaps partially responsible for enabling blacks to escape the high rates of lower-class dissolution. Yet, due to wide gaps in objective rewards vis-à-vis whites, blacks appear to be more prone to dissolution than whites who are comparably situated. A discussion follows of another major area of husband-wife interaction, i.e., authority relations and their impact on black family solidarity.

FAMILY AUTHORITY

Hostility was defined as "negative affect" and measured by frequency of "explosive interaction" between spouses. Authority refers more specifically to the issue of decision-making. Theoretically, hostility-type interaction may or may not enter into the processes of husband-wife decision-making. The vehicle for understanding authority relations is also exchange theory, or the notion of reciprocity. Numerous studies within white society and in other Western cultures indicate that the higher the social status of the husband, the more authority he has to make household decisions.[72] Through greater status, the husband is able to provide greater economic and prestige benefits, or resources. In turn, he exchanges these resources for authority in the family, or deference from his wife. The more of these kinds of rewards he provides, the more willing his wife is to allow him to exercise authority over decision-making within the family, i.e., to give him deference.

Because of responsibilities that historically have been thrust on the black American female, and because of her occupational activities and her alleged dominance within the black lower class, the applicability of the exchange model to black family authority is more problematic. In Detroit during the mid-fifties, Blood and Wolfe concluded that "Negro families . . . by and large . . . are affected by the same sources of power as white families," i.e., husband status and power are directly related.[73]

However, they found an "over-all picture of wife dominance in Negro families" that they attribute to the tradition of the "Negro wife [who] has become accustomed to having to hold the family together by hard work and responsible decision-making."[74] Many years have elapsed since that finding, and much has happened in black America. What is the picture of family authority that black husbands *and* wives (above the lower class) reveal today?

Conflict Resolution

Respondents were asked: "Thinking back over your married life, what is the *one* thing that you and your wife (husband) have disagreed about more than any other?" Upon naming the item, he (she) was then asked: "When you and your wife (husband) disagree over (*item*), who usually gets his way, you or your wife (husband)?" This kind of question measures *conflict resolution*. Whenever a contested issue arises, the object is to determine which partner has the ultimate "say-so" or authority.[75] Table 6–12 presents the relationship between who "gets his way" and husband's mean occupational status score (S.E.S.).

TABLE 6–12.   HUSBAND'S OCCUPATIONAL STATUS AND CONFLICT RESOLUTION

Husbands' Perceptions of Who Gets His Way	Husbands' Mean S.E.S. Scores	Wives' Perceptions of Who Gets His Way	Husbands' Mean S.E.S. Scores
Husband	54.8 (23)	Wife	43.5 (57)
Wife	41.8 (71)	Husband	49.3 (63)
Compromise	43.5 (80)	Compromise	45.0 (62)
	(df = 2 & 171		(df = 2 & 179
	F = 3.34; p < .05)		F = 1.32; n.s.)

First, we find that 46 percent of the husbands and about one-third of the wives could not reply that either spouse decided the issue alone. Instead, they said the issue was decided through "compromise," "give and take," etc. These proportions reporting *equality* in resolving conflicts are greater than those among white Indianapolis families, using an identical question.[76] Second, from the husbands' perspective, males with the *highest* mean S.E.S. score (54.8) are the ones most likely to resolve contested issues in their favor. Husbands with the next highest mean S.E.S. score (43.5) are likely to engage in compromise, and those with the lowest mean S.E.S. score (41.8) are most likely to have wives who decide contested questions in their own favor.

This pattern obviously fits the exchange model. Husbands with *most* status possess most authority, while those with *least* status have *least* authority. Husbands with an "in-between" status tend to *share* authority with their wives. Moreover, from the wives' perspective, we find the same pattern, only the differences are not as great (nor significant). Wives whose husbands have the lowest SES scores are the wives most apt to decide questions, and thus to reveal the greatest female authority. When their husbands have the highest occupational levels, wives see their husbands as having most authority. Compromise, from the female as well as from the male standpoint, occurs most often when male occupational levels fall somewhere in between these extremes. Females thus verify (though less strongly) the husband's perceptions: the greater the occupational status of her husband, the more "rewards" he provides to her, and the more deference she accords him. Thus, instead of any indication of "overall wife-dominance," we find a striking convergence (particularly from the husband's standpoint) between black and white families in this crucial area of authority relations.[77]

Authority-Participation

The same conclusion emerged when an index of "authority-participation" was constructed and run against occupational levels of husbands.[78] Table 6–13 shows that the higher the status of the hus-

TABLE 6–13. HUSBAND'S OCCUPATIONAL STATUS AND AUTHORITY-PARTICIPATION

		Husbands' Mean Authority-Participation Score	Wives' Mean Authority-Participation Score
Husband's Occupational Ranking	Low	2.36 (61)	4.14 (56)
	Medium	2.75 (61)	4.00 (62)
	High	3.69 (52)	3.50 (64)
		(df = 2 & 171	(df = 2 & 179
		F = 3.56; p < .05)	F = .6; n.s.)

band, the higher his mean authority score; the lower his status, the less his authority. For wives (though it is a far weaker relationship), the less their husbands' status, the more authority wives possess, and the higher his status the less authority they possess. However, none of the remaining objective or subjective indicators of economic-status rewards (income, satisfaction with husbands' job, or with life-style, and so on) produced any meaningful differences in the authority-participation index. Likewise, no differences in the index were found whether the wife worked or not. Nor were there any authority-participation differences among those who said they had thought about separation or divorce and those who said they had not.

Perhaps the picture can be summarized in this fashion. Although in the lower-class black family, the female may indeed have considerable power because the male has few resources to "earn" deference, this is not the case in the two-thirds of black American families above the underclass. Because the husband is working steadily, he has achieved a certain level of authority within the family. But in contrast to trends within the white family where females are pressing for egalitarian participation, it is the black male who is pressing for and has largely achieved equal authority with his wife. Indeed, it may be that equal participation in conflict-resolution is now generally more evident in stable black families than in comparable white families.

At the same time, both black and white families reveal strong similarity over the consequences of the husband's occupational position. Though income, education, or feelings of alienation do not, the status and prestige of his occupation do meaningfully delineate the amount of family authority possessed by the black husband, i.e., the more of one the more of the other. Now although we did not measure beliefs of those in the sample regarding family authority, we do know that among white wives, the higher her husband's status, the more strongly she believes he ought to have family authority.[79] Thus, the more he earns authority, the more she believes it is *legitimate* for him to exercise it. Very likely the same is true within black families. Not only does the higher status husband actually earn authority by virtue of his occupational position, it is quite probable that both sexes define this pattern as "desirable" and "right."

Nevertheless, the foregoing "picture" is somewhat more representative of the husband's perspective than the wife's. Black husbands see the situation right now as one in which status brings deference. Wives, on the other hand, merely reveal evidence of a trend in this direction. The tradition of female dominance dies as hard in black society as does the notion of male dominance in white society. The basic point, however, is that the tradition of female dominance appears to be expiring. The data give no indication whatsoever of traditional authority for the black female irrespective of male status. In black society above the underclass, the dominant pattern, based on a status-power linkage, is clearly emerging. This generalization is supported by another recent study of black husband-wife households. King found: (1) strong evidence of equal participation of both spouses in decision-making in both the working and middle-classes; and (2) "participation by the Negro father in the decision-making process in the family was more frequent than has been historically presented."[80]

Furthermore, Column 5 of Table 6–7 reveals that the best predictor of male participation in family authority (same index as

Table 6–13) is family income. His income is obviously related to his job status, and reinforces the critical theoretical point that as the black male is able to bring more economic and status resources into the family, he perceives his own authority to increase. Interestingly, from the wife's viewpoint, her authority-participation is increased most forcefully when her husband has only limited education (Column 6). If we consider education as a resource that the black husband may use to bargain for authority in the family, the less of it he possesses the more authority the wife perceives herself to possess.

Since we found no relationship between authority and feelings of conjugal solidarity ("wanting out"), we cannot be certain just what kinds of authority patterns are most conducive to black family stability. However, given the dominant trend in our society toward the relationship between husband job status and satisfaction with his authority, plus evidence of a status-power linkage among these blacks, we may suggest that not only is the dominant trend taking hold in black families, but also that this particular authority pattern is related to family stability more than any other.[81] We are assuredly not saying (for either blacks or whites) that "male headship" is "intrinsically right" and thus a "cause" of marital stability. This would be a veiled way of restating the "patriarchal ideology."

Rather, given the present order of things within the occupational and conjugal systems, males and females seem to define the exchange of status for deference as a suitable way to resolve the question of family leadership. (These definitions need not be overtly conscious nor imbued with any rational calculus.) Those social systems (of any sort) are most stable where power is defined as "legitimate" by those concerned. In contemporary marriage, authority based on resources provided by the husband is defined by blacks and whites as legitimate. It is precisely this notion of legitimate authority that helps to contribute to marital stability. In brief, as long as the authority question is defined in these terms, those who are able to conform most fully to the "preferred pattern" are the ones most likely to want to maintain their reward-producing situation. For instance, middle and higher status black wives receive prestige and economic benefits, and their husbands receive deference. Where is the momentum to "rock the boat"? However, in working-class black (or white) families (even above the "underclass"), both wives and husbands receive fewer desired rewards: wives, economic; husbands, deference. Hence there is greater likelihood of dissolution.

Effects of Wife-Employment

In this same vein, the working wife in white society has been found to have more authority than the nonworking wife.[82] Simply because the working wife brings more economic resources into the family than her nonemployed counterpart, she "earns" more authority in decision-making. Among families in the sample, however, whether the wife worked or not made no meaningful differences in the data of either Table 6–12 or 6–13.[83] Whether she worked or not, the scores and patterns in the tables remained about the same.

We may only speculate as to why employment changes the authority position of white wives but not of black wives. Possibly it is because the white wife starts from a position of relative "powerlessness" compared to her husband. Working can only increase her bargaining position in family "power-conflicts," and yet not necessarily threaten her husband. Conversely, the black wife stands in the wake of a long tradition that probably enables her to start from a position of equal bargaining "strength" vis-à-vis her husband. If, in addition to this tradition, she would utilize her "work resources" as a means to bargain for still more power, the result could be extremely threatening to the husband and to the total marital relationship. Perhaps, therefore, above the lower class the black wife does not use her work resources in this fashion. Power based on a more egalitarian tradition may be sufficient for her, whether she works or not. In the lower class, however, where the husband provides little or no resources, the employed wife very likely does add the full weight of her work resources to her traditional power in order to dominate almost totally.

Over all three core dimensions of husband-wife interaction—

primary relations, hostility, authority—many important similarities exist between blacks and whites, as well as some crucial differences. However, these differences are not due to anything *intrinsically distinctive* within either grouping. Instead, they are due to the traditional spectre of economic discrimination by whites against blacks. Before summarizing the several contrasts and similarities, we need to look at two additional salient aspects of the contemporary black family: fertility control and consumption rationality.

FERTILITY CONTROL

Taeuber and Taeuber comment that "social scientists have been rather unsuccessful in their attempts to explain reproductive behavior"[84] for both blacks and whites. In Chapter 2, we discussed briefly the fertility backgrounds of those in our sample and found that these patterns were representative of the black population in general. The same conclusion applies to the current fertility of couples in the sample. In 1966, the mean number of children per family among black households (husband-wife present) in the North and West of the United States was 1.86.[85] Among households in our sample there were 1.87 children currently living with these families.

Blacks in our study, therefore, appear to be representative of fertility patterns within the "dominant" black society. This condition does not include, of course, the black lower-class where a majority of households (75 percent) are headed by females.[86] Black families headed by females in the North and West contain 2.38 children per household.[87] Female-headed black families contain the most children but receive the lowest incomes of *any* type of family unit in our society—a median figure of $2,464 in 1965.[88] We saw earlier that even *whole* black families at *every* status level have lower incomes than whites. At the same time, whites in general have fewer children than blacks (a mean of 1.38 per family in the North and West.[89] (This figure includes all types of households.) Higher fertility leads blacks in being disadvantaged still further, since they must stretch *fewer* dollars over a *greater* distance to care for a greater number of bodies.

Much folklore and legend has grown up around alleged black "sexuality and fertility." Although black fertility was historically and is currently higher than white fertility, there is nothing biologically about *race per se* that accounts for this difference. On the contrary, "race is significant only as it involves the concentration of individuals with particular characteristics which are associated with high or low fertility."[90] One of the most crucial of these characteristics, for example, is education. Educated black women actually have less fertility than comparably educated white women. This situation is true for women who are high-school graduates, for those with 1–3 years of college, and especially for college graduates. For every 1,000 white women with college degrees, there are 2,235 offspring. A similar cohort of black female college graduates has only 1,649 children.[91]

Influence of Education

Since level of education is a major indicator of assimilation into the opportunity structure, what effect did it have on family fertility among those in our sample? First of all, we find that neither the job status of the husband, nor family income are associated with meaningful differences in fertility. (Fertility was measured in terms of the number of children the couple ever had.) Husbands, for example, with lowest job position, reported a mean of 3.3 children; medium status husbands, 3.0; high, 3.1. Wives at these three levels reported mean figures of 3.7, 3.1 and 3.0, respectively.[92] An analogous pattern emerged for income.

For education, however, it was quite different, at least for wives. Table 6–14 shows that although husband's own education makes little difference in family fertility, the wife's own education does. Significantly, those wives with some college or beyond indicate they have the fewest number of children. They show a sharp drop compared to high-school graduates who, in turn, have had fewer children than wives with less education. These findings

TABLE 6–14.   INDICATORS OF FAMILY FERTILITY

		Mean Number of Children-Husbands	Mean Number of Children-Wives
Years of Education of Respondent	0–8	3.50 (87)	3.15 (65)
	9–11	3.32 (43)	4.29 (65)
	12	2.27 (36)	2.88 (52)
	13+	3.15 (32)	1.85 (20)
		(df = 3 & 194	(df = 3 & 198
		F = 1.2; n.s.)	F = 4.34; p < .01)
How good are your chances to reach your success goals?	Excellent	2.44 (36)	2.77 (31)
	Average	3.70 (110)	3.57 (149)
		(df = 1 & 144	(df = 1 & 178
		F = 4.39; p < .05)	F = 1.8; n.s.)
Satisfaction with family life-style	Very satisfied	2.22 (76)	2.73 (71)
	Fairly satisfied	3.51 (92)	3.51 (94)
	Dissatisfied	4.63 (30)	3.97 (37)
		(df = 2 & 195	(df = 2 & 199
		F = 7.11; p < .001)	F = 2.36; n.s.)

support the previous observation that educated black women are highly successful in limiting fertility. Education is obviously a prime indicator of the degree to which one is a part of the opportunity system. On this basis, black women who are *most* a part of it, are most likely to be rational about contraceptive behavior.

Why husband's own education does not significantly reduce fertility is not totally clear. It may be, as some social scientists have observed, that the key to fertility control lies primarily with the wife rather than with the husband. For example, of all husbands in

Table 6–14 who have 13+ years of education, 53 percent of them are married to women with high school or less. Assuming that education engenders the motivation and rationality to limit births effectively and that it is the wife's education that is more crucial, then over half of these well-educated men are married to women whose lesser education is also *less* likely to result in the "most rational and effective" means to limit births. Consequently, in spite of the high education of these particular husbands, their family size is pretty much the same as husbands with less education.

Conversely, among those households where wives have 13+ years of education, obviously 100 percent of the wives are well-educated. So in spite of the fact that 55 percent of them have married "downward," these wives are able to limit family size quite effectively. Irrespective of the education of their husbands, therefore, it is wives' own education that seems to play the more vital role in terms of actual fertility. Clearly, however, much more work is needed among blacks and whites before we can speak with greater certainty about the different influences on fertility of husbands' versus wives' education. (The effects of "control" variables are discussed below in connection with Table 6–7.)

Economic Alienation

Some recent studies have suggested that a sense of alienation may be part of the reason for higher fertility among those (black and white) with lower social status.[93] Earlier in the chapter we saw how alienation may be linked to marital expressiveness and hostility. Hoffman and Wyatt, for example, talk about the "loneliness" and "alienation quality" of contemporary American life as a factor that precipitates high fertility.[94] They contend that if one feels "cut off" from meaningful relationships in society, a prime way to "compensate" for the feeling of "drift, meaninglessness, powerlessness, normlessness," is to have a larger family, a "ready-made primary group." Since those with lower status are the most alienated, they are the ones who generally seek for greatest "compensations." Feeling alienated not only generates desires for compensations in the form of more children, but also simultaneously undercuts the motivation and rationality inherent in contraceptive behavior.

The motivation to control births is linked to one's stake in the society. If one perceives that he and his children have a relatively large stake in society, he (she) is going to be more rational about contraception than if he perceives the opposite. Black Americans have been the ones least likely to perceive that they actually participate economically (or any other way) in our society. Lower-class blacks, especially females who head large families with minimal incomes, are least likely of all citizens to feel they are part of the society. They, therefore, possess least motivation to practice contraception effectively and are at the polar extreme from college-trained black women, who are apparently extremely effective in their contraceptive behavior.[95]

Judith Blake, for example, argues that high birth rates among the poor are not the result of lack of information ("the poor have no difficulty in gaining access to illegal narcotics despite their obvious 'unavailability' ") but rather the unavailability of alternative behavior patterns.[96] Since children are defined as such a major reward in our society, those women who perceive the potentiality of what they define as more valuable rewards will most effectively limit births. Lower-class blacks, perceiving they are blocked from almost all meaningful alternatives, possess no viable rationale to block the one set of rewards (i.e., children) that is readily available to them.

What of those in our sample who presumably represent blacks above the underclass? How does the alienation-fertility hypothesis apply to them? While all four alienation dimensions showed positive associations with family fertility, only the two listed in Table 6–14 revealed statistically significant differences for at least one sex. The data in the middle of the table are based on the question discussed in connection with Table 6–5. Only here the "good," "fair," and "poor" categories are grouped together under the row labeled "average." Husbands and wives who perceive their future chances to attain their success goals as "excellent" (and thus are less alienated) have fewer children than those who see their success chances as only "average" (those who are more alienated). Satisfaction with family life-style is also significantly related to family size. Husbands and wives who are "very satisfied" have fewer children than those who are "fairly satisfied," who in turn have less children than the "dissatisfied." The *greater* the satisfaction with life-style, the *less* one may be said to be alienated from the opportunity structure; therefore, the *less* the family fertility.

Table 6–7, Columns 7 and 8, shows the impact on fertility of all the "objective" indicators of economic articulation, plus the alienation index, along with years married (the longer the marriage, the greater the chances for more children) and whether the wife works or not. (In the sample, households with working wives possess fewer children than those with nonworking wives, a finding reported by virtually all such studies of blacks or whites.)[97] With all these other factors controlled, economic alienation appears to be the single most powerful predictor of family fertility, especially for wives, but also for husbands. That is, as a sense of alienation increases, the number of children in the family is likely to be greater; as alienation decreases, so should family size. In short, the argument made by some social scientists that children tend to function as a type of reward to compensate for feelings of alienation may have some validity among blacks (as well as whites) above the underclass. Especially from the wife's perspective, elements such as husband's education, family income, her own education, her own employment, may be viewed as rewards or compensations that help reduce painful feelings of economic alienation. Feeling rewarded in this sense, i.e., feeling she is (relatively, at least) a part of the opportunity system, there is less "need" for greater numbers of children to serve as rewards. Hence, *because* the opportunity structure is perceived as relatively open to them, blacks (or whites) then proceed to limit births. Alternatives to childbearing and caring must be seen as feasible *prior* to limiting the "gratifications" supplied by children. Some observers of the poor argue that if they would first limit births, then they would be better off economically. But this misreads the nature of the "deferred gratification syndrome," as seen also in Chapter 5. Before current rewards (children) are deferred or limited, present rewards (opportunity) and future expectations of more of the same must be substituted in their place.

This issue of alternative rewards to motherhood is also at the core of the question discussed above in connection with wife-employment, i.e., changes in the role definitions of American females. The suggestion was made there that blacks may be more "modern" and equalitarian in their conception of the female role than are whites. If this is indeed so, it might help to account for the lower fertility rates of educated black females versus white females. On the one hand, there are the compensations provided by a relative sense of participation in the opportunity structure. On the other side, educated black women, because they probably define the female role in less traditional terms than whites, may seek for fewer compensations through traditional means (i.e., motherhood), and instead seek for more "modern-type" compensations such as those found in employment. In Table 6–7, for example, wife employment-nonemployment is the best predictor of fertility besides alienation (and "years married" which is solely a "control" variable).

If reduced feelings of alienation through greater opportunity participation are viewed as one set of rewards, and "modern-type" compensations by means of female-employment are viewed as another, then in the long run one could predict that some of the current divergences between black and white fertility might decline. In the first instance, if the opportunity structure is opened wider to disadvantaged blacks, so that they are allowed to participate in the reward system on a more equal footing with whites, then we might expect black fertility to drop to the level of whites within comparable social strata. In the second instance, if highly educated white women become proportionately more numerous and more occupation (individual-achievement) oriented, then their fertility levels might also begin to drop to those of black women at comparable educational levels. In short, black "excess fertility" toward the bottom of the opportunity structure, and relative white excess toward the top, may eventually come to be diminished.[98] Whatever transpires, however, it is clear that racial or biological explanations regarding alleged greater "black sexuality and fertility" are nothing more than mythical. Fertility levels rest not on bio-racial, but on social, factors.

CONSUMPTION RATIONALITY

Besides primary relations, hostility, authority, fertility control, and the effects of wife-employment, we shall consider one additional dimension of husband-wife interaction. For want of a better term, we have labeled it "consumption rationality." Earlier in this chapter, consumption was discussed in connection with production of economic resources. It was suggested that as the husband provides greater resources, which make possible higher levels of consumption and thus status, marital expressiveness is increased; hostility is decreased; and authority patterns shift away from female-centeredness. The chief stress at that point was on the production of economic and status resources that made certain consumption levels possible. In that analysis, specifics regarding the consumption process *per se* were merely incidental to the idea of production levels. Here, instead, we want to put the focus specifically on the "consumption process" itself as it occurs between husbands and wives. Let us assume the couple has X number of dollars, i.e., a certain amount of resources. The question then becomes, what do they do with it, how do they arrive at decisions on how to use it?

Heretofore, this type of question has been dealt with mostly by what may be roughly termed "consumption economists." Their goal has been to analyze consumer behavior primarily with a view toward prediction. The obvious practical benefits to advertisers of this kind of enterprise are enormous. Being able to predict trends in tastes and desires within the "Negro market" referred to earlier is a case in point. This literature, however, while long on description, is very short on explanation or systematic theory. We know very little about (1) the processes whereby husbands and wives actually arrive at decisions about consumption, or even more significant, (2) how these processes and their outcomes affect marital solidarity and cohesion.

It is those kinds of issues we shall consider briefly here. Although these matters are obviously important in white families, they are perhaps even more central in black families above the underclass. For one reason, there is less money within most black families when compared to whites with comparable education or job status. Precisely because there are fewer dollars, how to spend them probably becomes more of an issue between black husbands and wives than between white husbands and wives at the same social status level.

A second reason lies with the exploitation that blacks have traditionally faced in the white-controlled market-place. Inferior merchandise, exorbitant prices, inflated credit charges, have all combined to shrink what dollars are available to the black family.[99] Hence this factor too makes spending decisions an extremely live issue. For in addition to there being "fewer dollars," the situations in which blacks expend these dollars are often exceedingly precarious in terms of the "family budget." Presumably, most black families above the lower class are aware (at least implicitly) of this exploitation and seek to cope with it as adequately as possible.

To try to explore the matter, we read an item to each respondent in the sample stating that "people have different ideas about how careful to be in spending money." We then asked how careful he (she) thought he himself (she herself) was in spending money. More important, however, was the next question, "Which of these is true about your wife (husband) when it comes to spending money? Is she (he) very careful, careful, not so careful, or careless about spending money?" Presumably, the person who is "very careful" about spending money is most *rational* about it; the person who is only "careful" is somewhat less rational; the one "not so careful" is even less rational; and the one who is "careless" is least rational of all.

Rationality or "care" simply imply such traditional notions as asking oneself *prior* to a purchase decision: "Do I really need this item?"[100] "If not, and I merely want it, why?" "Can I genuinely afford it?" "What about credit or finance charges?" "Can I get it for less money somewhere else?" "How will getting this affect other immediate family needs or desires?" "How will it influence attainment of long-term financial goals?" In Table 6–15, we find meaningful differences between husbands and wives concerning their respective consumption rationality. Husbands see themselves (Columns 1 and 2) as less rational about consumption than wives see themselves. At the same time, husbands are likely to perceive their wives to be quite rational about consumption (Columns 3 and 4); whereas, wives are not as likely to perceive their husbands as being rational in this regard. In other words, there is remarkable agreement between black husbands and wives that wives are indeed more careful, or rational, than husbands when it comes to spending money.

While we have no comparable data for whites, it is quite likely that a similar pattern would emerge for them also. Because the wife (black or white) in our society is the family's chief "consumption agent," she is generally concerned for the overall consumption needs of the family, particularly those of her children. The husband may take a more limited scope or viewpoint and thus be more will-

TABLE 6–15. HOW RATIONAL ARE RESPONDENTS AND SPOUSES IN CONSUMPTION BEHAVIOR?

	How careful in using money do respondents see themselves?		How careful in using money do respondents perceive their spouses to be?	
	Husbands	Wives	Husbands	Wives
Very careful	32.0%	46.3%	54.0%	35.3%
Careful	39.5	37.3	25.4	25.4
Not so careful	18.3	11.4	17.3	22.4
Careless	10.2	10.2	3.3	16.9
T	100%	100%	100%	100%
N	(197)	(201)	(197)	(201)
	($x^2 = 11.9$; p $<$ .01		($x^2 = 26.2$; p $<$ .001	
	3 df)		3 df)	

ing to expend dollars without taking into account as many contingencies as the wife. In that sense, he would be less rational or careful than she. Furthermore, he may feel that since he has, after all, earned most if not all the family resources, he should exercise the major discretion on how it is spent. We should note that the majority of respondents (Table 6–15) see both themselves and their spouses as at least "careful" in spending money. The frequency of this degree of rationality among these blacks is surely comparable to what would emerge in a sample of whites, and suggests further basic similarity between family patterns above the underclass.

Opportunity and
Consumption Rationality

We have posited that the capability to control births depends on deliberateness and rational calculation. This type of rationality appears to be linked directly to the family's position in the economic-opportunity system. Similarly, we would suggest that *the capability to exercise deliberateness and rationality over consumption behavior is likewise associated with economic position.* The more one is a part of the opportunity structure, the more rational control he will likely be able to exercise over family consumption.

To test this hypothesis two separate indexes were constructed based on the two questions discussed in Table 6–15.[101] The result is one index measuring the respondent's own care or rationality in spending, and a separate index measuring his perception of the care exercised by his spouse. When we ran the variables used earlier representing level of economic position (occupation, job satisfaction, and so on) against respondent's own rationality, no meaningful differences (either in pattern or statistical significance) emerged by economic position.

Table 6–16, however, reveals that most of these same variables do discriminate when the index used is perception of *spouse's* consumption rationality.[102] (The higher the mean score, the greater the perceived spouse rationality.) Interestingly, significant differ-

TABLE 6–16. ARTICULATION WITH THE OPPORTUNITY SYSTEM AND PERCEIVED CONSUMPTION RATIONALITY OF SPOUSE

		Degree of Spouse's Perceived Rationality in Spending Money (mean scores)			
		Husbands' Perceptions		Wives' Perceptions	
Husband's Occupational Ranking (S.E.S.)	Low	5.72 (66)	(F = .6; n.s.)	4.29 (62)	(F = 3.53; df = 2 & 194; p < .05)
	Medium	5.63 (66)		4.32 (68)	
	High	5.40 (65)		5.17 (67)	
Satisfaction with husband's job	Very satisfied	5.74 (108)	(F = 1.9; n.s.)	5.16 (107)	(F = 9.10; df = 2 & 196; p < .001)
	Fairly satisfied	5.54 (70)		4.06 (73)	
	Dissatisfied	4.89 (19)		3.42 (19)	
Satisfaction with family life-style	Very satisfied	5.57 (76)	(F = .0; n.s.)	5.28 (70)	(F = 7.23; df = 2 & 198; p < .001)
	Fairly satisfied	5.58 (92)		4.40 (94)	
	Dissatisfied	5.62 (29)		3.70 (37)	
Social class placement	High	5.95 (61)	(F = 2.1; n.s.)	5.11 (53)	(F = 4.15; df = 2 & 198; p < .05)
	Medium	5.17 (23)		5.14 (27)	
	Low	5.48 (111)		4.22 (121)	

ences emerge only for wives' perceptions of husbands, and not the other way around, although husbands' perceptions of wives are at least in the predicted direction, except for S.E.S.

In conjunction with the discussion concerning Table 6–15, these data both confirm and refine our hypothesis. First (comparing across the columns), at every level of each of the four dimensions in the table, the black wife is seen by both sexes to be a more

rational consumer than her husband. Second, the higher the family's
social and economic position, the more careful (in using money)
the black husband is perceived to be *by the wife*. Hence, in view of
the endemic husband-wife tension over consumption discussed
above, it would appear that the greater the economic position, the
less such tension occurs. If the husband is or at least feels more a
part of the opportunity system, he is evidently more rational or
careful in his consumption habits.

The reason is not merely that there are more resources to
expend at higher status levels. Higher status couples (black and
white) could easily become enveloped by a sense of "boundless-
ness," and expend their financial resources in a free-flowing and
relatively haphazard manner. Instead, just as fertility control seems
to be greater among those who perceive more of a stake in the
society, so "consumption control" would likewise appear to be
greater among those who perceive they are meaningfully linked to
the opportunity structure. The result is that increased economic
position generates greater convergence between black (or white)
husbands and wives in terms of the processes of consumption,
whereas lesser economic position results in greater divergence between spouses in terms of these kinds of behaviors.

Consumption Rationality and Solidarity

One consequence of these situations is seen in Table 6–17 where
we find that husbands and wives who considered dissolving their
marriages report a significantly lower score for spouse consumption
rationality, than those who say they have not considered dissolution.[103] The relationship is stronger for wives than for husbands,
but the data clearly suggest that the more rational or careful the
black husband or wife considers his *spouse* to be, the more cohesive
their marital relationship is. Conversely, the less the perceived rationality, the less cohesive the marital relationship. The fact that
consumption rationality, along with expressiveness (Table 6–8) and
hostility (Table 6–11), is meaningfully linked to feelings of marital

Table 6–17. Solidarity Feelings and Perceived Consumption Rationality of Spouse

		Degree of Spouse's Perceived Rationality in Spending Money (mean scores)	
		Husbands' Perceptions	Wives' Perceptions
Divorce or Separation Considered	Yes	4.95 (41)	3.81 (81)
	No	5.74 (155)	5.10 (120)
		(F = 6.87; df = 1 & 194; p < .01)	(F = 17.7; df = 1 & 199; p < .001)

solidarity, certainly underscores its import to marital stability. The husband (less often probably, the wife) who fails to spend money in a fashion deemed "careful" by his wife (husband) runs the risk of serious conflict with his spouse that undermines feelings of marital solidarity and potentially threatens the existence of the family unit. Although similar patterns probably exist among whites, black families may experience a greater frequency and special intensity of this type of tension, owing to their monetary deprivation and market exploitation vis-à-vis comparably situated whites. This condition too may help to account for higher rates of dissolution among blacks even above the underclass when compared with whites.

Although we have not considered the underclass in this particular discussion, we would assume that those persons (black or white) whose economic participation in the society is virtually nil, would be least rational of all in their use of money. It is not that such persons possess a "natural rejection" of "deferred gratification," but rather, as S. M. Miller et al. point out, all persons in our society ask, "deferred now for what payoffs later?"[104] Those who are in effect outside the opportunity structure, particularly blacks, see little sense in exercising care in the use of current funds in lieu of future advantage. Nothing in their precarious economic experience even remotely hints at the validity of such a process. Proponents of guaranteed family allowances argue, for example, that the relative certainty and security of that kind of program could perhaps provide a base on which to build some kind of meaningful consumption rationality. In any event, it would appear that consumption rationality is linked to one's sense of participation in the economic processes of the society. The more the participation, the more assured he is of continued payoffs; hence, the more careful he is in expending family resources.

Referring once again to Table 6–7 (Columns 9 and 10), we note that no one variable adequately predicts husbands' perceptions of spouse rationality. Yet for wives, the most powerful influence is clearly pervasive feelings of economic alienation, followed by husband's job status. As feelings of alienation decline (and husband's job status increases) the definition of her husband as a "rational consumer" tends to be more positive.

MULTIPLE EFFECTS ON MARITAL SOLIDARITY

Finally, in Table 6–18, we show the combined effects of all the key variables used in this chapter on feelings of marital solidarity and cohesion. Presumably, these variables represent some of the most critical factors that explain why some marriages (black or white) are maintained, while others are not. They point to the notion that there are certain rewards sought for in modern marriage which, if not gratified, undercut feelings of solidarity vis-à-vis one's spouse. Not surprisingly, for both husbands and wives, the strongest predictor of marital solidarity is the index of expressiveness or husband-wife primary relations. Clearly, blacks as do whites, seek from modern marriage, more than any other single element, fulfillment of the full range (not merely physical) of expressive needs and rights.

The path coefficient, however, between female expressiveness and solidarity is considerably greater than it is for males. Likewise, the multiple correlation (R^2) between all the independent variables and solidarity is stronger for females than it is for males. These

Table 6–18. Paths of Influence on Feelings of Marital Solidarity

	Husbands	Wives
Economic Alienation	− .132	− .145
Primary Relations	.197	.380
Husband's Job Status	.007	.090
Respondent's Education	.030	.079
Spouse's Education	.084	.041
Family Income	.076	.100
Wife-Employment	− .072	.185
Hostility	− .075	− .072
Authority	− .037	− .045
Consumption Rationality-Spouse	.109	.119
Fertility	− .044	− .061
Length of Marriage	− .084	.073
R^2	.35	.51
N	(127)	(154)

data continue to suggest the argument made throughout this chapter that wives' definitions of their marital situations are ultimately more critical with regard to conjugal cohesion and stability than are husbands'. Since in most instances the family remains the central focus of the wife's concern and activities, she is probably more likely to establish higher levels of expected rewards; and less likely to be willing to tolerate failures to reach those desired levels. Husbands, on the other hand, because their chief life-interests remain outside the family, are likely to expect and settle for less within the family. Therefore, predictions of "causal relationships" between rewards such as expressive gratifications and marital solidarity are much less firm for husbands than they are for wives.

Perhaps even more critical than the influence of expressiveness on solidarity is the influence of alienation on expressiveness and its influence on other components of husband-wife interaction. Figure 6–1 presents a simplified diagram tying together the most pertinent

WIVES

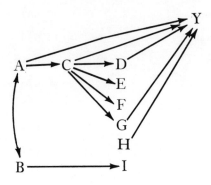

HUSBANDS

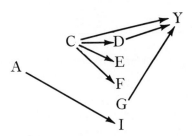

A = Family Income
B = Husband's Education
C = Economic Alienation
D = Expressiveness
E = Hostility

F = Fertility
G = Consumption Rationality
H = Wife-Employment
I = Authority-Participation
Y = Marital Solidarity

Fig. 6–1. Chain of influences on feelings of marital solidarity.

information from Tables 6–6, 6–7, and 6–18. It starts where Figure 5–1 left off at the objective status levels attained by respondents largely through tangible and intangible resources supplied mostly by their families of orientation. Although in Figure 5–1, husband's job status was the indicator of the family's "objective" social position, in this chapter it did not seem to have much direct influence on (though it was, at times, associated with) family interaction. This situation was attributed to systematic discrimination against black people so that in spite of certain educational achievements, blacks are denied job opportunities equal to whites with comparable education.

Consequently in Figure 6–1, we must begin with indicators of objective social status other than husband's job position.[105] For wives, the major paths of influence extend from income through economic alienation, through expressiveness and finally to marital solidarity. There are other less significant paths directly on marital solidarity, such as those from income, alienation, consumption rationality, and wife-employment.

For husbands, there is no clear path to explain their feelings of alienation. Perhaps for the black male, these feelings are accounted for in part by the all-encompassing reality of general, systematic economic discrimination. Nonetheless, the feelings are there and they exert a direct impact on male expressiveness that in turn affects solidarity. Thus, for both sexes the most salient feature of the diagrams is the centrality of feelings of economic alienation. At the conscious, overt level people marry and stay married because of perceived expressive rewards. But the definitions of these kinds of rewards are dependent in large measure on their definitions of economic and status rewards, and particularly so for wives. We cannot, therefore, explain marital cohesion apart from either economic or expressive reward levels. Specifically, in terms of black Americans, the economic deprivations they have experienced have had obvious consequences on those, for example, in the lower class. But in the more advantaged strata as well, discrimination has had its effects—perhaps more subtle but equally painful owing to a denial of earned achievements—on both major types of rewards that bind the conjugal unit in modern society.

SUMMARY

In this chapter, we have considered in some detail husband-wife relations within the black family above the underclass. It is reasonable to at least hypothesize that most of the generalizations made here could perhaps apply to many stable, urban black families. The basic thrust of the discussion was that husband-wife interaction is inextricably linked to the family's position in the economic-opportunity structure. As a result, we found many basic similarities with what we know of white families located at comparable status levels. In fact, the clear "drift" or trend within black family structure is toward convergence with family patterns existing in the dominant society. This is not necessarily conscious or planned, nor is it because dominant family forms are deemed "better." It is simply because family forms (black or white) in modern society are a response to the exigencies and demands of that kind of society.

The overwhelming majority of black Americans have made a value judgment, i.e., they want to participate in the economic benefits of a modern society. Inevitably, as a result of this goal, their family form takes a certain shape. As they increasingly enter into the dominant society economically, they also enter it conjugally. But owing to white discrimination which still hinders equal economic participation by blacks, black family patterns tend to diverge somewhat from dominant patterns. This situation is most obvious in the lower class. But the point is that these divergences are due to white economic discrimination, and not to intrinsic bio-racial differences, or to distinctive cultural patterns consciously chosen by blacks.

For example, increases in expressive gratifications and decreases in hostility are goals that white and black alike seek from modern marriage. In white marriages, "objective" resources such as husband's occupational status, education, and income tend to generate optimal attainments of these goals. Yet because blacks face discrimination in these three areas, we found it was more difficult for these kinds of factors to optimize desired marital goals. Other major differences between black and white family patterns centered on the meaning and consequences of wife employment, and on family authority and leadership. Although these particular differences have their roots in historical circumstances, both then and now the heart of the matter is economic discrimination. Historic and current black-white fertility differences can also be attributed to systematic exlusion of blacks from the opportunity structure and not to any "mystical Negro sexuality."

These several differences, however, should not obscure the main point, i.e., there are more similarities than differences in black and white conjugal relations, and that if blacks are permitted to participate more fully in the economic system, any existing differences will probably diminish in significance. Already there is evidence that over the several elements discussed in this chapter (husband-wife primary relations, wife-employment, family authority, hostility, wife employment, fertility, and consumption rationality), there is considerable movement toward a convergence of black-white behavior patterns.

The question of whether blacks "should" in the future develop their own unique conjugal patterns is something only blacks can answer for themselves. Up to this point in time, there is no evidence of any movement in that direction. If there is to be any significant trend of that sort in the next few decades, we would expect to find stirrings of it in the ways in which these parents socialize their own children to function in society. Examination of parent-child relations brings us full-cycle in our consideration of the developmental process within the "black family in modern society." We began by looking at family backgrounds of those in the sample, and now, in effect, we turn in Chapter 7 to certain background experiences of their own children.

NOTES

1. See Scanzoni, *Opportunity and the Family*.
2. See Robert F. Winch, *The Modern Family* (New York: Holt, Rinehart, Winston, 1963 rev.) pp. 709–13.

3. Scanzoni, *Opportunity and the Family*.

4. The remaining areas, discussed later in the chapter, are hostility relations, authority relations, fertility, and consumption rationality.

5. The exact wording was, "How do you feel about the companionship that you and your (husband-wife) have in doing things *together* during leisure or non-work time? Do you feel it's very good, ok, or not so good?" The question avoids all implications of "happiness, marital success, or adjustment." It is simply based on a fundamental sociological axiom, *viz.*, given a particular situation, persons in it will react to aspects of it in certain ways and evaluate these aspects accordingly. See Edwin L. Lively, "Toward Concept Clarification: The Case of Marital Interaction," *Journal of Marriage and the Family* 31 (February 1969) for a critique of "marital happiness" and related notions.

6. Male N = 154, 41, 3; Female N = 100, 65, 36; df = 2; x^2 = 44.8; p < .001.

7. Scanzoni, *Opportunity and the Family*.

8. "How do you feel about the love and physical affection that you receive from your spouse? Do you feel . . ." Males N = 152, 40, 5; Female = 122, 60, 20; df = 2; x^2 = 16.2; p < .001.

9. How do you feel about the way you and your (husband-wife) can confide in each other, talk things over, and discuss anything that comes up? Do you feel . . . ?

10. Male N = 147, 42, 9; Female = 111, 52, 37; df = 2; x^2 = 23.1; p < .001.

11. "How do you feel about the understanding that you receive from your (spouse.) of your problems and feelings? Do you feel . . . ?" Male N = 152, 36, 10; Female = 98, 67, 35; df = 2; x^2 = 34.8; p < .001.

12. John R. Seeley, R. Alexander Sim, Elizabeth W. Looseley, *Crestwood Heights* (New York: Basic Books, 1956), p. 178.

13. Pettigrew, *A Profile of the Negro American*, p. 187.

14. Ibid., pp. 191–92.

15. The index was constructed by assigning the following weights to the particular responses (very good = 5, ok = 3, not so good = 1) for each of the four questions. Each respondent then had a total score based on these four weights. For all husbands, $\bar{x}$ = 17.95, s.d. = 2.89. For all wives, $\bar{x}$ = 15.95, s.d. = 3.87.

16. "Low" rank in the table includes all households where the husband's S.E.S. score was 0–37; where their scores were 38–59 they were put in the

"medium" category; scores from 60–96 were put in the "high" category. The same procedure is followed in succeeding tables.

17. See our Chapter 5 (Table 5–3) for this discussion.

18. See Alvin Gouldner, "The Norm of Reciprocity: A Preliminary Statement," *American Sociological Review*, 1960.

19. Robert K. Merton, "Intermarriage and the Social Structure: Fact and Theory," in Ruth L. Coser, *The Family: Its Structure and Functions* (New York: St. Martin's Press, 1964), p. 149.

20. Ralph H. Turner, "Book Review," *American Journal of Sociology* 74 (September 1968): 198–99.

21. Andrew Billingsley, *Black Families in White America*, p. 170.

22. E. Franklin Frazier, *The Black Bourgeoisie*. Some critics claim that Frazier's points do not apply to black youth currently in college, i.e., to them, "black is beautiful, no matter what the white man thinks."

23. See Billingsley, *Black Families in White America*, pp. 167 ff.

24. J. Richard Udry, "Marital Instability by Race, Sex, Education, and Occupation using 1960 Census Data," *American Journal of Sociology* 72 (September 1966): 203–210. Jesse Bernard, "Marital Stability and Patterns of Status Variables," *Journal of Marriage and the Family* 28 (November 1966): 421–39.

25. Scanzoni, *Opportunity and the Family*.

26. Ibid.

27. Hyman and Singer, *Readings in Reference Group Theory and Research*, p. 11.

28. See J. F. Engel, D. T. Kollat, R. D. Blackwell, *Consumer Behavior* (New York: Holt, Rinehart, Winston, 1968), pp. 259–60; J. E. Stafford, K. K. Cox, J. B. Higginbotham, "Some Consumption Pattern Differences Between Urban Whites and Negroes," *Social Science Quarterly* 49 (December 1968): 619–630; Andrew F. Brimmer, "The Negro in the National Economy," in Davis, *The American Negro Reference Book*, pp. 275 ff.

29. A recent study of urban Negroes showed a relationship between status level of black reference group chosen and mental illness. See Seymour Parker and Robert J. Kleiner, *Mental Illness in the Urban Negro Community* (New York: The Free Press, 1966).

30. "There has been a lot of talk recently about social classes in the United States. If you were asked to use one of *these* names for your social class, which would you say you belonged in?" the lower class; the working class; the middle class (upper or lower); the upper class.

31. Scanzoni, *Opportunity and the Family*.

32. Ralph H. Turner, *The Social Context of Ambition* (San Francisco: Chandler Publishing Co., 1964), p. 217.

33. In another place life-style satisfaction was used as an *intervening* variable between alienation and expressiveness. Here it is used more as an *indirect* indicant of economic alienation. Satisfaction with family life-style is tied to the resources provided by the opportunity structure, and thus indirectly reflects articulation with it. Scanzoni, *Opportunity*.

34. See ibid., where this future-orientation was described as a form of *anomie*.

35. "Every person has some idea of what it means to be a success in our society. How good do you think your chances are to reach *your* success goals? Are they excellent, good, fair, or poor?"

36. Those conditions which influence choice of differing reference groups is of course a major issue in the whole area of "reference group theory." See Hyman and Singer.

37. Seymour Parker and Robert J. Kleiner, "Social and Psychological Dimensions of the Family Role Performance of the Negro Male," *Journal of Marriage and the Family* 31 (August 1969): 506.

38. Scanzoni, *Opportunity and the Family*. There is no necessary contradiction between this generalization and Goode's claim that the husband more often than the wife wishes to "escape" from the marriage. See Goode, *After Divorce*, p. 135. Even if the husband does wish to escape first (there is no clear empirical evidence for this) according to this reasoning, he must still *behave* so as to make the wife "want out." Interestingly, Goode acknowledges such male behaviors are not conscious or overt.

39. M. F. Nimkoff, "The American Family," in M. F. Nimkoff, *Comparative Family Systems* (Boston: Houghton Mifflin Co., 1965), pp. 330 ff.

40. William J. Goode, *World Revolution and Family Patterns* (New York: The Free Press, 1963), p. 57.

41. Each respondent receives an "alienation score" on the following basis. On the *"job Satisfaction"* item, assigned weights are very satisfied = 1; satisfied = 3, dissatisfied = 5. *Success Expectations:* Excellent = 1; good = 3; fair = 5; poor = 7. *Family Life-style Satisfaction:* very satisfied = 1; satisfied = 3; dissatisfied = 5. *Social Class Placement:* lower-class = 7; working-class = 5; lower middle-class = 3; upper middle-class = 1; upper-class = 0. Mean alienation score for males = 13.33, s.d. = 4.45; females = 13.77, s.d. = 4.47.

42. In the larger society, there is some indication that certain aspects of marital expressiveness become less satisfactory as the marriage wears on.

43. J. W. Thibaut and H. H. Kelley, *The Social Psychology of Groups* (New York: Wiley, 1959), pp. 21 ff. See also E. P. Hollander, *Principles and Methods of Social Psychology* (New York: Oxford University Press, 1967), pp. 204 ff.

44. Ibid.

45. This kind of question, though obviously not ideal, is widely used in the literature.

46. Male N: yes = 41, no = 156; female = 82, 120; df = 1, x^2 = 17.3; p < .001.

47. Males ever separated = 14; females = 33. Six of 7 males reported the wife had taken legal action; 7 of 8 females reported they had taken action.

48. Goode, *World Revolution*, 1963.

49. See Glen Cain, *Married Women in the Labor Force* (Chicago: U. of Chicago Press, 1966), for a discussion on increasing rates of female employment. For discussions of its marital consequences, see Scanzoni, *Opportunity and the Family*, also Susan R. Orden and Norman M. Bradburn, "Working Wives and Marriage Happiness," *American Journal of Sociology* 74 (January 1969): 392–407.

50. Scanzoni, *Opportunity and the Family*.

51. There is definitely a minority, among highly educated white women, who do define their employment as a *right*. See Robert Jay Lifton, ed., *The Woman in America* (Boston: Beacon Press, 1964).

52. Orden and Bradburn, *Working Wives*, argue further that an important factor in this syndrome is whether the wife feels "forced" into outside employment by financial exigencies.

53. Male N: wife work = 98; wife not work = 98; df = 1&194; F = 1.9; n.s. Female N = 83, 119; df = 1 & 200; F = .01.

54. *Male, wife works:* very satisfied $\bar{x}$ = 18.2; fairly = 16.6; dissatisfied = 18.5; df = 2&95; F = 3.7; p<.05. *Male, wife not work:* $\bar{x}$ = 18.9, 17.3, 15.6; df = 2 & 95; F = 6.9; p<.01. *Female, employed:* $\bar{x}$ = 16.7, 14.6, 12.9; df = 2 & 115; F = 6.1; p<.01. *Female, not employed:* $\bar{x}$ = 16.8, 14.2, 14.3; df = 2 & 79; F = 5.3; p<.01.

55. Steinmann, Fox, Farkas, "Attitudes Toward Marriage," op. cit. The discussion in the text draws from this report. For extensive data on conditions surrounding employment of black and white mothers, see Florence A. Ruderman, *Child Care and Working Mothers* (New York: Child Welfare League of America, 1968), pp. 129 ff. 152 ff. 194 ff. 215 ff.

56. Jeanne L. Noble, "The American Negro Woman," in Davis, 1966, p. 535.

57. Ibid., p. 526.

58. Ibid., pp. 533–34. Billingsley, however (*Black Families in White America*, pp. 79–88), notes that sex differences in black education and occupation are diminishing in the urban north and west.

59. Eli Ginzberg and Dale L. Hiestand, "Employment Patterns," pp. 216–17.

60. U.S. Bureau of the Census, *Current Population Reports*, Series P-23, special studies No. 27, "Trends in Social and Economic Conditions in Metropolitan Areas," Washington, D.C., February 7, 1969, p. 49.

61. Talcott Parsons, "The Social Structure of the Family," in Ruth N. Anshen, ed., *The Family: Its Function and Destiny* (New York: Harper and Row, 1959), pp. 241–74. This view, however, comes under strong attack by Alice S. Rossi, "The Road to Sex Equality," 1969, Towson College, Baltimore, Md. (Unpublished paper).

62. Cited in Walter L. Slocum, *Occupational Careers* (Chicago: Aldine Publishing Company, 1966), p. 163.

63. Ibid.

64. Ibid.

65. George C. Homans, *Social Behavior: Its Elementary Forms* (New York: Harcourt, Brace and World, 1961), p. 44.

66. See Scanzoni, *Opportunity and the Family*.

67. Male $N = 75$, 97, 23; female $= 8$, 13, 38, 83, 59; $df = 4$; $x^2 = 25.4$; $p < .001$.

68. Of those able to verbalize a response to the question, 27 percent replied in that fashion. (68 out of 248).

69. The responses to the item described in the text were weighted as follows: very often $= 9$; often $= 7$; sometimes $= 5$; seldom $= 3$; never $= 0$. For all husbands, the mean hostility score was 2.09, s.d. $= 1.7$; for females $\bar{x} = 2.74$, s.d. $= 2.1$. The items reported in Table 6–7 are the only "subjective" dimensions of alienation in which one or both spouses reported significant differences.

70. See Donald G. McKinley, *Social Class and Family Life* (New York: The Free Press, 1964), for an application of this hypothesis to father-son relations.

71. Male $N = 66$, 66, 63; $df = 2 \& 192$; $F = 0.3$. Female $N = 60$, 64, 66; $df = 2 \& 187$; $F = 2.2$; n.s.

72. Robert O. Blood and Donald M. Wolfe, *Husbands and Wives* (New York: The Free Press, 1960); David M. Heer, "The Measurement and

Bases of Family Power: An Overview," *Marriage and Family Living* 25 (May 1963): pp. 133–39; Scanzoni, *Opportunity and the Family*; Eugen Lupri, "Contemporary Authority Patterns in the West German Family: A Study of Cross-National Validation," *Journal of Marriage and the Family* 31 (February 1969): 134–144.

73. Blood and Wolfe, *Husbands and Wives*, p. 34.

74. Ibid., p. 35. Noble, "The American Negro Woman," pp. 538 ff., concurs with this assessment, but argues that it applies most strongly to the lower class.

75. See Scanzoni, *Opportunity and the Family*, Chapter 6, for a discussion of the differing ways to measure family authority. As in almost every study of white society, financial matters represent the area "disagreed about" most often.

76. Data from ibid., Males: $30/264 = 11\%$; Females: $21/334 = 6\%$.

77. None of the remaining objective or subjective indicators of opportunity articulation revealed significant differences for either sex in conflict resolution.

78. The index was constructed by assigning the following weights to responses to the item cited in the text. Who gets his way: if respondent = 8; if spouse = 0; if compromise = 4. Males reported an overall mean power score of 2.89, s.d. = 2.73. Wives reported an overall mean power score of 3.84, s.d. = 3.25.

79. See Scanzoni, *Opportunity and the Family*.

80. Karl King, "Adolescent Perception of Power Structure in the Negro Family," *Journal of Marriage and the Family* 31 (November 1969): 751–55.

81. See Chapter 8 for a detailed discussion of the fit between modern society and particular conjugal patterns.

82. David Heer, "Dominance and the Working Wife," *Social Forces* 36 (May 1958): 341–47. See Scanzoni, *Opportunity and the Family*.

83. *Table 6–12, Husband Response. Wife Works:* $\bar{x} = 54.0, 43.6, 48.2$; $N = 14, 35, 38$; df = 2 & 84; F = 1.1; n.s. *Wife not work:* $\bar{x} = 56.1, 40.0, 39.9$; N = 9, 35, 41; df = 2 & 82; F = 2.57, n.s. *Wife Response: Wife works:* $\bar{x} = 43.2, 47.3, 42.9$; N = 22, 26, 30; df = 2 & 75; F = 0.4; n.s. *Wife not work:* $\bar{x} = 43.6, 50.7, 47.0$; N = 35, 37, 32; df = 2 & 101; F = 1.0; n.s. *Table 6–13, Husband Response, Wife works:* $\bar{x} = 2.8, 2.2, 3.8$; N = 29, 28, 30; df = 2 & 84; F = 2.33, n.s. *Wife not work:* $\bar{x} = 2.5, 2.5, 3.4$; N = 31, 32, 22; df = 2 & 82; F = 1.0; n.s. *Wife Response, wife works:* $\bar{x} = 3.8, 4.0, 3.5$; N = 25, 28, 25; df = 2 & 75; F = 0.1; n.s. *Wife not work:* $\bar{x} = 4.3, 4.0, 3.4$; N = 31, 34, 39; df = 2 & 101, F = 0.6; n.s.

84. Karl E. Taeuber and Alma F. Taeuber, "The Negro Population in the United States," p. 154.

85. U.S. Bureau of the Census, *Current Population Reports*, Series P-20, No. 168, "Negro Population: March, 1966," Washington, D.C., 12–22–67, p. 30. The figure in the text includes all related children under 18.

86. See Noble, "The American Negro Woman," p. 540.

87. *Current Population Reports*, P-20, No. 168, op. cit., p. 30.

88. Ibid., see cover chart.

89. Ibid., p. 28.

90. Taeuber & Taeuber, "The Negro Population," p. 155.

91. Ibid., p. 153.

92. Male $N = 66, 67, 65$; $df = 2$ & 195; $F = 0.1$. Female $N = 63, 68, 67$; $df = 2$ & 195; $F = 0.9$.

93. H. Theodore Groat and Arthur G. Neal, "Social Psychological Correlates of Urban Fertility," *American Sociological Review* 32 (December 1967): 945–59; Lee Rainwater, *And the Poor Get Children* (Chicago: Quadrangle Books, 1960), pp. 167–68; L. Rainwater, *Family Design* (Chicago: Aldine Co., 1965), Ch. 6; Lois W. Hoffman and Frederick Wyatt, "Social Change and Motivations for Having Larger Families," *Merrill-Palmer Quarterly* 6, pp. 235–44.

94. Ibid.

95. Taeuber & Taeuber, "The Negro Population."

96. Judith Blake, "Population Policy for Americans: Is the Government Being Misled?" *Science* 164 (May 2, 1969).

97. *Males:* wife employed, mean no. of children $=2.61$ (98); wife not employed, $\bar{x} = 3.67$; $F = 5.39$; $df = 1$ & 194; $p < .05$. *Females:* employed, $\bar{x} = 2.95$; nonemployed, $\bar{x} = 3.57$; $F = 2.07$; $df = 1$ & 200; n.s.

98. Calvin Goldscheider and Peter R. Uhlenberg, "Minority Group Status & Fertility," *American Journal of Sociology* 74 (January 1969): 362–65, argue that as blacks become more advantaged they will have less rather than equal fertility to whites, due to "insecurities" of their minority group status.

99. Theodore L. Cross, *Black Capitalism* (New York: Atheneum, 1969), pp. 21–30; Frederick L. Sturdevant, *The Ghetto Market Place* (New York: The Free Press, 1969).

100. Much of the subsequent discussion is based on ideas drawn from Reuben Hill, "Patterns of Decision-Making and the Accumulation of Family Assets," in Nelson N. Foote, ed., *Household Decision-making* (New York: New York U. Press, 1961), pp. 57–80. Additional empirical information on the notions of "consumership" and "rationality," is found in a volume by Professor Hill, Schenkman Publishing Co., N.Y., in press.

101. A "very careful" response was weighted 7; careful = 5; not so careful = 3; careless = 1. This was done *separately* for respondent and for perceptions of his spouse. Males mean score for themselves = 4.87; For their spouses = 5.59. Females mean score for themselves = 5.50; for their spouses = 4.58.

102. Education, income, and "success chances," do not discriminate for either sex in statistically significant fashion.

103. No such relationship appeared for respondent's *own* consumption rationality.

104. See S. M. Miller et al., in Ferman et al., 1965, pp. 285 ff.

105. The correlation between family income and husband's education, represented by curved arrow in wife segment of the diagram is .25.

7

Parents
and Children

In certain previous chapters, we looked at some of the ways in which, as adolescents, blacks in the sample interacted with their own parents. We looked too at how they responded to their parents, how they identified with them, and how this identification alongside their education may have affected their subsequent position in the opportunity structure. The next step was to see how this very same position influenced their own marriages. In this chapter, we shall view them as *parents*, heading their own families of procreation. If we take seriously the idea that what their own parents did to them and for them substantially influenced their later lives, then we may likewise assume that how they relate to their own children will influence the next generation of blacks as well.

To be sure, this influence does not occur independently of the opportunity system. It is apparent from earlier chapters that what blacks can and actually try to do for their children is frequently limited, crimped, and frustrated by white-controlled educational and occupational structures. But precisely because this clash of white power and black aspirations occurs in part within the context of the conjugal family, it becomes all the more vital to examine the arena in which the tension is acted out.

A particular family system, and the cultural heritage it transmits, can be effectively undermined in one of two ways. One is by interrmarriage with members of out-groups, especially strongly dominant groups.[1] The other is by severe deprivation of the resources necessary to existence. When it comes to blacks American whites have eschewed the first alternative and embraced the second. During days of slavery and Jim Crow, murder and lynchings were the means to deprive blacks of even their lives. In this century, the deprivations (economic and social) have been less coarse but nonetheless painful. Therefore as Billingsley notes, the whole history of the black family in America has been one continuous effort to cope with these deprivations.[2] A large segment of the next generation of black Americans is presently part of a family system that has "come to terms" with white society in the manner described in Chapters 5 and 6. How is that next generation being socialized to cope with the kind of society in which it will live?

For example, given that whatever black leadership emerges will come from these strata rather than from the lower class, what kinds of attitudes toward white society are being communicated to these children?[3] Specifically, are they being encouraged to pursue dominant occupational and conjugal goals as their parents were and generally did? Or are they moving instead toward a repudiation of these goals and acceptance of alternatives as proposed by a few extreme militants? Answers to these questions are vital, not only because of their theoretical significance, but also because of their practical implications. For instance, the bulk of proposed government programs to "aid" blacks focus on the family—education, job training, guaranteed jobs, negative income tax (or family allowance). The fundamental assumption underlying these and other plans is that the opportunity structure must be opened wider to blacks.

Related to this assumption is the notion (right or wrong) held by most (white) policy-makers that the "healthy family" makes for a "healthy society." They usually define the "healthy family" as one where there is reasonable provision for the "good life." In this view possession of the "good life" reduces the likelihood that individuals will seek rewards through deviant means such as crime, riots, or looting. Absence of these events, it is thought, makes for a "healthy society." Two questions (among others) that naturally arise then are: Is this what blacks above the lower class actually want? And if so, how are children in these strata being prepared to seize (or to make) whatever opportunities come their way? It is to these dual questions of *goals* and *means* (to attain these goals) that this chapter is addressed. Certain issues were not included in this study, such as personality development of relatively advantaged black children. That and other questions must await future investigation.

GOALS FOR CHILDREN

Occupational Aspirations

We shall first look at goals that might specifically be termed "occupational." Respondents (who had sons) were asked if there were "any particular kind of job" they would like their "boys to have more than any other." The question was restricted to males, since the male in American society, more than the female, is expected to achieve, to fulfill the role of provider (see Chapter 6). Of those who did have a son, only about 34 percent replied "yes," they would like to see their son in a particular job. The remaining 66 percent said "no," but the great majority of these voluntarily supplied additional comments such as: "Just whatever job he wants." "Any *good* job he likes." "Anything so long as it is a professional job."[4] In hindsight, it would appear that although most black parents want to see their sons "move up" occupationally, they do not particularly care what specific job the son eventually takes. Had we listed categories or general types of jobs, undoubtedly many more parents would have been able to identify desired goals for their sons. Incidentally, there was no significant difference in family social status between those who could name a specific job and those who could not.[5]

Those blacks responding "yes," were asked what kind of job

they had in mind for their sons. Typical replies were occupations such as physician, minister, lawyer, teacher, professor, social worker, artist. Obviously, these particular parents want their sons to have occupations with very high status or incomes. In fact, 76 percent of those responding to this question want occupations for their children that the Census Bureau places in its highest prestige category, i.e., professional and technical.[6] When we compare occupations desired for children with those presently held by parents who express these desires, we find wide differences in status levels. Desired jobs for their sons are at a much higher status and income level than their own. Within the households responding, the mean S.E.S. score of husbands' actual job is 47.8; while the mean S.E.S. score of *desired* job for son is 75.5.[7] This finding respresents a desired upward gain in job status of about 28 points on the S.E.S. scale.

From Chapter 5, we recall that the mean S.E.S. score of males from all households in the sample is around 45. This figure is quite close to the 47.8 SES score for those expressing a job preference for their sons. Presumably, therefore, those expressing a job preference are representative of those not doing so insofar as desired job level is concerned. That is, had we listed "kinds of occupations" and asked respondents to choose from the list, the difference between father's actual job level and desired job for son would probably be about the same for almost all parents in the sample, i.e., around 28 points.

Blau and Duncan define an S.E.S. gain of from 6 to 25 points as a "short distance upward" in social mobility.[8] The parents of these respondents had a mean S.E.S. score of around 30 (see Chapter 5), as compared to the mean S.E.S. score of around 45 for respondents themselves. Thus they themselves have moved a "short distance upward," around 15 points. What they want for their children, however, is the level of mobility Blau and Duncan define as a "long distance upward," 26+ points.

Within the dominant (white) society, those with the lowest social origins tend to move the longest distance upward.[9] Likewise 25 percent of males in the Blau and Duncan national sample had in fact moved a "long distance upward."[10] However, these researchers also found that "a Negro's chances of occupational success in the United States are far inferior to those of a Caucasian."[11] Nonetheless, parents in the sample are evidently using whites as a reference point to measure the kinds of jobs they want their own children to have. They are apparently aware that many white children with social origins comparable to their own (relatively low to moderate) are experiencing substantial social mobility. *They want for their own children what white children have had and continue to have.*

Using past attainment levels of the majority of blacks as a reference point, however, plus the perennial hesitancy of white society to implement the kinds of policies that could help gain these attainments, it might be argued that these occupational goals for their children are perhaps in many cases unrealistic.[12] Still these appear to be the goals which they hold. The fact this is so suggests, among other things, a basic commitment to the American occupational system, and there is no indication of a repudiation of that system. For example, parents give no evidence of thinking their children should "forget about Whitey's occupational world and do their own thing—whatever that might be." Instead, these parents evidently concur with many serious advocates of "black self-determination." This view implies opportunity for the black person to be able to pursue any economic route now open to white citizens. Such a notion is congruent with the report of McCord et al., that most black leaders do not envision total independence from white economic processes, but rather the evolution of a type of "symbiotic interdependence."[13]

Occupational Expectations

Perhaps even more significant than goals or aspirations in assessing commitment of this sort is the degree of *expectation* that these goals will actually be realized. For if, in spite of high aspirations, there is little confidence that they can be attained, then there is serious question as to just how much commitment actually exists toward the occupational structure and the "American Dream."

Limiting ourselves to those who named a specific desired job for their own sons, we asked what "the chances are that he will ever have that kind of job? Of this group, 44 percent said the chances are "excellent," 30 percent replied "good," and 26 percent said "fair" or "poor."[14] Though judged by past standards, it might be unrealistic to think black males can actually achieve the kind of mobility their parents hope for them, nonetheless three-quarters of those holding such hopes feel strongly they will be attained. Hence, there is no indication that these black parents are disillusioned about the "Dream" or their children's chances to participate in it.

Children's Success Chances

The same absence of disillusionment or despair was evidenced when we asked a more general question of everyone in the sample with children. "What do you think your children's chances are to get ahead in life?" Forty percent replied the chances were "excellent," 43 percent said "good," while only 17 percent replied "fair" or "poor." Once again there were no significant differences in kind of response by status of husband's job.[15] Regardless of present social status, better than 80 percent of these black parents are quite optimistic about their children's chances to advance within the status structure of our society.

Even more overwhelming is the conviction that their children will participate more generously in the "Dream" than they have been able to. We asked these parents to compare the chances to "get ahead" that they had with their children's chances to do the same. Eighty-two percent affirmed that their children's prospects were "much better" than theirs had been. About 16 percent replied their children's chances were "somewhat better," and only 2 percent said they were "about the same." Here too there were no meaningful differences in responses by occupational level of husband.[16] Thus, whatever the actual or relative deprivation experienced or felt by these adult black citizens, as parents they are certainly convinced their children are going to experience far less deprivation than they themselves have. Whether this belief represents a kind of "false consciousness" or not, in view of the cumulative discriminations practiced by whites against blacks, we cannot be sure. What does seem evident is that these parents strongly believe that the opportunity structure is "opening up" ever more widely to their children.

College for Children

One reason they hold such strong expectations for this particular goal is found in their beliefs regarding a related goal, e.g., their children's chances of going to college. When we asked about their children's college chances, 28 percent said they were "excellent," 33 percent replied they were "good." About 17 percent indicated "fair," and 22 percent said "poor."[17] So better than 60 percent of those responding are quite optimistic about higher education for their children. Higher education, of course, although a vital goal per se, is also an (if not "the") important vehicle for black mobility.

Nevertheless, we should not assume that those parents who see their children's college chances as less than "good," do not at the same time perceive them becoming mobile in some fashion. It may be that they would like to see them entering the skilled blue-collar ranks, or certain civil service positions, etc., where college is not requisite for entrance or advancement. Finally, as we have found consistently in examining these success goals, there are no differences, with regard to husband's job status, in level of college expectations for children.[18]

In summary, these black parents—representative presumably, of those strata above the lower-class—appear "tuned in" to the success goals of American society as far as their children are concerned. They do not appear to have repudiated the goals nor to deprecate them. Instead, they seem to have embraced them personally both for themselves and for their children. Significantly, this is a striking convergence with white society. The great majority of black and white parents approve the "American Dream" for their children. Indeed both groups generally have high aspirations *and* high expectations that their progeny will advance substantially beyond their parentage.

A further important convergence with white society is that

these strongly held goals do not seem to vary by the social position of the family. There is considerable evidence that within the dominant society, both in terms of goals for themselves and for their children, the goals are rather uniformly distributed throughout the class structure.[19] Here within a specifically black sample, we find the same uniformity of goals regardless of class position. On the basis of evidence reported elsewhere, it seems likely that even the black lower-class shares these success goals with those in the strata above them.[20] It would appear, in short, that there is considerable homogeneity of shared success goals for self and children throughout all levels of black and white society.

MEANS FOR GOAL-ATTAINMENT

It is one thing for goals to be shared equally, and quite another when it comes to the *means* to attain these goals. Within the dominant society, it appears that the lower the status of the family, the less it provides those means that actually enable its children to "get ahead." Hence in spite of shared success goals, since higher status families are usually more adept at providing the means to attain these goals, their children generally attain higher status jobs than those from lesser status homes. In earlier chapters, these means were described as resources that are part of the process of parent-child socialization. They included such things as values, attitudes, and actual behaviors that would "help" their children in and through school, and would also aid them in penetrating the opportunity system. We have seen that, as adolescents, respondents' parents provided them with substantial amounts of these kinds of resources. Now that they are adults are they doing the same for their children, and are there differences by their social position?

Contact with School

We shall first look at those respondents who currently have children in school. Parental interest in the child's school is presumably an important incentive to the child to take his studies more seriously.

By meeting the child's teachers, for instance, the parent has a personal link with someone who is quite important in the life of the child. Not only does the parent thus have a more intimate check on the child's progress, it also reinforces in the child's mind his parents' direct and genuine concern with his academic efforts.

Therefore, we asked those with children currently in school if they had "met and talked with any of your children's school teachers this school year?" Seventy percent replied "yes" which is probably quite similar (perhaps even more) to what we might find in a sample of white parents.[21] Also like white parents, it is wives more than husbands who make this kind of personal contact with teachers. While only 57 percent of husbands said "yes," 80 percent of wives replied affirmatively. However, no meaningful differences for either sex emerged by occupational level of husband as far as these personal contacts were concerned.[22] Social position does not discriminate among black husbands and wives in this regard.

The fact that blacks with relatively lesser status are just as active in this type of behavior as those with more status, underscores the earlier conclusion that ambition for children is rather uniform throughout the black class-structure. Blacks traditionally have seen the school as *the single most important* means whereby their children can attain "success." Drake and Cayton point this out in their classic study of the black community in Chicago and in Chapter 3 we saw how many of the parents of these respondents stressed education as "doubly important" for blacks.[23] When they, in turn, assume the role of parent we find concrete evidence of their own concern for the academic progress of their children. We have no way of testing whether, as some allege, the lower-class parent takes no interest in the school activities of his (usually "her") child. But above the underclass, this interest is strong regardless of social position.

Evaluation of School

A frequent complaint of urban blacks interested in their schools is that *de facto* segregation leads to inferior education for their children. "Inferior education" of course influences later achievement and so it seemed important to discover how these parents felt about their schools compared to white schools. We asked, "How do you think the school your oldest child goes to compares with most other schools in this city: better, about the same, not as good?" Fifty-nine percent of those responding said the schools were "about the same," 24 percent said "better," and only 17 percent said "not as good." Husbands were significantly more optimistic than wives about their children's schools; however, there were no meaningful differences for either sex in school evaluation by occupation level of husband.[24]

Each respondent was asked *why* he felt as he did, and answers centered on quality of teachers, of physical facilities, and of curricula. Specifically, those who felt their schools were "better" said it was these three basic kinds of things that were superior; those who had said "same" or "not as good" (worse) indicated it was these kinds of things that were either equal or else inferior to the situation in other schools. Hence, the great majority of these parents of school-age children are clearly satisfied with the three core elements of any school situation. They evidently feel that the teachers, facilities, and curricula to which their children are exposed are "sufficient" to enable their children to attain the kinds of occupational and success goals they hold for them.

We cannot be certain whether *in fact* the schools to which their children go are as "sufficient" as these parents believe them to be. The point is that they define them as such, which supplies additional evidence of commitment by black adults to the dominant society. In view of their great concern that their children participate fully in the "Dream" we would expect that they would give their schools extremely close scrutiny, as witnessed by the high proportion who have had teacher contact. To the extent this is so, they evidently perceive their schools as providing an adequate entrance for their children into the opportunity structure. There is a degree of congruence between their high child-aspirations, child-expectations, and positive views of the schools. No matter how much they do or do not see the society closed to them personally, they perceive it as substantially open to their children. That is not the kind of society these parents are likely to want to see "burned down."

Choice of Peers

Intimately linked to school experiences is the matter of peer influence. Traditionally, minority groups seeking "corporate advancement" have sought to escape the characteristics and behaviors
of the "lower-class way of life." Black Americans have in the past
been no exception in this.[25] The current stress on middle-class blacks
"helping" the (lower-class) "brothers" does not extricate black
parents from the long-standing dilemma of how to seek to influence
their children's peer choices. On the one hand, if they allow their
children to maintain friendships with lower-class children, the
latter might in fact be "helped." On the other hand, such friendships could impede the achievement goals held for their own children. Vivid descriptions of these kinds of role conflicts are found
in Frazier, Lewis, Davis and Dollard.[26]

Given this parental dilemma, we asked parents: "Do you give
your children specific counsel or instruction on what kinds of friends
to go around with?" Seventy-nine of them said "yes," they did;
only 21 percent said they did not. Wives were slightly more apt
than husbands to say "yes," and again there were no differences by
social position.[27] When we asked *what* they told their children,
responses were on this order: "Tried to point out detrimental things
to them—that they should not run with people that will tear them
down." "Did not want her to run with the low class of people."
"Not to run around with bad class of people—respect yourself."
"Go around with people you know and don't mess with low class
of people." "Always pick the best class of friends or no friends at
all." "I make them bring their friends home so I can see and talk
to them." "Not to follow the leader." "Don't be around children
that will do things you will be blamed for—if you see children
stealing get away from them." "Told them to think before they
pick a new friend—did they want to be like him?" "Associate
with the best people." "Stay away from hoodlums."

While black youth on college campuses are (rightly) concerned about ways to aid the lower class, black parents are in a
totally different situation. Most of the year college youth are

physically removed from the often unpleasant realities of the situation in black neighborhoods, whereas black parents must actually live with it day by day. It is critical to note that many black non-lower-class parents, as a result of segregated housing, find that their children experience much more extensive physical proximity with lower-class children than do white parents at similar social levels.[28] Moreover, the black parent must be involved with the immediate and long-range consequences of his own child's behavior in a way that the unmarried, college-age student, unbeset by such responsibilities, cannot be. If criticized, these parents might respond, in their defense, that if the parents of black youth now in college had not influenced their own children in the same ways as described above, those youth might not have gotten where they are. In any event, the vast majority of black parents in the sample resolve the dilemma of how to guide impressionable adolescents by urging them to take a *long-range, individualistic* stance toward peers.

They apparently feel that if the child's friend can contribute to his social, academic, and economic goals both currently and potentially, then the friendship should be cultivated. If the friend gives evidence of being an impediment to any of these goals, then he ought to be "dropped." This is precisely the orientation that is transmitted in white families and the convergence is significant. What is uppermost is the friend's contribution to the child in terms of "socially accepted" goals. The assumption, of course, is that one's own child can make similar contributions to receptive peers, and that what is maintained is a mutually beneficial relationship.[29]

The desired benefit or outcome is the "advancement" of the individual child into and through the opportunity structure. Parents (black and white) do not ordinarily stress to their children that they ought to "help" and "become involved with" lower-class children in an intimate primary-type relationship, chiefly because they fear (rightly or wrongly) that it will boomerang in terms of their own child being "dragged down." Although parents might encourage "social concern" in a general or objective sense (or perhaps even "acquaintanceship") they do not appear likely in most cases to encourage friendship with lower-class children. They apparently believe that adolescents, reaching *across* to their age equals (but social inferiors), are much less likely to have the positive impact that say, campus youth might have, reaching *downward* both in status position and age.

Religious Instruction

Closely allied to and supportive of stress on "suitable" peer choice is the question of religious instruction. In earlier chapters, we saw something of the historical and current importance of the church to black Americans. A good deal of religious teaching within the black community has been socio-ethical in nature, i.e., reinforcing the kinds of goal-oriented behavior encountered in the discussion on the selection of friends. We know that most respondents in the sample are relatively involved in organized religious activity. Fifty-one percent attend *at least* once a week, 13 percent attend "every other week," 29 percent attend "about once a month" or "occasionally," while only 7 percent never attend.[30] Nonetheless, recalling Chapter 2, this represents less behavioral involvement in church than their own parents displayed.

The question is do these respondents, as parents, maintain the tradition within black society of transmitting religious instruction that has the effect of reinforcing the quest for achievement and success—an orientation to which many of them were exposed (see Chapter 3). We asked: "Compared to other families you know, how much religious training do you give your children—more, less, same?" (Presumably most of the "other families" are also black.) Sixty-seven percent of those responding indicated they gave the "same" amount of religious training, 28 percent said "more," and 5 percent said "less." Once again, there were no differences by husband's occupational level.[31]

While these limited data necessarily restrict the scope of our inferences we can make one major point. Almost all these parents acknowledge some effort at religious instruction for their children.

These efforts are perceived as equal to or in some cases greater than those of others in the black community. Most significantly, these parents do not reject the notion that they or other contemporary black parents are seeking to instill religious values into their children. Instead, they are likely maintaining the socio-ethical religious tradition described earlier, in spite of clear trends toward lessened church attendance.

This finding provides one more bit of evidence that the majority of black adults have not radicalized vis-à-vis the larger society. Some militants, for example, argue that one of the elements in black society that absolutely must "go" is the "white man's" religion. But given the fact that "American religion" is so intimately bound up with the success ethos (for whites and blacks) it seems unlikely that most blacks are about to give up either though formal church attendance may decline. Indeed there is clear evidence that when a group of lower-class blacks did give up "Whitey's" Christianity and became Black Muslims, they were better able than nominal Christians to fulfill dominant marriage patterns as well as the American success ethos.[32] Thus a "nonwestern" religion, with a strong separatist ideology, but set in the fabric of American society, has identical economic consequences for blacks as does a particular variety of Christianity. The point is that socio-ethical religion, as one more *means* to enable black youth to achieve and succeed, is still very much a part of the black family system in America.

So far in looking at the school, peers, and religion as *means* toward success goals we have found no differences by social position. That is, regardless of the family's location in the class structure (remember that all are above the lower-class) there was equal utilization of these particular means, just as there was equal emphasis at all class levels on dominant success goals. However, we come now to two final "means" whereby families encourage "success" in their children and in which we do find meaningful differences by social position. Furthermore, it could be argued that these "means" are perhaps more basic and important than those just considered.

College-Encouragement

The first of these has to do with the emphasis that the parent places on college for his children. Blau and Duncan have demonstrated definitively what much earlier evidence and common sense had pointed to, i.e., the more the education, the greater the chances for high occupational achievement. This finding was replicated for our sample of blacks. Education is the key to later attainments: Whatever impedes education impedes mobility, whatever supports it contributes to success. One of these "supports" would be definite encouragement to youth from parents to make college a realistic goal. Although all youth in our society may know college is a "good thing," not all may believe it is "personally possible for me," especially if they are black, which is synonymous with disadvantage. The more the parent makes it a "personal possibility" the more likely it is to be eventually attained.[33]

In our study, parents were asked: "Have you ever specifically encouraged your children to go to college?" Seventy percent said "yes," 30 percent said "no," with wives slightly more active in this than husbands.[34] So the great majority of parents have tried to make college a "personal possibility," but as Table 7–1 shows, parents with greater status are more apt to do this than those with lesser status.[35]

In Chapter 5, we saw that male respondents who came from higher status homes tended to have higher status jobs than those from lower status homes. This is true of white as well as of black society. Here we have some indication that this pattern may con-

TABLE 7–1.   ENCOURAGEMENT FOR CHILDREN TO ATTEND COLLEGE, BY OCCUPATION LEVEL OF MALE HEAD OF HOUSEHOLD

		Father's Mean S.E.S. Score
Do Mothers and Fathers Encourage Children to Go to College?	Yes	47.7 (213)
	No	41.9 (93)
		(df = 1 & 304 $F = 5.47$; $p < .05$)

tinue into the next generation. Presumably, those children (black or white) who are encouraged to go to college are more likely to get there than those who are not. And, subsequently, they will attain higher status jobs. However, it is not merely a matter of the value-impetus. Higher status families are also better able to promise and provide more financial help to their children. Nothing encourages a relatively disadvantaged child (in this case, "black") more in terms of college than some assurance of financial aid. In addition, higher status parents are probably better educated and thus can provide more *genuine* help with lessons, as well as provide a home atmosphere more conducive to study, learning, and inquiry.

College-encouragement, and all that is implied in it in terms of college being made personally realistic, and financially and academically feasible, is a means vital to achievement and success. In a very real sense, this one means provides a justification for the other means previously discussed. Without this specific stress on college, the other three lose some of their force and meaning. Parents get personally involved in their children's school, teach their children to "watch" their friends, and use socio-religious instruction. Why? They wish their children to internalize a "bent" toward occupational achievement. But for maximum attainments this bent is incomplete without the stress on college. So no matter how active the parent may be in the other three areas, unless he is also active here, mobility for his child is more problematic. Yet while college as a desirable *goal* is distributed rather uniformly throughout black and white society, specific encouragement as a *means* to attain that goal is found more often among those families with higher status. And it is their children who will probably eventually attain higher job status.

Value-Transmission

The remaining and probably most vital "means" of all, in terms of later achievement, also varies by occupational level of parents. This particular "means" might be called the "basic values" or "fundamental orientations toward life" that parents transmit to children.

Over the past years, in a series of papers, Kohn has argued that certain kinds of parental values for children are intimately related to social class.

In one statement he and Pearlin say:

> Occupation stands out as a critical dimension of class. . . . By occupation we refer to . . . how the structure of work imposes constraints and imperatives on their behavior. Three features of occupational life [closeness of supervision; whether one works with things, people, or ideas; degree of self-reliance] account for a very large part of the difference between middle- and working-class fathers' values.[36]

What Kohn and his associates have found is that father's occupational position is related to a stress on child-obedience as over against what he calls "self-control" or what Lenski calls "intellectual autonomy."[37] Their studies have included samples of white and black Americans, plus a sample from an industrialized West European city. The conclusion is (and, it has empirical validity due to extensive replication) that working-class fathers (and mothers) in industrial society tend to believe that the "most important thing" their children can learn in life is to *obey*, or to conform to outward authority. On the other hand, most middle-class parents tend to believe that the most vital thing their children can learn is to exercise "self-control," "think for themselves," "respond to inner controls," i.e., to be "intellectually autonomous." According to Kohn, these radically different orientations are the result of differing job situations of the husband: in the working-class job setting obedience to outward prescription is requisite, whereas in the middle-class one's job more often requires autonomous decisions.[38]

Both in his studies and in Lenski's (where religion is also found to differentiate between the two sets of values) there is clear implication that autonomy promotes achievement and mobility, whereas obedience impedes it. For instance, children who learn to *think for themselves* can rationally weigh their school performance, the influence of peers, benefits of certain religious principles, parental stress on college, and then finally decide for themselves the meaning of these things for their success goals. Given that success goals are equally distributed, the autonomous child will likely be better able to plan and to order his life rationally to attain those goals. The "less autonomous" or primarily "obedient" or "conforming" child, on the other hand, may be less able to distinguish between harmful and helpful influences on those goals, and thus be less "successful." Obviously, the fact that middle-class children are more successful is not due solely to this type of value. But it is an intrinsic part of the syndrome that includes stress on education and financial resources. Besides, of all the "means to success" discussed, this one is probably the most crucial because it represents the pinnacle or apex into which the others ultimately feed. Given the essence of the American occupational structure, the child who is most autonomous is most likely to reach the greatest attainments.

Respondents in our sample were asked: "What is the most important thing for a child to learn to prepare him for life?"[39]

> To obey
>
> To be well liked or popular
>
> To think for himself
>
> To work hard
>
> To help others when they need help

Thirty-seven percent replied "think for himself" (autonomy), 33 percent said "obedience," 14 percent said "work hard," 11 percent "help others," and 5 percent "popularity." There were no meaningful differences by sex.[40] Because of their small numbers and also because of their theoretical superfluity compared to autonomy and obedience, the remaining three categories of responses are combined into the "other" row in Table 7–2.

The first column in the table suggests that our respondents fall under the same rubric that earlier studies have shown applies to white and black Americans and which probably applies to industrial societies in general.[41] Mothers and fathers with the highest status (in terms of father's occupation) are the parents most likely to stress intellectual autonomy for their children. Interestingly, not far behind in social status are parents who stress "other" values. Those with *least* status are the ones *most* likely to stress *obedience* (or

TABLE 7–2. CHILD VALUES BY OCCUPATION LEVEL OF MALE HOUSEHOLD-HEAD, AND ALSO BY WIFE'S OCCUPATION LEVEL

		Father's Mean S.E.S. Score (Responses of Husbands and Wives)	Mean S.E.S. Score of Wife's Occupation (Husbands' Responses)	Mean S.E.S. Score of Wife's Occupation (Wives' Responses)
Most Important Thing Child Should Learn	Obedience	40.9 (130)	24.9 (48)	29.1 (55)
	Autonomy	48.7 (147)	46.2 (58)	45.8 (63)
	Other	46.0 (119)	38.6 (51)	30.7 (53)
		(df = 2 & 393 F = 4.97; p < .01)	(df = 2 & 154 F = 9.01; p < .001)	(df = 2 & 168 F = 7.01; p < .001)

conformity to outward controls) to their children. As we saw under "educational stress," it is the higher status black home (as well as white) which is most likely to contain fathers and mothers who transmit the kinds of autonomy values that promote achievement. Presumably, as Kohn argues, this result is due to the greater independence and autonomy characteristic of higher status jobs.

Kohn has also examined the consequences of wife-employment on child values. He has found that among homes where the wife is employed, there is greater stress by both parents on autonomy than on obedience; where she is not employed, obedience seems to be more valued than autonomy. Parental stress on autonomy also increases with increases in the wife's job status.[42] The data in Table 7-2 (Columns 2 and 3) based on the job status of black wives in the sample, tend to confirm Kohn's findings. Column 3 indicates that the greater her own job status, the more likely she *herself* is to transmit autonomy values; and, the greater the wife's *own* occupational status, the more likely it is for her husband likewise to transmit autonomy values (Column 2).

In Table 7-3, we extend this analysis by asking which element among the several listed (husband's occupation, respondent's education, family income, economic alienation, wife-employment, length of marriage, college-encouragement) is the single best predictor of parental emphasis on autonomy-type values. We included college-encouragement in the equation because there seems to be some relationship between it and autonomy. Of those parents who replied "yes," they did stress college, 42 percent also thought child-autonomy was most important, whereas only 29 percent of them felt obedience was most vital. On the other hand, of those parents who replied "no" to the college question, 42 percent said obedience was most crucial and only 33 percent underscored autonomy. (One could expect that black children from homes where *both* college and intellectual autonomy are stressed simultaneously are the ones most likely eventually to achieve the highest status. Those from homes where obedience is stressed but college is not are least likely to achieve highest status. Children from homes where other combinations of these two elements exist likely fall somewhere in between.)

TABLE 7–3. INFLUENCE OF CERTAIN FAMILIAL FACTORS ON AUTONOMY
VALUES FOR CHILDREN

	Husbands		Wives	
	p	r	p	r
Respondent's Education	.226	.11	.143	.36
Husband's Occupation	.116	.41	.128	.11
Family Income	.140	.03	.012	.21
Economic Alienation	.047	.07	− .107	.02
Wife-Employment	.153	.09	.014	.11
College-Encouragement	.014	.01	.068	.17
Length of Marriage	− .156	.06	.040	.01
R^2	.30		.25	
N	(113)		(137)	

In any case, Table 7–3 indicates that for both husbands and wives it is their *own* education which has the strongest path of influence on autonomy values transmitted to children. For wives, their husband's occupational level follows next in degree of impact; but for husbands, family income and wife-employment seem to be somewhat more potent than their own job status. (It would also appear that the longer husbands are married, and are therefore older, the more likely they are to stress obedience rather than autonomy.)

In earlier chapters, it was made clear that there are various indices of a family's integration with the opportunity structure, e.g., husband's job status, education, income, a sense of economic alienation. Viewed in that theoretical light, Tables 7–2 and 7–3 complement each other. In the first place, there is a correlation between husband's occupation and his education (r = .30), and between wife's education and husband's occupation (r = .26). And beyond that, both sets of data suggest that the more fully parents (black or white) become part of the opportunity structure, the more strongly they tend to transmit autonomy-type values to their children.[43] Conversely, those who are less a part of it, are more likely to emphasize child-obedience. Parental attainment evidently, therefore, generates efforts to seek to instill individualism in children. At the same time, lesser attainments seem to undercut somewhat the strength of this kind of parental orientation toward children. The positive impact of economic-integration with the opportunity system on child-values is clearly analogous to its positive consequences for the several aspects of husband-wife interaction (see Chapter 6).

Figure 7–1 is the last of a series of simplified diagrams attempting to trace structure and process within the black family system above the underclass. Factors which have an impact on child values, i.e., education and occupation, were themselves accounted for in Figure 5–1 by earlier tangible and intangible family influences. Therefore, just as our respondents utilized parental resources to help attain certain socioeconomic and conjugal goals, we may assume that most of their children will probably attempt to do

A = Father's Education
B = Mother's Education
C = Husband's Occupation
D = Mother's Employment
E = Family Income
Y = Parental Emphasis
      on Child-Autonomy

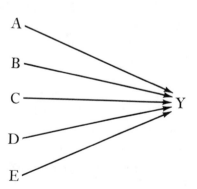

Fig. 7–1. Chain of influences on child autonomy values.

the same. Students of the black lower-class family refer often to the "cycle of poverty" transmitted from generation to generation. But above the lower-class there would appear to exist a "cycle of relative advantage," also transmitted from generation to generation. Needless to say in this late chapter, the advantage possessed and transmitted is *relative*—it is far less than that enjoyed by whites at comparable "objective" status levels.

ACTUAL AND PROJECTED CHILD-ATTAINMENT

We set out, in this chapter, to try to discover whether relatively advantaged black families share dominant patterns with regard to child-success goals and the means for their attainment. The weight of evidence seems to indicate that in both instances they do. We wanted to know if certain current black socialization practices differ from practices of an earlier day in such a way as to separate consciously the next generation of blacks from the white-dominated occupational-opportunity structures. There is no indication of this. But neither was there any indication of this on the part of their own parents, and yet adult respondents do not experience anywhere near equal participation with whites in the abundance promised by the "Dream." Moreover, as we saw in Chapter 5, the ironic situation was that children from families that provided most resources actually attained less occupational status than children receiving fewer rewards. As suggested there, this strange turn of events was due primarily to the intractability of the white-dominated opportunity structure.

Will black children who are currently exposed to the maximum *means* to attain success *goals* actually achieve lesser status than those who are exposed to fewer such resources? We do not know, but given the apparent continued intransigence of the opportunity system, it is at least a possibility. So in spite of the fact that black parents seem committed to the "American Dream," and to preparing their children for a place in it, their efforts may continue to be frustrated by the capriciousness of white society. The dominant society, in effect, communicates to black parents that they should socialize their children to participate in the economic mainstream. And so they do socialize in this fashion, yet their children are not able to participate as fully as do whites.

Nonetheless, absolute gains were made by our respondents compared to their own parents, and there is some indication that their own children may in general penetrate further into the opportunity structure than they have been able to do. To begin to determine this, all parents were asked what the highest grade was that each of their children (separately) had completed in school. We also asked whether each child was in school during "this current year." We thus arrived at a subsample of 132 cases of children *above 10 years of age who were not now in school.* Most of these presumably had therefore completed all the education they would ever get. Some perhaps would return for more training, but these undoubtedly represent a minority of the 132 offspring.

Table 7–4 shows a comparison of the educational attainments of all adults in the sample vs. those of children who have (probably) completed their education. These black children have made substantial gains over adults with regard to entering high school

TABLE 7–4.   EDUCATION OF ADULTS AND EDUCATION OF THEIR CHILDREN
WHO HAVE COMPLETED SCHOOL

Years of Education	Adults	Children
0–4	9.3% (37)	1.5% (2)
5–7	12.5 (50)	3.0 (4)
8	16.3 (65)	3.7 (5)
9–11	27.0 (108)	44.0 (58)
12	22.0 (88)	39.3 (52)
13 +	12.9 (52)	8.5 (11)
T	100.0% (400)	100.0% (132)

and also completing it. Only 27 percent of adults as compared with 44 percent of children have 9 to 11 years of schooling, and only 22 percent of adults compared with 39 percent of children have a high-school diploma. Very noticeable and perhaps the most significant element in the table is the slight proportion of children (8.2 percent) compared to adults (38.1 percent) who have only a *grade-school* education or less. Blacks seem clearly to be leaving the ranks of the radically sub-educated.

While less than 9 percent of these particular offspring have gone beyond high school (compared with 13 percent of adults), this condition may simply reflect the fact that some of the children in the larger sample were currently in post high-school training. When this number is combined with those now in grade and high school and who will eventually enter college, we may expect that when all offspring from the sample have finally completed their education, the total proportion will exceed the 13 percent of adults who have gotten as far as college.

The fact that these children are going further than their parents educationally almost certainly means that they will likewise exceed them in occupational position and in income. It would thus appear that the pattern of intergenerational gains within the black community (above the underclass) described in Chapter 5 is an ongoing phenomenon. This possibility seems reinforced by national census data showing substantial gains by blacks in school enrollment at all educational levels including college.

Of those enrolled in college in 1968, 434,000 were Negroes, or 6 percent of total college enrollment. The number of Negroes in college in 1968 was an 85 percent increase over the number enrolled in 1964.[44]

In all likelihood it is this realization of at least some steady gains which, *up until this point in time at least,* has preserved faith in and commitment to the American occupational structure on the part of black adults.[45] Awareness of the possibilities of these absolute gains is what probably accounts for similarities between black and white family systems in terms of acceptance of success goals and the means to attain them. It is this which has perhaps prevented a large-scale repudiation by black adults of dominant achievement and success goals for themselves and especially for their children. One outcome of giving some benefits to an underprivileged people, along with the promise of more to come, is to reinforce their support of the reward system.

Deprivation and Conflict

An alternative outcome, however, is that those who have tasted some benefits and who, at the same time, realize they remain severely deprived compared to the dominant group, will seek to undermine the reward system by tactics such as violence.[46] Several studies, for example, show that—

the participants in recent urban riots apparently did not represent the most disadvantaged people in the slum areas involved. . . . educational achievement [of] the rioters [was] slightly better . . . than [that] of their peers . . . and . . . the great majority . . . were currently employed. . . . the Watts rioters were in the mainstream of modern Negro urban life. They were not simply seeking jobs but better ones. . . . the typical prisoner [from the Detroit riot] was employed . . . in a manufacturing plant, where he earned an average of $120 per week. Two out of every five of the prisoners had a high school education or better, *but only . . . 1 out of 10 had a skilled or white-collar job, commensurate with this level of education.*[47] (Italics supplied)

It is this last element (discussed also in Chapters 5 and 6) that is evidently so devastating to blacks, and that is probably at the root of their painful feelings of relative deprivation. For in spite of conformity to an essential requirement of the "Dream" (education) they are not rewarded equally with whites for their conformity. Specifically, as far as offspring from the sample are concerned, as well as for black youth generally, in spite of the fact that they will exceed their parents in education, occupation, and income, the next generation of blacks will, for the most part, probably remain economically deprived relative to whites with comparable education.

In short, the pattern of "absolute gains-relative losses" which Pettigrew sees in the *present* generation of blacks, gives indication of continuing into the next as well. Indeed it may even become more pronounced simply because the educational system through programs such as "Headstart," "Upward Bound," and other similar forms of compensatory training both in and out of the ghettoes, gives evidence of becoming more responsive to certain black needs than it was heretofore. At the same time it is not at all certain that this larger number of better-educated blacks will necessarily face a less hostile job market. What the results of that type of potentially explosive situation might be, can only be conjecture.

For the time being at least the fact that better educated blacks are overly represented among alleged looters and rioters, should not result in their being lumped together with those whom McCord et al., label as "revolutionaries," persons who vocally advocate "dismantling" of the total society with the nature of its replacement (if at all) left uncertain.[48] In the former case, there is little if any conscious avowal to destroy the establishment, or any rational planning to that end. For the most part apparently, they participated in the riots because they were swept along by the chaos of the moment—immediate chaos that fed on their long standing feelings of relative deprivation.

As one recent study puts it:

> Rioters can be drawn from almost any stratum of urban Negro society. Once inflamed, the oppression of centuries breaks out in a revolt which makes no distinction of age, "respectability" or income. . . . one may make a distinction between three types of rioters: "violent" rioters (. . . who . . . are truly out to "get Whitey"); "carnival" rioters who simply enjoy the excitement of the riot and may also wish to get a share of the loot; and "ideological" rioters, who act on the basis of a more or less coherent doctrine which condemns the status quo.[49]

To the extent that our sample is representative of this mass of American blacks, i.e., the nonrevolutionaries, it would appear that nonviolent yet fundamental change within and of the system is what they desire rather than its demise. They apparently concur with McCord et al., who argue that "the only answer to ghetto problems, we believe, lies in the political realm. Blacks must exert political power and the socioeconomic structure will change."[50] For instance, each respondent was asked, "As you see it, what is the best way for Negroes to try to gain their rights in our society—use laws and persuasion, use non-violent protests, or be ready to use violence?"[51] Forty-six percent of our sample said "laws and persuasion"; 49 percent replied "non-violent protests;" and only 3 percent referred to violence. There were no significant differences by social status.[52]

There is no contradiction between these data and those which show that a large proportion of blacks feel the use of violence is justified for "self-defense" or is "justified for other reasons."[53] These latter data (as blacks themselves point out) simply reflect an orientation held as well by most white Americans that one may respond to force in kind. Hence the allegation by many blacks and Europeans that America is a "violent society" is in that specific sense correct. On the other side, it is an equally strong tenet of our society that genuine political, social, and economic goals can and should be attained by non-violent means. Paradoxical as they may seem, these dual orientations are held by the dominant society, and they appear to be held in the same fashion by blacks above the underclass as well. In short, conclusions based on our sample confirm those drawn by McCord et al., in an intensive nationwide study of the black community. They contend that "most urban Negroes simply reject" revolutionary ideology. Blacks "have basically the same aspirations and values as other Americans. . . . in the 1960's most Negroes seem concerned above all with political and economic, 'bread and butter' issues."[54]

In this vein one of the most basic and pressing changes that blacks would like to see brought about is equitable occupational and income rewards *for educational attainments equal to those of whites*. In the meantime, while waiting and pressing for this and other fundamental changes within the opportunity structure, the majority of the present generation of blacks firmly believes their children are going to obtain far more rewards than they have gotten; consequently this helps retain commitment to the existing structure and to those socialization processes that foster occupational success in their children.

SUMMARY

In this chapter we have examined the commitment of black parents to the American occupational structure insofar as this is manifested in child socialization for achievement and success. We have found that these parents hold high aspirations and expectations for their children's attainments. Likewise, they use means common to those used by the dominant society to seek to ensure these attainments. While their children are likely to exceed them socially and economically, it is not all clear that they will significantly close the gap that now separates blacks and whites above the underclass. Nonetheless there is strong indication that the next generation of blacks is being socialized to seek to participate in the "American Dream." Hence, this and other studies indicate that the beckoning of revolutionaries toward violence and certain amorphous goals is, *up until this point in time,* largely unheeded by the vast majority of American blacks.

NOTES

1. See Marshall Sklare, "Intermarriage and the Jewish Future," *Commentary,* 1964, where the author contends that unique Jewish identity and heritage are being lost as a result of extensive marital exogamy by Jews.

2. Billingsley, *Black Families in White America;* see also Bernard, *Marriage and Family,* pp. 73–77.

3. That such leadership usually emerges from other than the lower strata, see William McCord, John Howard, Bernard Frieberg, Edwin Harwood, *Life Styles in the Black Ghetto* (New York: W. W. Norton & Co., Inc., 1969), Ch. 11.

4. yes = 90; no = 171; T = 261.

5. Mean S.E.S. of head of household of those replying "yes" = 47.0; "no" = 44.7; df = 1 & 257; F = 0.6; n.s.

6. 63 out of 83 who were able to verbalize a job title.

7. $t = 6.64$; $p < .001$; $N = 53$.

8. Blau and Duncan, *The American Occupational Structure*, p. 160.

9. Ibid., p. 402.

10. Ibid., p. 154.

11. Ibid., p. 404.

12. Similar conclusions emerge in Aaron Antonovsky and Melvin J. Lerner, "Occupational Aspirations of Lower-Class Negro and White Youth," *Social Problems* 9 (Fall 1959); Theodore V. Purcell, "The Hopes of Negro Workers for Their Children," pp. 144–53.

13. McCord et al., *Life Styles in the Black Ghetto*, p. 287.

14. $N = 38, 26, 22$, respectively.

15. $N = 125, 134, 55$ respectively. S.E.S.: $\bar{x} = 47.7$; 44.7; 44.2; $df = 2 \, \& \, 307$; $F = 0.9$; n.s.

16. $N = 261, 47, 11$, respectively. S.E.S.: $\bar{x} = 45.0$ ($N = 257$); $\bar{x} = 48.9$ ($N = 58$); $df = 1 \, \& \, 313$; $F = 1.6$, n..s

17. $N = 61, 72, 38, 47$, respectively.

18. S.E.S.: $\bar{x} = 47.3$ ($N = 130$); $\bar{x} = 46.1$ ($N = 84$); $df = 1 \, \& \, 212$; $F = 0.1$.

19. See Ralph H. Turner, *The Social Context of Ambition* (San Francisco: Chandler Publishing Co., 1964), pp. 80 ff.; Scanzoni, *Opportunity and the Family*.

20. Liebow, *Tally's Corner*, pp. 59 ff.

21. The assumption is that the meetings and conversations were in connection with other than severe disciplinary or attendance problems. Yes $= 142$; no $= 62$.

22. Chi Square $= 11.1$. Husband ($N = 94$), wife ($N = 110$); 1 df; $p < .001$. Mean S.E.S. of husbands replying "yes" $= 49.7$ ($N = 54$); "no" $= 46.0$ (40); $df = 1 \, \& \, 92$; $F = 0.7$; n.s. Wives: $\bar{x} = 45.8$ (86); $\bar{x} = 54.0$ (21); $df = 1 \, \& \, 105$; $F = 2.6$, n.s.

23. St. Clair Drake and Horace R. Cayton, *Black Metropolis*, p. 666.

24. Total N: better $= 39$; same $= 94$; worse $= 27$. Husbands: 27% (20), 64% (47), 8% (6); wives: 22% (19), 54% (47), 24% (21); $df = 2$; $x^2 = 7.1$ $p < .05$. Mean S.E.S. of husbands replying "better": 46.2 (20), same $= 53.5$ (47), worse $= 40.1$ (6); $df = 2 \, \& \, 70$, $F = 1.7$; n.s. Wives: $\bar{x} = 50.1$ (19), 46.9 (46), 42.1 (20), $df = 2 \, \& \, 82$; $F = 0.7$; n.s.

25. Drake and Cayton, *Black Metropolis*, p. 710.

26. Cited in and elaborated on by Bernard, *Marriage and Family*, pp. 58–59.

27. Total N: yes = 251; no = 67. 82% of wives said "yes," 76% of husbands, n.s. Mean S.E.S. of those saying "yes" = 46.6 (247); no = 44.0 (67); df = 1 & 312; F = 0.8; n.s.

28. Evidence for this is found in Karl E. Taeuber and Alma F. Taeuber, *Negroes in Cities* (Chicago: Aldine Publishing Co., 1965), pp. 2–4, *passim*.

29. This is yet another application of exchange theory used extensively throughout the volume.

30. N = 400.

31. More (N = 89), Less (15), Same (214). Mean S.E.S. for "more" = 47.8; "same" = 45.4; df = 1 & 297; F = 0.9; n.s.

32. Harry Edwards, "Black Muslim and Negro Christian Family Relationships," *Journal of Marriage and the Family* (November 1968), pp. 604–11; see also McCord et al., *Life Styles in the Black Ghetto*, pp. 118 ff., for a discussion of "Protestant-Ethic Muslims."

33. See Elizabeth Douvan and Carol Kaye, "Motivational Factors in College Entrance," in Nevitt Sanford, *The American College* (New York: John Wiley and Sons, 1962), p. 200.

34. Yes = 216; no = 94. Husbands, yes = 65% (96); wives = 74% (120), n.s.

35. For further evidence of this same pattern, see William H. Sewell and Vilmal P. Shah. "Social Class, Parental Encouragement, and Educational Aspirations," *American Journal of Sociology* 73 (March 1968): 559–70.

36. Leonard I. Pearlin and Melvin L. Kohn, "Social Class, Occupation, and Parental Values," *American Sociological Review* 31 (August 1966): 466–79.

37. Gerhard Lenski, *The Religious Factor* (New York: Doubleday & Company, 1963 edition), p. 222.

38. Pearlin and Kohn, "Social Class, Occupation and Parental Values," see Scanzoni, *Opportunity and the Family*, chapter 7 for analogous orientations labeled as "passivity" and "mastery."

39. This is the form used by Lenski, but it is a variation on forms used by Kohn.

40. N = 148, 132, 55, 42, 23, respectively.

41. For a discussion of class as a more powerful predictor of parental values than "race," see Melvin L. Kohn, *Class and Conformity: A Study in Values* (Homewood, Ill.: Dorsey Press, 1969), pp. 59–60, 63–65, 69, 72. Also see Rose Stamler, "Acculturation," p. 288.

42. Kohn, *Class and Conformity*, pp. 30–31, 69.

43. The same conclusion is suggested in Scanzoni, *Opportunity and the Family*.

44. U.S. Bureau of the Census, *Current Population Reports*, Series P-23, No. 30, "Characteristics of American Youth," Washington, D.C., February 6, 1970, p. 2. See also *Current Population Reports*, Series P-20, No. 194, February 19, 1970.

45. See Blau and Duncan, *The American Operational Structure*, p. 439, for a discussion of the association, in a democracy, between social mobility and societal stability.

46. Ralf Dahrendorf, *Class and Class Conflict in Modern Society* (Stanford, Calif.: Stanford University Press, 1959), pp. 215–18. See also McCord et al., *Life Styles in the Black Ghetto*, p. 217.

47. *Manpower Report of the President* (Washington, D.C., U.S. Department of Labor, April 1968), p. 102.

48. McCord et al., *Life Styles in the Black Ghetto*, p. 233.

49. Ibid., p. 269.

50. Ibid., p. 287.

51. This is an item used previously in several surveys conducted by *National Opinion Research Center*.

52. N = 185, 194, 12 respectively. Two percent did not reply. Mean S.E.S. in each category = 47.0, 43.3, 51.6; df = 2 & 384; F = 1.9, n.s.

53. McCord et al., *Life Styles in the Black Ghetto*, p. 88.

54. Ibid., p. 283.

8

Substance, Theory, and Policy

For it must be said with all candor that the social scientists who have recently discovered the Negro family have not yet produced a study of that 75 percent of Negro families who have stable marriages, or that half of Negro families who have managed to pull themselves into the middle-class, or that 90 percent of all Negro families who are self-supporting, or that even larger portion who manage to keep out of trouble, often despite the grossest kinds of discrimination and provocation.[1]

Billingsley bases this indictment of social science research on several factors.

1. White concern with "deviant behavior"—especially black deviant behavior. Certain whites assessed the black lower-class family to be "deviant," and thus "automatically" worthy of study.

2. Because of the lack of a meaningful theoretical approach to the family (black or white) in modern society, white social scientists tended to transfer their psychologically oriented, individual adjustment approach to the black family.

3. When it appeared that this approach to blacks was inadequate, the "culture explanation" evolved. This development meant that the black family was understood as a "cultural type," i.e., it was the way it was because of "culture," including unique slave experiences. Few really bothered, however, to try to "account" for culture, or to draw clear distinctions between

> the variations of family patterns that exist within black society itself.

4. The feeling grew (especially among certain welfare and religious groups) that what was "needed" was to socialize blacks into "accepted" patterns of family interaction.

Lewis remarks that

the answer to the problem of family disorganization is not one of inculcating marriage and family values in young couples; there is ample evidence that they exist. The critical test is to find ways and means for the young adult male to meet the economic maintenance demands of marriage and family life.[2]

Through this unpretentious assertion, Lewis has put his finger on the theoretical (or explanatory) notion most central to the understanding of family structure and interaction (black or white) in modern society. This notion of socioeconomic resources has been the prime idea followed throughout this volume. The book, moreover, represents one attempt to respond to Billingsley's indictment regarding the paucity of research into what is, in fact, the contemporary picture of dominant conjugal patterns within the black community.

It is difficult to sort out the theoretical, substantive, and practical implications of a study such as this, since overlap inevitably occurs. Overlap, however, is not necessarily undesirable. It has been noted that the most powerful theory is also the most practical because of its capability to explain phenomena, thereby helping to bring about both understanding and control. Our plan is to examine the major theoretical, and then the salient practical (or policy) points that are suggested in earlier chapters. But first we need to briefly review the major substantive conclusions of Chapters 2 through 7.

SUBSTANTIVE CONCLUSIONS

In an effort to combine the structural-functional, interactional and developmental frameworks, we began by examining some of the background experiences of our respondents. *Structurally,* they appeared to have had a status advantage over the black population nationally. Many also had an advantage in terms of residence in and length of exposure to the urban milieu. With respect to *functionality*, or parental benefits, the great majority of respondents perceived their parents (fathers and mothers) to have provided them with ample resources for both economic and conjugal attainments. In addition, many of them encountered support and aid from community figures such as clergymen and school teachers. Most were highly involved with the church, which they also defined as beneficial. Their experiences in the school system and their own view of themselves as students tended to be quite positive.

When it came to the matter of *identification*, the majority of respondents chose their parents both as role model (positive or negative) and reference person. We found that identification was directly related to the level of rewards provided by parents. Of great significance was the finding that there had been substantial identification with fathers, which strongly suggests that the black father above the lower class, who is regularly employed, maintains a position little different from that of the comparably situated white father.

In Chapter 5, we began to examine the current stage of the life-cycle of these families. In terms of job status, education, and income, it was evident that they had made substantial gains compared to their parents. The sample also paralleled national trends among urban blacks in the same three dimensions, indicating that generalizations drawn from the study may be considered hypotheses applicable to dominant and prevailing patterns within the black community above the underclass. In spite of certain gains, however, it is clear that blacks in the sample and nationally remain relatively deprived when compared to equally educated whites. When trying to relate background resources to degree of occupational achievement, we found that those who had received most benefits from their parents did not fare as well as those who had received comparatively fewer resources. This phenomenon was attributed to patterns of discrimination practiced by the white-dominated opportunity structure.

The relative deprivation that black Americans experience also seemed to pervade husband-wife relationships. Unlike most studies of white marriages which consistently reveal that education, occupation, and income are positively related to marital expressiveness, such was not generally the case for blacks in the sample. However, as is so for white families, alienation from the opportunity structure was found to be inversely linked to expressiveness. In other areas of husband-wife interaction—hostility, authority, fertility—there was substantial convergence with what we know about dominant family patterns. Where there is divergence, it appears to be the result of white economic discrimination and thus black deprivation. Interestingly, one realm where whites appear to be moving in the direction of black family patterns is in the extensiveness and also definition of wife employment.

Moving finally to the child-training stage of the life-cycle, we discovered that most black parents want their children to participate in the "American Dream," and fully expect that they will do so to a greater extent than they themselves have been able to do. Consequently, they are socializing their children by means calculated to achieve these valued ends. There was some indication that their children might exceed the social status of their parents, thereby continuing the pattern of intergenerational gains that some American blacks seem to be making.

The fact that these parents were as active and vigorous in the socialization of their own children as their parents were toward them brings us full-cycle in this study of black family patterns above the underclass. The inescapable conclusion (and the notion that gradually edges us into a discussion of theoretical implications) is that the black family in America, as much as the white family, is shaped by its relationship to the economic-opportunity structure. This relationship is mediated primarily via the occupation of the male head-of-household. Where he is not present, as is often the case in the lower class, this has certain negative consequences for the family. And where he is present, the degree of his integration with the opportunity system influences most, if not all, aspects of husband-wife and parent-child interaction.

That there is a "black community" and a "white community" reflects in part differential access to the economic rewards of the total society. That there are certain "black family patterns" which may differ somewhat from "white family patterns" reflects this same differential economic access.

Gordon has coined the term "ethclass" to try to apprehend certain differences between groups at the same social-class level who in many other ways are quite similar. Throughout this book, we have documented basic similarities between black and white family patterns at the same class level, but have noted several dissimilarities as well. These divergences are largely the result of ethnically based discrimination against black-skinned people. They are prevented from attaining the preferences, values, and goals that they share in common with most members of our achievement-oriented society. Although our study has generated numerous hypotheses for further investigation, one important direction that future research might take is to focus on these divergences and their consequences for the family as a unit and for individual family members. We asked our respondents: "Do you think Negro men and women have the same kinds of problems in marriage that white men and women have, or do they have different problems?" Sixty-nine percent replied the problems were the "same," 23 percent said they were "different," and 8 percent said they "did not know." Of those replying "different," better than 90 percent indicated that the differences were in the economic realm (jobs, family finances, etc.). We did not ask the 69 percent what they perceived the "common problems" of whites and blacks to be, but we might hypothesize that if we had these would center on socioeconomic factors and their impact on family processes.

Future research, therefore, should look very closely at samples of black and white families whose educational levels are equal and whose ages are similar. To what degree do disparities continue to exist between these black and white families in terms of job status (for the male, and for the female when she works), and of income? What are the consequences, in black families, for husband-wife and for parent-child interaction when the inequities are great, and when they tend to be small? In this study, we have offered the broad outlines and some of the details of black family structure and process above the underclass. We have shown the processual inter-relationships between family background, family functionality, identification with parents, achievement and mobility, husband-wife relationships, and certain aspects of child-rearing. It is now neces-sary to test these conclusions and modify them where necessary. It is especially important to take note of convergence and divergence in family forms between blacks and whites, and to see whether increased economic access for blacks (if such indeed occurs) tends in the future to lead toward greater convergence of family patterns.

THEORETICAL IMPLICATIONS

Perhaps the most central and all-encompassing question we have considered is the evolution or "choice" of family form by black Americans. Some younger persons in our society have recently come to question the whole of what they call "middle-class values." Among many other things, they disparage the idea of a conjugal family, based on a more or less permanent arrangement, in which stability is the ideal. They point to some "liberated" young couples who are currently living together solely because of "love"—couples who have no legal or contractual obligations to each other.[3] In this situation, it is claimed, the façades and role-playing of "bourgeoisie marriage" are gone. In their place reign spontaneity and person-hood. Others claim to see the emergence of a stratum of highly educated, sophisticated, self-supporting, upper middle-class females, who choose to live alone or with any offspring, apart from any permanent resident male. Still others point to people living to-gether in varied types of "group marriage."[4] Therefore, since there is such wide variation in our society, argue these critics, why should blacks be burdened by "white family" traditions.

The reply, of course, is that no one is "burdening" blacks nor anyone else when it comes to marriage patterns. Instead, what we know about blacks from more advantaged strata support Lewis' conclusion regarding the lower class: "The evidence suggests that Negro mothers from the low-income category, as much as mothers in any category of our population, want and prefer their men to be strong and supportive in marriage, family, and community relationships."[5] The vast majority (probably better than 95 percent) of blacks and whites in our society clearly prefer the dominant form of the household consisting of husband, wife and dependent children, if any. There is no mystique about this preference; the conjugal family as several theorists contend, is simply the form "best suited" to the demands and opportunities of a modern industrial society such as our own. Those who make the choice to participate in the economic and status benefits of the society, almost inevitably, therefore, find themselves moved toward the *dominant* family form.

Furthermore, it is not accurate to use the term "middle class" in a pejorative sense to describe this family form, as if it were a hideous creature of some stagnant, tradition-bound, "bourgeoisie" culture. Nor is it accurate to call it "white" as if it were part of a conspiracy by ethnocentric whites to inflict their values on unsuspecting blacks. Neither allegation is true any more than saying the black lower-class matriarchy is the result of "Negro culture." Quite the contrary. The *dominant family form* represents those patterns that tend to emerge within the context of a modern, individualistic, achievement-oriented, acquisitive society. It is not a coincidence, for example, that the Black Muslims, once they adopted a work ethic virtually indistinguishable from that of the dominant society, have likewise evolved an identical family form.

Theorists, who in recent years have examined the association between economy and family, have largely focused on the erosion of the extended family form, and the emergence of the conjugal form in industrial society.[6] They have responded to those who argue that the conjugal family is in its turn being eroded, by contending instead that all available evidence points to the contrary.[7] Fewer people remain single than ever before in our history; the divorced remarry in greater proportions than formerly; and with so many households producing high numbers of babies, our population is growing at a rapid (same say "alarming") rate. While the "humanist" may argue that such quantitative data are superficial—that they do not measure the "quality" of family interaction —there is evidence as well that indicates that evaluation of family experiences by those involved is quite positive and substantial.[8]

The kibbutz represents the one contemporary family form that best approximates the ideals of those young Americans who seriously question typical conjugal patterns. However this exception proves the rule, for the uniqueness of kibbutzim marriage and family patterns lies precisely in their communal-agricultural type of economic system.[9] At the same time, most members of the "extreme left" who advocate certain varieties of "family experimentation" also verbally reject dominant achievement and success values. Hence they are consistent, but their position too reinforces the point that economic and conjugal forms are inextricable. And aside from the relatively few young blacks who are part of this extreme fringe, most blacks want the American Dream, i.e., they want to participate fully in American abundance and affluence.

What is the nature of the linkage between industrial and family systems? First, the *family* (*kin*) *does not directly control job or job rewards for its members.* "The prime social characteristic of modern industrial enterprise is that the individual is ideally given a job on the basis of his ability to fulfill its demands, and that . . . the same standards apply to *all who hold the same job.*"[10] Ideally, the kin (any relatives beyond husband, wife, dependent children) or wider family does not guarantee or give jobs to its offspring within industrial bureaucracies apart from merit. And even if a certain amount of nepotism does occur in terms of job-placement, once in the organization promotion and rewards must be chiefly on the basis of merit, else the bureaucracy itself may go under owing to competition.

Second, *the family substantially influences opportunities and achievements for its offspring.* American society leaves it primarily up to the family to prepare its offspring to compete within modern society. As a result, some are better prepared than others. Usually, the ones better prepared come from homes where the parents themselves have attained relative advantage.

Third, *the conjugal family serves as the established social vehicle whereby status and prestige are assigned in the community.* Since family name and tradition count for little in a fluid society characterized by great geographic mobility, certain consumption symbols displayed by the family *qua* unit and as individuals identify their standing in the community and in society. This process serves to convey a sense of worth and respect to those displaying the symbols.

Fourth, *the conjugal family is the prime unit which provides expressive satisfactions* or "psychological intimacy . . . such as comradeship, security, dependency, succorance."[11] While kibbutz couples (or couples in a "hip commune") may enjoy expressive benefits without concern for points 1, 2, or 3, it is not quite so simple for those enmeshed in achievement-oriented society. A recent account of college couples who "cohabit" more or less permanently without the "strings" of legitimate marriage, points out that finances become the "stickiest" tangle of their "idyllic" experiment.[12] Once the dominant goals of individual achievement and success are accepted, then all four elements are inevitably juxtaposed.

In this regard, one question that perenially puzzles European intellectuals is why American blacks are not socialists, why the overwhelming majority embrace a "market economy" and "private enterprise." A French journalist, after a participant-observer type of investigation of the most radical elements in the American black community, wrote for his countrymen:

> I had expected to meet revolutionaries of pure, hard purpose, who were preparing to overthrow the American capitalist system from within. Instead I found that the most "fanatical" revolutionaries were unconditional defenders of private enterprise and the American way of life. . . . They have taken as their own the traditional American ideology. . . . This is difficult for a European to understand.[13]

Decline of Kin Control

Assuming that blacks embrace the "Dream," let us trace, in terms of the findings of this study, how living in a modern, industrial society shapes the contemporary black family. To assist us we shall expand the four linkages just discussed between economic and family systems. First, blacks (and whites) have little option but to accept the reality that the kin unit does not *control directly* the economic destiny of its members. In view of the relative disadvantage of blacks, this condition is of course in their interest, as it is for any minority group.

More specifically for blacks however, it diminishes the "functional significance" of the (predominantly lower-class) matriarchate. Several generations under one roof, living at the behest of the eldest female, is an adequate means for survival in a hostile milieu. But because in a modern society that arrangement cannot guarantee more than survival, its continued existence is problematic. The same principle, of course, applied in the past to European and white American kin structures.[14] Once economic rewards are taken out of the control of the kin and placed in the hands of an impersonal formal organization, the focus of family organization gradually shifts from the kin to the nuclear or conjugal unit. Since the modern industrial setting promises not mere survival but also abundance and affluence, there is no compelling reason to maintain a traditional type of extended kin structure.[15]

At the same time, the fact that geographic mobility is often necessary to enjoy this abundance further depresses the desirability of living as part of the kin and greatly enhances living as part of a conjugal family. Therefore, it is not surprising to find that the vast majority of our respondents grew up without other relatives living with them in the same household, and that probably very few of them, as adults, had relatives staying with them on other than a temporary basis. As children, they learned the conjugal form; as adults, they sought to maintain that same form.

Influence of Conjugal
Family on Children

But while their families of orientation could not guarantee their destiny, they could try to influence it. And we saw that indeed their families provided substantial "resources and benefits" to help enable them to attain dominant economic and conjugal goals. Additional benefits were also provided to them by community figures such as teachers and clergy, as well as by relatives. But the greatest resources of quantitative and qualitative significance were supplied by fathers and mothers. This conclusion is borne out by the high degree of both specific and general identification that respondents made with their own parents.

Their parents felt very keenly the responsibility to socialize their children as they did, because if they did not, *there was (is) no other societal agency that could or would do it.* In an individualistic, achievement-oriented society, the conjugal family is the agency charged with the responsibility to prepare children to enter and to compete within the opportunity structure.

Obviously, the wider kin as well as private and government agencies, can and do provide benefits to the offspring of conjugal units. These benefits, however, are almost always intended to strengthen the conjugal unit *qua* unit, not to supplant it or to undercut its influence. At the same time, there is a proportion of American households "broken" by death or divorce. Nevertheless, it is quite likely that most adults who live alone with children consider this setting "less than ideal," and would want the "right" partner to help share the task of child-rearing. This desire is undoubtedly one reason for the high rates of remarriage in American society.

But most important of all is the issue of other agencies that might be the "functional equivalent" of the conjugal family to socialize children. If, for example, the couple who live together primarily to "find themselves and each other" could give any offspring to a "superb" state agency and be assured that the child would be "properly cared for," this would uncomplicate matters for them in the event that they became bored with their "mutual quest." In the kibbutzim, the larger community does in fact officially assume this function, thereby releasing the parents from prime responsibility for child socialization. Why not do the same in the United States?

Perhaps the strongest reason in favor of such a national program is that it would have a great leveling effect on opportunity. Aside from native intelligence, factors such as nutrition, exposure to books, development of reading and reasoning skills, economic benefits, quality of academic instruction, and so forth, would be more or less equalized throughout the society. Such a proposal might be thought to be particularly appealing to disadvantaged groups such as black Americans. The major implication of this idea is spelled out by Blau and Duncan:

> If parents, having achieved a desirable status, can *ipso facto* do nothing to make comparable achievement easier for their offspring, we may have "equal opportunity." But we will no longer have a family system—at least not in the present understanding of the term. (This point has not been misunderstood in radical, particularly Marxist, ideologies.)[16]

In short, if parents were actually put in the position of being unable to aid their children's attainments, it would signal a very different kind of family and also a very different type of society—one in which individualism and occupational achievement were far less central than they are now. Such a society is found in the kibbutz, which is the most successful experiment to date in communal ownership of property *and* communal socialization of children. But in American society where compensatory programs to aid opportunity (such as Headstart) or day-care centers for working mothers are encouraged as adjuncts to the family, it is nonetheless the conjugal unit *per se* that maintains primary responsibility for the training of children.

Consider the generational span of blacks in our sample. When they were children, these blacks were earnestly and effectively trained, primarily by their parents, to achieve. Now as parents themselves, they most willingly and eagerly take on this same task. Why? Because, for one reason, in a modern, achievement-oriented society, children and their attainments are viewed (sometimes unconsciously) as rewards, as compensations. Some parents (regardless of color) bask openly in the reflected glory of their children's academic, athletic or occupational attainments, while other parents may simply feel gratified in more unobtrusive fashion. In any case, the achievements of the children reflect back on the parents and provide a certain amount of prestige and status for them. Children, in effect, become another status symbol in a society whose status order rests on the display of just such symbols. The blue-collar parent may boast that his child is getting *A's* in high school and has won a scholarship to college. The white-collar parent is equally gratified by such outcomes, as well as by more subtle attainments, e.g., "my child is skilled on the violin or piano," "he's unbeatable at chess," "he's interested in abstract art."

The structure of the situation becomes quite clear when compared to the kibbutzim. In American society, it is believed that there is a great variety of occupations open to the child, and that whichever one he chooses he is "free" to do as well (whether in terms of money, or prestige, or power) as he possibly can. Therefore, it is in the interest of parents to aid their children, as much as they possibly can, to "do as well as possible." The more "successful" or at least "respectable" their child is, the greater the degree of reward and gratification this provides to parents. Therefore, most parents (black or white) will resist strongly any efforts to remove this source of gratification (which is so strongly embedded in the warp and woof of the society) from their control. It thus becomes apparent why, from this reward standpoint, the conjugal (or dominant) form of the family and an individualistic-type society are intrisically linked.

On the other hand, when the modern form of occupational structure is removed from the scene, such as in the kibbutz, children are no longer the reward incentive to parents that they are in industrial societies. Consequently, parents have no reason to object to communal socialization. Since neither they nor their children aspire to "upward social mobility," and since their goal is "to create a socialist enterprise in which all persons would experience the deep satisfactions to be derived from working the soil,"[17] it makes more sense, in fact, to ensure this goal through collective child-training. Once again, the point is that there exists an inextricable link between type of economic system and family patterns, specifically here, socialization.

Significantly in certain kibbutzim, family patterns including parent-child ties tend to take on a "Western" shape.[18] Shepher, for example, in a recent study, compared two types of kibbutzim—one with a *collective*, the other with a *familistic* system of housing the children. In the latter type, the children sleep in the houses of their parents; in the former type, they sleep away from parents in "children's houses." Obviously, the familistic system approximates the conjugal form of the household more closely than does the collective system. Shepher concludes:

> The most prominent differences between the two systems appeared in the field of consumption. People of the familistic system seem to be more "consumption-minded." . . . [They have] an outspoken tendency to extend further the range of discretion of the family in consumption matters.[19]

Shepher's point is that there is an association between personal responsibility for children and a desire to consume in their behalf, i.e., to provide them with certain material benefits and advantages. Why the association? Shepher remarks that the founders and leaders of familistic kibbutzim have always been more individualistic in their ideologies. Owing, therefore, to their own preferences and values they *prefer* a familistic system; they prefer the pattern of providing as great a level of benefits as possible to their own children that inevitably results in differences and inequities. What is it about their individualism that accounts for these preferences? One explanation is that they too view their children as a source of "status-rewards" reflecting back on the parent's own prowess in providing for them at both the tangible and intangible levels. In sum, even among some kibbutzim, there would appear to be a connection between individualism, the approximation of a distinct and clearly definable conjugal-type family unit, and children as a kind of "status-symbol" for that unit.

Status Order and
Husband-Wife Economic Interdependence

The preceding discussion moves us into the third major factor which accounts for the linkage of modern society with the conjugal family. In trying to explain why, once American blacks embrace the "Dream" and its corresponding ethos they then tend to evolve the dominant family form, we have focussed chiefly on parent-child relations. We turn next to husband-wife relations. Much of the essence of what the conjugal family is "all about" hinges on the fact that it is the *center* for the display of consumption symbols that accord status and thus personal worth. Given the stress in American society on "visible success," some "center" or focal point must exist. Conversely, in some kibbutzim because such emphasis is relatively absent, there is less need for any such structure.

Consider, for example, a black couple who are representative of that great majority of the black community who want to participate in the "Dream," they want to "get ahead," to "succeed," to have certain levels of money. The purpose of the income is not merely to maximize gain (in the Marxist sense) but primarily to be able to "prove" to significant and "community-others" that one is "worthy," or "respectable" (as described by Max Weber). To accomplish this, the income is used to obtain appropriate consumption symbols. Obviously, single men and women (black or white) engage in a similar process, and are formally recognized through Census Bureau terms as "single-person households."

When, however, a male and female engage in this process *conjointly*, they become *ipso facto* economically interdependent. The female takes on the male's status since it is his occupation and income that largely determines the life-style which, in turn, gives rise to their jointly shared status. And as chief "consumption agent" for the family, she generally participates heavily in the distribution of family resources, thus making exceedingly personal and intense her involvement in the family's economic position. And if she works, her involvement is increased still further. Often, for instance, her income is used to enhance the life-style of the family. (In spite of that embellishment, however, the actual class level of the American family continues to rest chiefly on the occupation of the male head-of-household.) By definition, according to Murdock, this type of economic interdependence constitutes one essential half of what marriage is (the other being sexual access, discussed below).[20]

Central to this discussion is the premise that the particular couple (black or white) wishes to participate fully in the American "success syndrome," and that implicit in this must be some way to "show to others" that they are in fact doing so. If this premise is granted, then the conjugal form of the household, based on the economic interdependence described above, tends to emerge almost inevitably within American society. This condition has been true for whites, and it appears to hold also for blacks. Given the nature of American society, this conjugal form is the dominant and by far the *predominant* form of the family. No other form, up to this point in time, has "fit" the modern character of American society quite so well.

Regarding the future, there is one factor that could engender certain changes in the dominant family form with regard to economic interdependence. But this would have nothing to do with race, ideology, or culture. It would not be something peculiarly black or white. It would rest instead on the changing definition of the role of woman. Such change, significantly (were it to occur), would emerge straight out of the historic and "constant" stress on individualistic achievement. Women, of course, are working in increasing numbers, but as yet except for a tiny minority (black or white), few define this as a life-interest comparable in significance and scope to domestic interests. If a greater proportion of women come to define occupational achievement as equal (or perhaps greater) in import to domestic behaviors, then it is possible that certain alterations could occur in terms of the economic and status interdependence discussed above.

One thing that seems apparent is that such a trend would be accompanied by a sharp decline in fertility among these women. Occupational efforts evidently tend to be seen by some females as a viable alternative to "excessive" childbearing. Although much more research is needed to assess this whole area, the point is that the existence of such trends should not differ markedly in either black or white society. There are, in short, no "cultural" or "racial" differences in this regard either. If anything, as suggested in Chapter 6, black women are more "tuned in" to such a trend than white women. In view, however, of the ever-enlarging proportion of white women going to college, the likely prospect is for convergence (not divergence) in future role definitions by black and white females.

Expressive Gratifications

Fourth, and finally, the majority of black (and white) youth continue to define the conjugal relationship as ideally the prime means to obtain expressive (including but not solely sexual) gratifications. Although there is some evidence of increased sexual permissiveness, particularly among engaged couples, there is no indication of wholesale sexual promiscuity nor repudiation of marriage *per se*.[21] Most people continue to prefer marriage over nonmarriage. Most people marry consciously to obtain expressive rewards.[22] Whether black or white, they stay married as long as these rewards are forthcoming; they seek "out" when the rewards fall below a certain level.

Many observers have contended that most modern Americans continue to choose contemporary marriage because it is evidently the most effective means to cope with the loneliness and impersonality of modern society. To the extent this is so, it suggests yet another reason why blacks prefer and choose the dominant family form. Most Americans appear to believe that it is the "most acceptable means" to obtain these kinds of valued primary relations.

We found, however, that for blacks (and whites) expressive rewards do not exist independently of economic-status rewards. And, we found too that although blacks have made genuine economic gains over the past decade, they continue to lag substantially behind whites. This lag is due primarily to economic discrimination by whites. The fact that blacks with education comparable to that of whites are nevertheless underrewarded tends to have deleterious effects on marital primary relations and, hence, on marital stability. This theme of economic inequity is the key to understanding whatever differences there are between black and white family structures.

Rewards and Family Forms

In trying to summarize why American blacks are evolving the dominant family form, it helps to think of the four linkages just considered as "systems" of rewards. Each one suggests a way in which the conjugal family is more attractive than any other alternative, i.e., it provides greater rewards than any other perceived possibility. And since human beings (black or white) will inevitably tend to gravitate toward rewarding situations and eschew neutral and especially punishing ones, it makes sense to see why the conjugal form is the preferred family pattern among blacks as well as whites.

1. In modern society, the extended kin has lost most of its reward-functions. Therefore, the conjugal family is the one primarily looked to for rewards. 2. "Effective socialization" by the conjugal family which produces "respectable" or "successful" children provides substantial rewards to parents. Thus socialization by the conjugal unit is a coveted prerogative. 3. As the center for display of consumption symbols, the conjugal family form mediates status to both husband and wife—a crucial and highly significant reward in our society. 4. The conjugal form provides sought-after expressive rewards to both partners. Since in each of these four areas the conjugal family seems to be the pattern "best suited" or able to provide these kinds of valued rewards, it is the family

form which tends to predominate in both black and white society. What the future will bring in terms of other patterns that could channel these valued rewards in similar or superior fashion, no one yet can tell. For now, since the conjugal family is the structure best able to offer *all* these rewards *simultaneously*, it is the form toward which most black (and white) persons gravitate.

Before moving on to some practical implications, we first must stress the obverse of the foregoing discussion. We have discovered fundamental similarities between black and white family patterns, and we have found certain dissimilarities between these patterns. These differences, however, are not the result of culture, race, or of black ideology. They are, pure and simple, the consequence of white discrimination, especially against black males. For example, in Chapters 2, 3, and 4 we found that parental socialization and child-identification are both present and vigorously carried on within the black family above the lower class. In Chapters 5, 6, and 7 we saw that black adults make ample use of childhood resources to attain economic and conjugal goals, and to train their children to do the same.

Yet from Chapters 5 and 6 it was readily apparent that white discrimination places the working- and middle-class black family in a relatively disadvantaged position compared to whites. It is ironic that while many American blacks are attempting to fulfill the "demands" of the dominant work and success ethic, they are denied equal fruits thereof. Hence, when we focus on policy matters as we shall below, there are several points to keep in mind. One is that we need no schemes to "strengthen" the black family above the underclass.[23] It is already as "strong" and "viable" as the white family at similar strata. What is called for are programs with a totally different objective. By the same token, rather than thinking in terms of "strengthening" the lower-class black family, a radically different perspective is also in order. What are these policy perspectives and objectives? Whatever they are, they must be based on the cardinal theoretical principle that the conjugal family is inextricably linked to the American economic-opportunity structure, chiefly through the *husband's* occupational role. Correlatively, it follows that the greater the economic-status resources possessed by the family unit: (1) the more cohesive will tend to be the bonds between husbands and wives; (2) the more effectively will the family be able to prepare its children to function in the larger society.

PRACTICAL IMPLICATIONS

In view of the enormous literature that has been produced over the past few years offering a wealth of suggestions to alleviate black suffering in white America, it may seem presumptuous and perhaps unnecessary to add still more verbiage of this sort. Nevertheless, because we have viewed black society from a relatively novel perspective, i.e., its prevailing family patterns, it seems useful to iterate points made elsewhere and connect them to conclusions reached in this study.

Perhaps the foremost question is one of overall strategy. Will blacks employ self-initiated violence to gain equality and justice, or will they choose some other means? At this point in time, at least, the answer seems to be in the latter direction.[24] *This does not mean that there will not be considerable black-white violence over the next few years.* Huey Newton, founder of the Black Panther (political) Party, says the symbol of his party describes its basic outlook. He claims the black panther is not an aggressive animal, that it becomes violent only when provoked.[25] His party, he insists, will operate only in a retaliatory fashion. Members of the party do carry weapons, however, and there have been pitched gun battles between party members and police. The Panthers claim that in these situations they were provoked by the police.[26]

This kind of erratic violence, plus spontaneous riots and looting, are likely to erupt spasmodically for some time to come. Nonetheless, McCord et al., report that most black leaders and almost all black people do not see violence (either random or guerrilla-type) as an effective means to attain their goals.[27] Aside from the temporary sense of urgency and crisis that violence creates among white politicians, little of lasting significance seems to be accomplished other than the proliferation of commissions that produce endless "reports" on the violence. The reports in turn are then promptly ignored, e.g., the widely acclaimed *Kerner Report*.[28] The violence may even induce reactionary behavior on the part of some whites, leading to heightened white fear and repressiveness.

What other means then are open to blacks given their widespread and serious determination to participate fully in the "Dream"? Poussaint remarks:

> The Negro, like other Americans, has accepted the belief . . . that individuals succeed or fail solely as a result of their individual efforts. . . . The acceptance by the Negro of this idea of individual merit has worked to his detriment—for it has operated to sustain a delusion in the face of a contradicting reality.[29]

Does Poussaint then argue that blacks should give up their strong adherence to individualistic occupational achievement in favor of something else? Not in the least. Instead, he contends that an *additional* factor must be inserted to enhance individual achievements. This factor, he claims, is "black power" or "black consciousness."[30] For example, in Chapter 5, our data confirmed those of Blau and Duncan that blacks are "cheated" in terms of income and job status. According to Poussaint, this type of situation could be changed through ". . . expending greater group assertiveness for social and political action. . . ."[31] The goal remains the same, i.e., greater economic resources for the black—especially the male head-of-household. But if acting alone, he still cannot gain these ends, then he ought to work together in concert with other blacks to assert social, economic, and political pressures to attain these ends.

Such organization, or "black self-determination," is analogous to the organization of labor unions by whites many decades ago. An enormous difference, however, between the job situation then and now is the reality of automation. In Chapter 2, we noted that the black (or white) who migrated to the city a generation or two ago found access to a host of unskilled or semi-skilled jobs. Currently, the best estimates are that "about 1.5 million American jobs a year are abolished by automation."[32] The problem of joblessness is, of course, linked primarily to the plight of the lower-class black family. It is the basic issue to be resolved if the hopelessness of those involved is to be alleviated.

A prime issue facing the non lower-class black family, those who have been in the urban milieu for some time and/or who have background advantages, is that of equal rewards for equal effort. At present, universalistic criteria do not apply even to well-trained blacks, and this has enormously negative consequences for pride and self-respect. If rewards (monetary and advancement) were made available equally to all regardless of skin color, this would be a significant boon to black self-respect, and would go a long way toward easing structural tension within non-lower-class families (see Chapter 6). Furthermore, it would probably contribute to a lowering of the black working- and middle-class divorce rates, and bring them more into line with white divorce rates of the same social strata.

In brief, "in the 1960's most Negroes seem concerned above all with political and economic 'bread and butter' issues."[33] Economic improvement is the key to the plight of the underclass black family and the particular tensions of black families above the lower-class. But the key to genuine economic improvement is "political power" or black self-determination. Blacks must participate fully in the decisions that affect their economic destiny. Repeatedly throughout the blook, the point has been made that money alone will not resolve the uneasy situation of blacks, especially in the middle class. Frazier noted this during the fifties. There is some indication that now more middle-class blacks realize this too. One black militant is quoted as saying:

> The black bourgeoisie is in the process of coming over to our side en masse. This has been happening unnoticed, over the last few years. It's pretty difficult to find a black today who contests the idea of "Black Power."[34]

Billingsley puts it this way:

As important and indeed indispensable as are jobs, job training, and a minimum income floor for Negro families, nothing in any of these programs necessarily speaks to ownership, control, management, independence, high status, or power. . . . [thus the programs] could fail to solve the essential problems of economic, social, and psychological dependence and the sense of alienation which accompany these phenomena.[35]

Hamilton says essentially the same thing.[36] Pfautz agrees but goes a step beyond and states that:

Power is but a proximate aim of the Negro revolution. In the long run, the goal is the goal of all human beings—*status*. I refer here not to status in the narrow sense of prestige but in the broader sense of having a place and function in, of being a member of "the" community. To be a member of the community . . . is to have one's concept of self validated by significant others . . . [it] is to be able to cash in one's educational, income, and occupational gains for status.[37]

Pfautz goes on to contend that self-determination is the means best able to foster this "sense of status" among black Americans. So that ultimately, the future course of the black family in America is tied to the capability of black society to participate fully in the decisions that affect its own destiny, plus the destiny of the society as a whole. To the extent such participation actually occurs, we would expect to see as first steps such measures as a guaranteed annual income and the abolishment of current welfare programs that are demeaning to all Americans forced to resort to them. We would expect to see blacks helping to restructure elementary and secondary schools to meet the particular needs of black children. We would expect to see black interests being met in terms of local, state, and federal, political, legal, and legislative processes. Measures would be taken by blacks themselves to encourage their entrance into the professions, into the ranks of management, into small business, and into wide-ranging forms of entrepreneurship.[38]

Many other programs and developments would be sure to emerge, with blacks participating fully in their inception and execution. Since so much of this would be in the nature of experimentation, some of it would be bound to prove ineffectual. But black self-determination, if it is to be genuinely free from white paternalism, requires the right not only to innovate, but also at times to fail and to be able to start over.

Put very simply, the identical political and economic opportunities for attainment and self-determination now open to whites must be opened wide to blacks. The promise of the American Dream—that achievement, not ascribed characteristics such as skin color, determines rewards—must finally be made a reality. Up to this point in time, blacks have been clearly committed to the *promise* of the Dream. From now on they are determined to obtain its *reality*. It seems remarkable that in spite of such limited reality most blacks have nonetheless maintained the viable, functionally efficient, and rewarding (to its participants) family system described in these pages. Barring unforeseen catastrophe, we may only hope that whites will support (even if grudgingly, out of self-interest) black efforts at political and economic power. If such is the case, we may expect the black family, at each class level, eventually to become structurally indistinguishable from the dominant form of the family.[39] If such support is not forthcoming, then no one can now tell what the ensuing sense of black frustration will mean for either white or black society.

NOTES

1. Billingsley, *Black Families in White America*, p. 206.
2. Hylan Lewis, "Culture, Class and Family Life Among Low-Income Urban Negroes," in Arthur M. Ross and Hebert Hill, eds., *Employment, Race and Poverty* (New York: Harcourt, Brace and World, 1967), p. 158.
3. In the absence of scholarly research into recent developments, the interested reader might consult "Experiments in Marriage: Sweden and Denmark," *Life* (August 15, 1969), pp. 38ff.
4. See *The Futurist* IV (April 1970) for several articles on the "future of marriage," including "group marriage."

5. Lewis, "Culture, Class and Family Life," 1967.

6. The best known work is Goode, *World Revolution*.

7. See Talcott Parsons, "The Stability of the Small Family System," in Norman W. Bell and Ezra F. Vogel, *A Modern Introduction to the Family* (New York: The Free Press, 1968, rev.), pp. 97–101.

8. See Scanzoni, *Opportunity and the Family*.

9. Melford E. Spiro, "Is the Family Universal?—The Israeli Case," in N. W. Bell and E. F. Vogel, eds., *A Modern Introduction to the Family* (New York: The Free Press, 1968), pp. 68–79.

10. Goode, *World Revolution*, p. 11.

11. Spiro, "Is the Family Universal?", p. 72.

12. "Student Cohabitation Means Problems as Well as Fun," *Indiana Daily Student*, October 15, 1968, p. 4.

13. Guy Sitbon, "Discovery of Black America," *Atlas* 17 (June 1969): 43. Translated from *Le Nouvel Adam* of Paris.

14. Goode, *World Revolution*; Cloward and Ohlin, *Delinquency and Opportunity*, pp. 79–82.

15. This by no means implies that Americans (black or white) do not interact with the kin. See our Chapter 4 for additional discussion along this line.

16. Blau and Duncan, *The American Occupational Structure*, p. 205; Kohn, *Class and Conformity*, pp. 201–3.

17. Leslie, *The Family in Social Context*, p. 143.

18. Ibid., pp. 147–50.

19. Joseph Shepher, "Familism and Social Structure: The Case of the Kibbutz," *Journal of Marriage and the Family* 31 (August 1969): 567–73.

20. George P. Murdock, *Social Structure* (New York: The Free Press, 1949), p. 8.

21. Ira L. Reiss, *The Social Context of Premarital Permissiveness* (New York: Holt, Rinehart and Winston, 1967), Chapter 10; Gerhard Neubeck, ed., *Extra-Marital Relations* (Englewood Cliffs, N.J.: Prentice-Hall, 1969).

22. Michael M. McCall, "Courtship as Social Exchange: Some Historical Comparisons," in Bernard Farber, ed., *Kinship and Family Organization* (New York: John Wiley & Sons, 1966), pp. 190–200.

23. See S. M. Miller and Frank Riessman, "Social Change Versus the 'Psychiatric World View'" in their *Social Class and Social Policy*, pp. 261–74.

24. See McCord et al., *Life Styles in the Black Ghetto;* also Sitbon, "Discovery of Black America."

25. In a television interview with black newsman on NET-produced, *Black Journal*, June 23, 1969.

26. Much in the news at the turn of the decade was the deaths of both police and Panthers in several "Shoot-outs" across the country. See the account by Gordon Parks, *Life* (February 6, 1970), pp. 18ff.

27. McCord et al., *Life Styles in the Black Ghetto*, pp. 274ff.

28. See *One Year Later:* An Assessment of Response to the Kerner Report (New York: F. A. Praeger Publishing Co., 1969).

29. Alvin F. Poussaint, "The Psychology of a Minority Group with Implications for Social Action," in Charles U. Daly, ed., *Urban Violence* (Chicago: University of Chicago Press, 1969), p. 37.

30. Ibid.

31. Ibid.

32. Cross, *Black Capitalism*, p. 76.

33. McCord et al., *Life Styles in the Black Ghetto* p. 283.

34. Sitbon, "Discovery of Black America," p. 43.

35. Billingsley, *Black Families in White America*, p. 171.

36. Charles V. Hamilton, "The Politics of Race Relations," in Daly, *Urban Violence*, pp. 47–55.

37. Harold W. Pfautz, "The American Dilemma: Perspectives and Proposals," in Daly, op. cit., p. 61. This is also the point made by Kenneth Clark before Congress—see Billingsley, *Black Families*, p. 169–70.

38. One current example of a pragmatic and effective source of organized black economic pressure on the white "power-structure" is *Operation Breadbasket* founded by Dr. Martin Luther King, Jr., and headed by the Rev. Jesse Jackson.

39. This is totally compatible with the current stress on Afro heritage and black distinctives. Such "ethnic" identities can be preserved by blacks while still participating fully in the dominant political and economic processes. The Jewish population in America is a prime example of the capability of doing both well.

Appendix:
Sampling Procedures

The task of drawing a sample for this study was carried out by the *National Opinion Research Center*, Chicago. What follows is the sampling report prepared by their office. NORC also trained their interviewers (all of whom were black) in the details of sampling requirements. NORC also supervised the total process of data collection from beginning to end.

SAMPLE DESIGN FOR STUDY OF STABLE NEGRO FAMILIES IN INDIANAPOLIS

The universe for this study consists of husbands and wives in families who have lived together for five years or more and who are now living in Indianapolis.

The sample is selected in three stages. At the first stage, Census Tracts were selected in Indianapolis with probabilities proportionate to the number of married Negro men. At the second stage, blocks were selected with probabilities proportionate to the number of Negro households. A total of 80 selections were made.

At the third stage, within each block a random starting point was selected, and a travel pattern designated. Quotas were set by sex, and interviewers called at consecutive households until they filled their quotas. Since only couples married more than five years were eligible, those married a shorter period of time or divorced or single were excluded, as were not-at-home households and those where the occupants were not Negro. Within each block, approximately five cases were obtained so that the total sample size was 400.

Bibliography

ADAMS, BERT N. *Kinship in An Urban Setting.* Chicago: Markham Publishing Co., 1968.

ANTONOVSKY, AARON, and MELVIN J. LERNER. "Occupational Aspirations of Lower-Class Negro and White Youth," *Social Problems* 9 (Fall, 1959).

BALL, RICHARD A. "A Poverty Case: The Analgesic Subculture of the Southern Appalachians." *American Sociological Review* 33 (December 1968): 891–94.

BERNARD, JESSIE. *Marriage and Family Among Negroes.* Englewood Cliffs, N.J.: Prentice-Hall, 1966.

BERNARD, JESSIE. "Marital Stability and Patterns of Status Variables." *Journal of Marriage and the Family* 28 (November 1966): 421–39.

BILLINGSLEY, ANDREW. *Black Families in White America.* Englewood Cliffs, N.J.: Prentice-Hall, 1968.

BLAKE, JUDITH. "Population Policy for Americans: Is the Government Being Misled?" *Science* 164 (May 2, 1969).

BLALOCK, HUBERT M. *Social Statistics.* New York: McGraw-Hill Book Co., 1960.

BLAU, PETER M., and OTIS DUDLEY DUNCAN. *The American Occupational Structure.* New York: John Wiley & Sons, Inc., 1967.

BLOOD, ROBERT O., and DONALD M. WOLFE. *Husbands and Wives.* New York: The Free Press, 1960.

BOYLE, RICHARD P. "Path Analysis and Ordinal Data." *American Journal of Sociology* 75 (January 1970), Part 1, pp. 461–80.

BRIMMER, ANDREW F. "The Negro in the National Economy," in John P. Davis. *The American Negro Reference Book,* Englewood Cliffs, N.J.: Prentice-Hall, 1966.

BRINK, WILLIAM, and LOUIS HARRIS. *Black and White.* New York: Simon and Schuster, 1967.

CAIN, GLEN. *Married Women in the Labor Force.* (Chicago: University of Chicago Press, 1966).

COLEMAN, JAMES S. "Implications of the Findings on Alienation." *American Journal of Sociology* 70 (July 1964): 76–78.

CLOWARD, RICHARD A. and LLOYD E. OHLIN. *Delinquency and Opportunity.* New York: The Free Press, 1960.

CROSS, THEODORE L. *Black Capitalism.* New York: Atheneum, 1969.

DAHRENDORF, RALF. *Class and Class Conflict in Modern Society.* Stanford, Calif.: Stanford University Press, 1959.

DALY, CHARLES U. (ed.) *Urban Violence.* Chicago: University of Chicago Press, 1969.

DAVIS, ALLISON, and JOHN DOLLARD. *Children of Bondage.* New York: Harper & Row, 1964 edition.

DAVIS, JOHN P. (ed.) *The American Negro Reference Book,* Englewood Cliffs, N.J.: Prentice-Hall, 1966.

DEUTSCH, MARTIN, IRWIN KATZ, A. R. JENSEN. (eds.) *Social Class, Race, and Psychological Development.* New York: Holt, Rinehart and Winston, 1968.

DOUVAN, ELIZABETH, and CAROL KAYE. "Motivational Factors in College Entrance," in Nevitt Sanford (ed.) *The American College,* New York: John Wiley & Sons, 1962.

DRAKE, ST. CLAIR, and HORACE R. CAYTON. *Black Metropolis.* New York: Harper & Row, 1962 edition, Vol. 2.

DUNCAN, OTIS DUDLEY. "Methodological Issues in the Analysis of Social Mobility," in Neil J. Smelser and Seymour M. Lipset. (eds.) *Social Structure and Mobility in Economic Development.* Chicago: Aldine Publishing Co., 1966.

DURHAM, MICHAEL. "Experiments in Marriage in Sweden and Denmark." *Life* (August 15, 1969): 38–46.

ECKLAND, BRUCE K. "Social Class and College Graduation: Some Misconceptions Corrected." *American Journal of Sociology* 70 (July 1964): 36–50.

EDWARDS, HARRY. "Black Muslim and Negro Christian Family Relationships." *Journal of Marriage and the Family* (November 1968): 604–11.

ELDER, GLEN H. JR. "Adolescent Socialization and Development," in E. F. Borgatta and W. W. Lambert (eds.) *Handbook of Personality Theory and Research.* Chicago: Rand McNally Co., 1968, pp. 330–31.

ENGEL, J. F., D. T. KOLLAT, R. D. BLACKWELL. *Consumer Behavior.* New York: Holt, Rinehart and Winston, 1968.

FARLEY, REYNOLDS. "Fertility Among Urban Blacks." *The Milbank Memorial Fund Quarterly* (April 1970), Part 2, pp. 183–214.

FEIN, RASHI. "An Economic and Social Profile of the Negro American," in *Daedalus,* Fall 1965.

FERMAN, LOUIS A. et al. *Poverty in America.* Ann Arbor: University of Michigan Press, 1965, 1968.

FRAZIER, E. FRANKLIN. *The Negro Family in the United States.* Chicago: The University of Chicago Press, 1939, 1948, 1966.

FRAZIER, E. FRANKLIN. *Black Bourgeoisie.* New York: The Free Press, 1957.

FRAZIER, E. FRANKLIN. *The Negro Church in America.* New York: Schocken Books, 1964.

GANS, HERBERT J. *The Urban Villagers.* New York: The Free Press, 1962.

GINZBERG, ELI, and DALE L. HIESTAND. "Employment Patterns of Negro Men and Women," in John P. Davis, *The American Negro Reference Book,* Englewood Cliffs, N.J.: Prentice-Hall, 1966.

GLAZER, NATHAN, "Foreword," in Frazier, *The Negro Family in the United States.* Chicago: The University of Chicago Press, 1966.

GLICK, PAUL C. "Marriage and Marital Stability Among Blacks." *The Milbank Memorial Fund Quarterly* (April 1970), Part 2, pp. 99–125.

GOLDSCHEIDER, CALVIN, and PETER R. UHLENBERG. "Minority Group Status and Fertility." *American Journal of Sociology* 74 (January 1969): 362–65.

GOODE, WILLIAM J. *After Divorce.* New York: The Free Press, 1956.

GOODE, WILLIAM J. *World Revolution and Family Patterns.* New York: The Free Press, 1963.

GOODE, WILLIAM J. "Family and Mobility," in Reinhard Bendix and Seymour Martin Lipset (eds.) *Class, Status, and Power.* New York: The Free Press, 1966 edition, pp. 582–601.

GOODE, WILLIAM J. "Family Disorganization," in Robert K. Merton and Robert A. Nisbet (eds.) *Contemporary Social Problems.* New York: Harcourt, Brace and World, 1966 edition.

GORDON, MILTON. *Assimilation in American Life.* New York: Oxford University Press, Inc., 1964.

GOULDNER, ALVIN W. "The Norm of Reciprocity: A Preliminary Statement." *American Sociological Review,* 1960.

GREENFIELD, SIDNEY M. *English Rustics in Black Skin.* New Haven, Conn.: College and University Press, 1966.

GROAT, H. THEODORE, and ARTHUR G. NEAL. "Social Psychological Correlates of Urban Fertility." *American Sociological Review* 32 (December 1967): 945–959.

HAMILTON, CHARLES V. "The Politics of Race Relations," in Charles U. Daly (ed.) *Urban Violence.* Chicago: University of Chicago Press, 1969.

HEER, DAVID M. "Dominance and the Working Wife." *Social Forces* 36 (May 1958): 341–47.

HEER, DAVID M. "The Measurement and Bases of Family Power: An Overview." *Marriage and Family Living* 25 (May 1963): 133–39.

HILL, REUBEN. "Patterns of Decision-Making and The Accumulation of Family Assets." in Nelson N. Foote (ed.) *Household Decision-Making.* New York: New York University Press, 1961.

HILL, REUBEN, and ROY H. RODGERS. "The Developmental Approach," in Harold T. Christensen (ed.) *Handbook of Marriage and the Family.* Chicago: Rand McNally and Co., 1964, pp. 204–05.

HIMES, JOSEPH S. "Some Work-Related Cultural Deprivations of Lower-Class Negro Youth." *Journal of Marriage and the Family* 26 (November 1964): 447–49.

HOFFMAN, LOIS W., and FREDERICK WYATT. "Social Change and Motivations for Having Larger Families." *Merrill-Palmer Quarterly* 6 (1960).

HOMANS, GEORGE C. *Social Behavior: Its Elementary Forms.* New York: Harcourt, Brace and World, 1961.

HYMAN, HERBERT H., and ELEANOR SINGER. (eds.) *Readings in Reference Group Theory and Research.* New York: The Free Press. 1968.

KAMII, CONSTANCE K., and NORMA L. RADIN. "Class Differences in the Socialization Practices of Negro Mothers," *Journal of Marriage and the Family* 29 (May 1967): 302–10.

KANDEL, DENISE B., and GERALD S. LESSER. "Parental and Peer Influences on Educational Plans of Adolescents." *American Sociological Review* 34 (April 1969): 212–21.

KING, KARL. "Adolescent Perception of Power Structure in the Negro Family." *Journal of Marriage and the Family* 31 (November 1969): 751–55.

KOHN, MELVIN L. *Class and Conformity: A Study in Values.* Homewood, Ill.: Dorsey Press, 1969.

LENSKI, GERHARD. *The Religious Factor.* New York: Doubleday & Co., 1963 edition.

LESLIE, GERALD R. *The Family in Social Context.* New York: Oxford University Press, 1967.

LEWIS, HYLAN. "Child Rearing Among Low-Income Families," in L. A. Ferman, et al., *Poverty In America,* Ann Arbor: University of Michigan Press, 1965, pp. 342–53.

LEWIS, HYLAN. "Culture, Class, and Family Life Among Low-Income Urban Negroes." in Arthur M. Ross and Herbert Hill (eds.) *Employment, Race and Poverty.* New York: Harcourt, Brace and World, 1967.

LIEBOW, ELLIOTT. *Tally's Corner.* Boston: Little, Brown and Company, 1967.

LIFTON, ROBERT JAY (ed.) *The Woman in America.* Boston: Beacon Press, 1964.

LIPSET, SEYMOUR MARTIN, and REINHARD BENDIX. *Social Mobility in Industrial Society.* Berkeley, Calif.: University of California Press, 1960.

LITWAK, EUGENE. "The Use of Extended Family Groups in the Achievement of Social Goals: Some Policy Implications." *Social Problems* 7 (1959–60): 177–87.

LIVELY, EDWIN L. "Toward Concept Clarification: The Case of Marital Interaction." *Journal of Marriage and the Family* 31 (February 1969).

LOTT, J., and BERNICE E. LOTT. *Negro and White Youth.* New York: Holt, Rinehart and Winston, Inc., 1963.

LUPRI, EUGEN. "Contemporary Authority Patterns in the West German Family: A Study in Cross-National Validation." *Journal of Marriage and the Family* 31 (February 1969): 134–44.

McCALL, MICHAL M. "Courtship as Social Exchange: Some Historical Comparisons." in Bernard Farber (ed.) *Kinship and Family Organization.* New York: John Wiley & Sons, 1966, pp. 190–200.

McCORD, WILLIAM, JOHN HOWARD, BERNARD FRIEBERG, EDWIN HARWOOD. *Life Styles in the Black Ghetto.* New York: W. W. Norton & Co., Inc., 1969.

McKINLEY, DONALD G. *Social Class and Family Life.* New York: The Free Press, 1964.

McMILLAN, SYLVIA R. "Aspirations of Low-Income Mothers." *Journal of Marriage and the Family* 29 (May 1967): 282–301.

MERTON, ROBERT K. *Social Theory and Social Structure.* New York: The Free Press, 1957 (rev.)

MERTON, ROBERT K. "Intermarriage and the Social Structure: Fact and Theory," in Ruth L. Coser. *The Family: Its Structure and Functions.* New York: St. Martin's Press, 1964.

MILLER, S. M. "The American Lower Classes: A Typological Approach." in Arthur B. Shostak and William Gomberg (eds.) *Blue Collar World,* Englewood Cliffs, N.J.: Prentice-Hall, 1964, pp. 9–23.

MILLER, S. M., and FRANK RIESSMAN, "The Working-Class Subculture: A New View," in Shostak and Gomberg, 1964.

MILLER, S. M., FRANK RIESSMAN, ARTHUR A. SEAGULL, "A Critique of the Non-Deferred Gratification Pattern," in Louis A. Ferman, et al. *Poverty in America.* Ann Arbor: The University of Michigan Press, 1965, pp. 285–302.

MILLER, S. M., and FRANK RIESSMAN. *Social Class and Social Policy.* New York: Basic Books, 1968.

MILLER, S. M., MARTIN REIN, PAMELA ROBY, and BERTRAM M. GROSS. "Poverty, Inequality and Conflict," in Bertram M. Gross (ed) *Social Intelligence for America's Future.* Boston: Allyn and Bacon, Inc., 1969.

MIZRUCHI, EPHRAIM H. *Success and Opportunity.* New York: The Free Press, 1964.

MOYNIHAN, DANIEL P. "Employment, Income and the Ordeal of the Negro Family." *Daedalus* (Fall 1965): 745–69.

MURDOCK, GEORGE P. *Social Structure.* New York: The Free Press, 1949.

NEUBECK, GERHARD. *ExtraMarital Relations.* Englewood Cliffs, N.J.: Prentice-Hall, 1969.

NEWCOMB, THEODORE M. *Social Psychology.* New York: Dryden Press, 1950.

NIMKOFF, M. F. "The American Family," in M. F. Nimkoff (ed.) *Comparative Family Systems.* Boston: Houghton-Mifflin Co., 1965.

NOBLE, JEANNE L. "The American Negro Woman," in John P. Davis, *The American Negro Reference Book.* Englewood Cliffs, N.J.: Prentice-Hall, 1966.

ORDEN, SUSAN R., and NORMAN M. BRADBURN. "Working Wives and Marriage Happiness." *American Journal of Sociology* 74 (January 1969): 392–407.

PARKER, SEYMOUR, and ROBERT J. KLEINER. *Mental Illness in the Urban Community.* New York: The Free Press, 1966.

PARKER, SEYMOUR, and ROBERT J. KLEINER. "Social and Psychological Dimensions of the Family Role Performance of the Negro Male." *Journal of Marriage and the Family* 31 (August 1969).

PARKS, GORDON. "The Cycle of Despair," in Louis A. Ferman et al. *Poverty in America*. Ann Arbor: University of Michigan Press, 1968, pp. 513–18.

PARKS, GORDON. "Black Panthers: The Hard Edge of Confrontation." *Life* (February 6, 1970).

PARSONS, TALCOTT, "The Social Structure of the Family," in Ruth N. Ansher (ed.) *The Family: Its Function and Destiny*. New York: Harper & Row, 1959, pp. 241–74.

PARSONS, TALCOTT, "The Normal American Family," in S. M. Farber, P. Mustacchi, Roger H. L. Wilson (eds.) *The Family's Search for Survival*. New York: McGraw-Hill, 1965, pp. 31–59.

PARSONS, TALCOTT. "The Stability of the Small Family System," in Norman W. Bell and Ezra F. Vogel (eds.) *A Modern Introduction to the Family*. New York: The Free Press, 1968, pp. 97–101.

PEARLIN, LEONARD I., and MELVIN L. KOHN. "Social Class, Ocupation, and Parental Values." *American Sociological Review* 31 (August 1966): 466–79.

PETTIGREW, THOMAS F. *A Profile of the Negro American*. Princeton, N.J.: D. Van Nostrand Co., Inc. 1964.

PFAUTZ, HAROLD W. "The American Dilemma: Perspectives and Proposals," in Charles U. Daly (ed.) *Urban Violence*. Chicago: University of Chicago Press, 1969.

PIERCE, CHESTER M. "Problems of the Negro Adolescent in the Next Decade," in Eugene B. Brody (ed.) *Minority Group Adolescents in the United States*. Baltimore: Williams and Wilkins Co., 1968.

POUSSAINT, ALVIN F. "The Psychology of a Minority Group with Implications for Social Action," in Charles U. Daly (ed.) *Urban Violence*. Chicago: University of Chicago Press, 1969.

PRICE, DANIEL O. *Changing Characteristics of the Negro Population*. Washington, D.C.: U.S. Bureau of the Census, 1969.

PROSHANSKY, HAROLD, and PEGGY NEWTON. "The Nature and Meaning of Negro Self-Identity," in Deutsch. *Social Class, Race, and Psychological Development*. New York: Holt, Rinehart and Winston, 1968.

PURCELL, THEODORE V. "The Hopes of Negro Workers for Their Children," in Shostak and Gomberg (eds.) *Blue-Collar World*, Englewood Cliffs, N.J.: Prentice-Hall, 1964, pp. 144–53.

QUEEN, STUART A., and ROBERT W. HABENSTEIN. *The Family in Various Cultures*. J. B. Lippincott Co., 1967, chapter 15.

RAINWATER, LEE. *And The Poor Get Children*. Chicago: Quadrangle Books, 1960.

RAINWATER, LEE, and GERALD HANDEL. "Changing Family Roles in the Working Class," in Shostak and Gomberg (eds.) *Blue-Collar World*, Englewood Cliffs, N.J.: Prentice-Hall, 1964.

RAINWATER, LEE. *Family Design*. Chicago: Aldine, 1965.

RAINWATER, LEE. "Crucible of Identity: The Negro Lower-Class Family." *Daedalus* 95 (1966): 172–216.

RAINWATER, LEE. "Work and Identity in the Lower Class," in Sam Bass Warner, Jr. (ed.) *Planning For a Nation of Cities*. Cambridge, Mass.: The M.I.T. Press, 1966.

RAINWATER, LEE, and WILLIAM L. YANCEY. *The Moynihan Report and the Politics of Controversy*. Cambridge, Mass.: The M.I.T. Press, 1967.

RAINWATER, LEE. *Behind Ghetto Walls: Black Family Life in a Federal Slum*. Chicago: Aldine, 1970.

REISS, IRA L. *The Social Context of Premarital Permissiveness*. New York: Holt, Rinehart and Winston, 1967.

RICHARDSON, HARRY V. "The Negro in American Religious Life," in John P. Davis (ed.) *The American Negro Reference Book*. Englewood Cliffs, N.J.: Prentice-Hall, 1966.

ROSENBERG, MORRIS. *Society and the Adolescent Self-Image*. Princeton, N.J.: Princeton University Press, 1965.

ROSENTHAL, ROBERT, and LENORE JACOBSON. "Self-Fulfilling Prophecies in the Classroom: Teachers' Expectations as Unintended Determinants of Pupils' Intellectual Competence," in Deutsch, *Social Class, Race and Psychological Development*. New York: Holt, Rinehart and Winston, 1968.

ROSSI, ALICE S., "The Road to Sex Equality," unpublished paper, Towson College, Baltimore, Md., 1969.

RUDERMAN, FLORENCE A. *Child Care and Working Mothers*. New York: Child Welfare League of America, 1968.

SAFA, HELEN ICKEN. *An Analysis of Upward Mobility in Low Income Families*. Youth Development Center, Syracuse University, Syracuse, N.Y., 1967.

SCANZONI, JOHN. *Opportunity and the Family*. New York: The Free Press, 1970.

SCHEINER, SETH M. "The Negro Church and the Northern City," in W. G. Shade and R. C. Herrenkohl. (eds.) *Seven On Black*. New York: J. B. Lippincott Co., 1969.

SCHULZ, DAVID A. *Coming Up Black*. Englewood Cliffs, N.J.: Prentice-Hall, 1969.

SEELEY, JOHN R., R. ALEXANDER SIM, ELIZABETH W. LOOSLEY. *Crestwood Heights*. New York: Basic Books, 1956.

SEWELL, WILLIAM H., and VILMAL P. SHAH. "Social Class, Parental Encouragement, and Educational Aspirations." *American Journal of Sociology* 73 (March 1968): 559–70.

SHEPHER, JOSEPH. "Familism and Social Structure: The Case of the Kibbutz." *Journal of Marriage and the Family* 31 (August 1969): 567–73.

SHOSTAK, ARTHUR B., and WILLIAM GOMBERG (eds.) *Blue-Collar World*. Englewood Cliffs, N.J.: Prentice-Hall, 1964.

SITBON, GUY. "Discovery of Black America." *Atlas* 17 (June 1969). Trans. from *Le Nouvel Adam* of Paris.

SKLARE, MARSHALL. "Intermarriage and the Jewish Future." *Commentary*. 1964.

SLOCUM, WALTER L. *Occupational Careers*. Chicago: Aldine Publishing Co., 1966.

SPIRO, MELFORD E. "Is the Family Universal? The Israeli Case," in N. W. Bell and E. F. Vogel (eds.) *A Modern Introduction to the Family*. New York: The Free Press. 1968.

STAFFORD, J. E., K. K. COX, J. B. HIGGENBOTHAM. "Some Consumption Pattern Differences Between Urban Whites and Negroes." *Social Science Quarterly* 49 (December 1968): 619–30.

STAMLER, ROSE. "Acculturation and Negro Blue-Collar Workers," in Shostak and Gomberg (eds.) *Blue-Collar World*. Englewood Cliffs, N. J.: Prentice-Hall, 1964.

STEINMANN, ANNE, DAVID J. FOX, RUTH L. FARKAS. "Attitudes Toward Marriage, Family Relationships, and Childrearing in Samples of Negro and White Female and Male College Undergraduates in the United States," paper read at *Seventh International Congress on Mental Health*, London, England, August 1968.

STURDEVANT, FREDERICK L. *The Ghetto Marketplace*. New York: The Free Press, 1969.

SUSSMAN, MARVIN B., and LEE BURCHINAL. "Kin Family Network: Unheralded Structure in Current Conceptualizations of Family Functioning." *Marriage and Family Living* 24 (1962): 231–40.

TAEUBER, KARL E., and ALMA F. TAEUBER. *Negroes in Cities*. Chicago: Aldine Publishing Co., 1965.

TAEUBER, KARL E., and ALMA F. TAEUBER. "The Negro Population in the United States," in John P. Davis (ed.) *The American Negro Reference Book*. Englewood Cliffs, N.J.: Prentice-Hall, 1966.

TENHOUTEN, WARREN. "The Black Family: Myth and Reality." *Psychiatry* 2 (May 1970): 145–73.

THIBAUT, J. W., and H. H. KELLEY. *The Social Psychology of Groups*. New York: John Wiley & Sons, 1959.

TURNER, RALPH H. *The Social Context of Ambition*. San Francisco: Chandler Publishing Co., 1964.

TURNER, RALPH H. "Book Review." *American Journal of Sociology* 74 (September 1968): 198–99.

UDRY, J. RICHARD. "Marital Instability by Race, Sex, Education, and Occupation using 1960 Census Data." *American Journal of Sociology* 72 (September 1966): 203–210.

VEROFF, JOSEPH, and SHEILA FELD. *Marriage and Work in America*. New York: Van Nostrand Reinhold Co., 1970.

WAKIN, EDWARD. *At the Edge of Harlem*. New York: W. Morrow & Co., 1965.

WESTLEY, WILLIAM A., and NATHAN B. EPSTEIN. *The Silent Majority*. San Francisco: Jossey-Bass, Inc., Publishers, 1969.

WINCH, ROBERT F. *Identification and its Familial Determinants*. Indianapolis: Bobbs-Merrill Co., 1962.

WINCH, ROBERT F. *The Modern Family*. New York: Holt, Rinehart and Winston, 1963.

YETT, DONALD E. "The Cash Value of College—for Negroes and for Whites." *Trans-action* 5 (November 1967): 44–49.

YOUNG, DONALD R. "The Socialization of American Minority Peoples," in David A. Goslin. *Handbook of Socialization Theory and Research*. Chicago: Rand McNally and Co., 1960.

Census Working Paper #15, "Methodology and Scores of Socioeconomic Status," Population Division, Bureau of the Census, Washington, D.C., 1963.

Community Service Council of Metropolitan Indianapolis. *The Negro in Indianapolis: A Summary of Local Data*. 1967.

Current Population Reports, Series P-20, No. 194, February 19, 1970.

Current Population Reports, Series P-23, No. 26, BLS Report #347. "Recent Trends in Social and Economic Conditions of Negroes in the U.S." July 1968.

Current Population Reports, Series P-23, Special Studies, No. 27, "Trends in Social and Economic Conditions in Metropolitan Areas." February 7, 1969.

Current Population Reports, Series P-23, No. 29. "The Social and Economic Status of Negroes in the United States, 1969."

Current Population Reports, Series P-23, No. 30. "Characteristics of American Youth." Washington, D.C., February 6, 1970.

Manpower Report of the President. U.S. Department of Labor, Washington, D.C. April 1968.

One Year Later: An Assessment of Response to the Kerner Report. New York: F. A. Praeger Publishing Co., 1969.

"Student Cohabitation Means Problems as Well as Fun." *Indiana Daily Student* (October 15, 1968) p. 4.

U.S. Bureau of the Census. *Current Population Reports.* Series P-20, No. 168, "Negro Population: March, 1966." Washington, D.C., December 22, 1967.

U.S. Bureau of the Census: *Current Population Reports,* Series P-60, No. 71, July 16, 1970.

U.S. Bureau of the Census. *Measures of Overlap of Income Distributions of White and Negro Families in the United States.* Technical Paper 22, 1970.

U.S. Bureau of the Census: "Social and Economic Conditions of Negroes in the United States," BLS Report No. 332, *Current Population Reports,* Series P-23, No. 24, October 1967.

U.S. Bureau of the Census. *U.S. Census of Population: 1960.* Detailed Characteristics. Indiana Final Report PC(i) 16D., p. 382.

U.S. Public Health Service. "Trends in Divorce and Family Disruption." *Health, Education and Welfare Indicators.* Washington, D.C., September 1963.

Index of Names

Adams, B., 151 (fn.)
Antonovsky, A., 303 (fn.)

Ball, R., 151 (fn.)
Bendix, R., 146, 178, 184; (fnn.): 100, 148, 149, 150
Bernard, J., vii, 209; (fnn.): xi, 57, 150, 267
Billingsley, A., 2, 3, 11, 12, 43, 84, 87, 89, 116, 120, 131, 137, 147, 167, 209, 275, 306, 307, 328; (fnn.): xi, 26, 27, 57, 99, 100, 149, 150, 193, 267, 270, 302, 329
Blake, J., 250; 272 (fn.)
Blalock, H., 101 (fn.)
Blau, P., 32, 34, 42, 46, 67, 70, 110, 134, 154, 158, 161, 162, 166, 167, 168, 169, 171, 179, 207, 277, 288, 317, 326; (fnn.): 29, 55, 56, 57, 99, 100, 148, 149, 191
Blood, R. O., 329; 270 (fn.)
Borgotta, E. F., 56 (fn.)
Borland, M., 193 (fn.)
Boyle, R., 101 (fn.)
Bradburn, N., 269 (fn.)
Brimmer, A. F., 155; (fnn.): 192, 193
Brody, E. B., 149 (fn.)

Burchinal, L., 150 (fn.)

Cain, G., 269 (fn.)
Cayton, H. R., 17, 51, 282; (fnn.): 28, 57, 150, 303
Clark, K., 331 (fn.)
Cloward, R., (fnn.): 99, 330
Coleman, J., 33, 35; 56 (fn.)
Cross, T., (fnn.): 195, 272, 331

Dahrendorf, R., 305 (fn.)
Daly, C., 331 (fn.)
Daniel, J., x
Davis, A., 284; 150 (fn.)
Davis, J. P., (fnn.): 58, 193
Deutsch, M., (fnn.): 149, 150
Dollard, J., 284; 150 (fn.)
Douvan, E., 304 (fn.)
Drake, S. C., 17, 51, 282; (fnn.): 28, 57, 150, 303
Dubois, W. E., 49
Duncan, O. D., 32, 34, 42, 46, 67, 70, 110, 134, 154, 158, 161, 162, 166, 167, 168, 169, 171, 179, 207, 277, 288, 317, 326; (fnn.): 29, 55, 56, 57, 99, 100, 148, 149, 191, 192
Durkheim, E., 64

Index of Subjects

Achievement aid, 78-81, 90
Achievement values, 74-78, 280, 289-96
African family patterns, 4, 5
Alienation (economic), 210-19, 220-26,
    233-36, 249-53, 262-63, 294, 309
Assimilation, 8, 9, 12, 34, 40, 62-63,146
Authority, 239-46

Black Panthers, 325
Black power (self-determination), 326 ff.

Child autonomy, 290 ff.
Companionship, 201-2
Comparison levels, 223-26
Conflict resolution, 240-41
Consumption rationality, 253-60
Consumption and social status, 76, 199,
    212-16, 314, 319
    and family structure, 320-22

Economic resources and black family
    structure, 1, 2, 4, 7, 8, 11 ff.,
    32-33, 53, 62, 84-85, 87, 93-98,
    134-35, 152-53, 169, 174, 199-200,
    204-10, 224-26, 229, 246, 263-64,
    307, 309-10, 312, 313-14, 318 ff.
Economic and status deprivation of

blacks relative to whites, 9, 10, 40,
    65, 70, 80, 98, 124, 146-47,
    153-55, 161-63, 165-66, 184 ff.,
    205, 207-10,.236, 246, 254, 263,
    274, 278, 296, 308-9, 323-25,
    326 ff.
and conflict, 299 ff.
Education, 9, 39-40, 159-63, 206, 221,
    235, 247-49, 280, 288-89, 294, 299
Education attainment of children, 297-99
Educational help (support), 68-74,
    126-33, 282, 288-89
Educational values, 65-68, 282
Empathy (communication-understand-
    ing), 202-4
Ethnic identity, 11 ff., 63-64, 98, 136,
    153, 162, 191, 310-11, 331
Expressive behavior, 105-12, 119,
    199-226, 227-28, 236-38, 260-63,
    309, 322-23

Father in black family, significance of,
    96-97, 110, 138, 145, 172-73, 308
Female employment, 165, 170-71,
    173-74, 182-84, 204, 226-32,
    236-38, 245-46, 251, 321
Female mobility, 158-59, 168-70, 180-82

351

Parental hindrance, 73-74, 81, 86, 91
Peers, choice of, 284-86
Physical affection (including sex), 202
Policy, social, 2, 8, 62-63, 147, 209, 275,
278, 300-2, 317, 324-29
Power (see Authority)
Primary relations (see Expressive
behavior)

Reference group, 103, 208-10, 212-13,
218, 223
Reference person, 103, 136 ff., 171,
176 ff.
Religion and black family structure,
48-53, 120-26, 286-87
Resources from outside the conjugal
family, 116, 316
and kin, 133-36
and persons, 117-20
and religion, 120-26
and school, 126-33
Role:
duties, 83-88, 121-22, 199, 210, 218,
220
options, 227, 229
rights, 84-88, 199, 220, 229, 237
Role differentiation, male-female, 72-73,
110, 203-4
Role model, 103-16, 137 ff., 171, 176 ff.
Rural southern experience, 32 ff.

School integration, 133
School quality, 282-83
School Teachers, 117-18, 126-33, 281-82
Self-concept (image, esteem), 5, 10, 119,
128
Self-fulfilling prophecy, 127, 130
Siblings of respondents, 45-48
Slavery and family patterns, 5, 306
Social exchange (reciprocity), 102, 112,

137, 142, 184, 198-200, 207, 219,
232-33, 239-40, 244, 304
Social system analysis of family, 21-22,
115-16, 174, 224, 232, 244
Socialization, 60-64, 65 ff., 203, 274 ff.,
309, 318-19
anticipatory, 78-79, 185
in means to attain success goals,
281-96, 301-2, 313-14
Status advantages, 36-40
Status-estrangement, 213-16
Structure-function and interactionist
approaches, 307-8
Success expectations and aspirations,
217-18, 276-80

Theory, Social, vii, 4, 62, 94, 102-3, 180,
187, 199 ff., 253, 294, 306-10,
311-24
Trends and changes:
in black family structure, 264-65,
308-11
in dominant conjugal patterns, 311 ff.,
321-22, 324-25

Urbanization, 6, 7, 31-36

Violence, 299-302, 314, 325-26

White bias in social science research, x, 2,
306
White "deviations" from dominant
family patterns, 136
White immigrant mobility, 185
Work and success ethos, black acceptance
of, 74-75, 79, 123-25, 279, 283,
287, 296, 298-99, 301, 320, 326
Working-class blacks, 7, 8, 13, 15, 16, 54,
82, 89, 108-9, 114, 131, 155, 169,
179, 290